SONGS OF SORROW

ALSO BY SAMUEL CHARTERS

MUSIC

Jazz: New Orleans 1885–1963
The Country Blues
Jazz: A History of the New York Scene
The Poetry of the Blues
The Bluesmen: The Story and the Music of the Men Who Made the Blues
Robert Johnson
The Legacy of the Blues: Art and Lives of Twelve Great Blues Men
Sweet as the Showers of Rain
Spelmannen (The Swedish Fiddlers)
The Roots of the Blues: An African Search
The Blues Makers
The Day Is So Long and the Wages So Small: Music on a Summer Island
Blues Faces: A Portrait of the Blues (with Ann Charters)
Walking a Blues Road: Notes and Writings 1956–2004
New Orleans: Playing a Jazz Chorus
A Trumpet Around the Corner: A History of New Orleans Jazz
A Language of Song: Journeys in the Musical World of the African Diaspora

POETRY

The Children
The Landscape at Bolinas
Heroes of the Prize Ring
Days, or Days as Thoughts in a Season's Uncertainties
To This Place
From a London Notebook
From a Swedish Notebook
Of Those Who Died: A Poem of the Spring of 1945
In Lagos
The Poet Sees His Family Sleeping
Things to do Around Picadilly
What Paths, What Journeys: Selected Poems

FICTION

Mr. Jabi and Mr. Smythe
Jelly Roll Morton's Last Night at the Jungle Inn
Louisiana Black
Elvis Presley Calls His Mother After the Ed Sullivan Show
The Harry Bright Dances

Songs of the FREEDMEN of Port Royal.

Collected and Arranged by MISS LUCY Mc KIM.

1. POOR ROSY, POORGAL.	2. ROLL JORDAN ROLL.
3.	4
5.	6
7.	8

Geo. Swain.

Philadelphia.

Ent. according to Act of Congress AD 1862 by Miss Lucy McKim in the Clerks Office of the Dist Court of the Eastn Dist of Pa.

SONGS OF
SORROW

Lucy McKim Garrison and
Slave Songs of the United States

SAMUEL CHARTERS

University Press of Mississippi / Jackson

www.upress.state.ms.us

The University Press of Mississippi is a member
of the Association of American University Presses.

All black-and-white photographs courtesy of the
Samuel and Ann Charters Archives of Vernacular African
American Music and Culture unless otherwise indicated

All color photographs by Samuel Charters

First printing 2015

∞

Library of Congress Cataloging-in-Publication Data

Charters, Samuel, 1929– author.
Songs of sorrow : Lucy McKim Garrison and Slave songs of the United
States / Samuel Charters.
    pages cm. — (American made music series)
Includes bibliographical references and index.
ISBN 978-1-62846-206-7 (cloth : alk. paper) — ISBN 978-1-49685-210-6
(trade paperback) — ISBN 978-1-62674-530-8 (ebook) 1. Garrison, Lucy
McKim, 1842–1877. 2. Ethnomusicologists—United States—Biography.
3. Slave songs of the United States. 4. Spirituals (Songs)—History and
criticisim. I. Title.
ML423.G24C53 2015

782.42162'96073—dc23   2014037771

British Library Cataloging-in-Publication Data available

For

Kristin Eshelman,
indispensible associate and valued friend—
who shares the life's spirit this
book describes.

Of the Sorrow Songs

They that walked in darkness sang songs in the olden days—Sorrow Songs—for they were weary at heart. And so before each thought that I have written in the book I have set a phrase, a haunting echo of these weird old songs in which the soul of the black slave spoke to men. Ever since I was a child these songs have stirred me strangely. They came out of the South unknown to me, one by one, and yet at once I knew them as of me and of mine . . .

Little of beauty has America given the world save the rude grandeur God himself stamped on her bosom; the human spirit in this new world has expressed itself in vigor and ingenuity rather than in beauty. And so by fatal chance the Negro folk-song—the rhythmic cry of the slave—stands today not simply as the sole American music, but as the most beautiful expression of human experience born this side of the seas. It has been neglected, it has been, and is, half despised, and above all it has been persistently mistaken and misunderstood, but notwithstanding, it will remain as the singular spiritual heritage of the nation, and the greatest gift of the Negro people.

—W. E. B. Du Bois
from *The Souls of Black Folk*, 1903

CONTENTS

ACKNOWLEDGMENTS

Slave Songs of the United States has been part of my life since I first encountered it in the research for my early book *The Country Blues* in 1959. In turning finally to write about this pioneering work I feel as though I am completing a long, circular journey, and as with most journeys I couldn't have found my way without guidance along the path. The work of three scholars and writers has been particularly helpful.

Dena Epstein, one of the most diligent and respected scholars in the field of African American musical culture, published a small monograph on Lucy McKim Garrison in 1963, as well as writing the entry for her in the *Encyclopedia of American Women*. Only two years earlier Epstein's research had led her to the discovery of the correspondence between Lucy McKim and Ellen Wright that made this book possible. Epstein's own analysis of the backgrounds of *Slave Songs of the United States* in her classic study *Sinful Tunes and Spirituals: Black Folk Music to the Civil War* was of crucial importance in pointing directions for my own research. Willie Lee Rose, with her definitive, prize-winning work *Rehearsal for Reconstruction*, enabled me to place the Port Royal experiment in the South Carolina Sea Islands in a historical perspective. Harriet Hyman Alonso's patient efforts in telling the complex story of the family of William Lloyd Garrison in *Growing Up Abolitionist* saved me months of labor with its painstaking detail of Lucy McKim's life as the wife of Wendell Phillips Garrison, William Lloyd Garrison's third son.

I am indebted to many people at the research libraries that I visited in my work. Kristin Eshelman at the Dodd Research Center at the University of Connecticut in Storrs, Connecticut was unfailingly helpful with finding source materials and contacts for other archives I visited. She had an intuitive sense of what information I might need and where it might be found, and her cheerful patience softened many perplexing moments. I found that at every institution where I searched for materials I was met with courtesy and a friendly interest in assisting my efforts. I usually never learned the names of the persons so generously helping me, but to the staffs of the Sophia Smith Collection at Smith College, Northampton, Massachusetts; the Manuscript Division of the New York Public Library,

Forty-Second Street and Fifth Avenue, New York City; the university library at Cornell University, Ithaca, New York; the periodical archives of the Mugar Library at Boston University in Boston; and also to Alex Bartlett at the Historical Society of Germantown, Pennsylvania, I offer my sincere thanks and gratitude.

I would particularly like to thank Lee Grady at the Wisconsin Historical Society, in Madison, Wisconsin, for his assistance with the manuscript diary of William Francis Allen. I had no personal contact with the staff of the Penn School during my visit to St. Helena Island in South Carolina, but I found my visit there to be an inspiring experience, and it brought me closer to the lives and the work of Laura Towne, her life's partner Ellen Murray, and their fellow teacher in the early days on St. Helena, Charlotte Forten.

There have been two readers of the manuscript as it neared completion. One was blues scholar and friend David Evans who made a number of suggestions to sharpen the focus of the story. His long interest in the subject made him a particularly insightful reader. The other was my wife, Ann Charters, with whom I have collaborated on several books in the past, and whose editorial skills and sympathetic reading were as ever invaluable. She also spent many hours sharing the arduous work of transcribing the original correspondence between Lucy McKim and Ellen Wright at the Smith College library. Finally she agreed that a winter journey to South Carolina and St. Helena Island to visit the places where Lucy McKim had heard the slave songs was a reasonable idea in the middle of a long New England winter. My deepest gratitude, as always.

I promised myself, during a confused night journey through the dark streets of north Philadelphia trying to find my way from Germantown Square to the Pennsylvania Turnpike, that I would acknowledge the assistance of the many friendly people I encountered in all-night cafes and gas stations who patiently directed me further on my way. They also helped make this book possible.

—Samuel Charters
Storrs–Stockholm, 2011–2014

SONGS OF SORROW

1

With Voices to Sing!

Roll, Jordan Roll

March, angels, march! March, angels march!
My soul am rise to heav'n Lord,
where de heav'n'e Jording roll.

March, angels march! March, angels march!
My soul am rise to heav'n Lord,
where de heav'n' Jording roll.

    Little chilen sittin' on de Tree ob Life,
    Where de heav'n' Jording roll, Oh!
    Roll Jording, roll Jording, Roll, Jording, roll!
    Little chilen sittin' on de Tree ob Life,
    Where de heav'n' Jording roll.
Oh! Roll, Jording, roll Jording, Roll, Jording, Roll!

—Collected on St. Helena Island, South Carolina, July 1862, by Lucy McKim

In his groundbreaking work *The Souls of Black Folk* W. E. B. Du Bois introduced in his chapter titled "Of the Sorrow Songs" the circumstances of the discovery of black song in the South in the early years of the Civil War.

> ... in war-time came the singular Port Royal experiment after the capture of Hilton Head, and perhaps for the first time North met the southern slave face to face and heart to heart with no third witness. The Sea Islands of the Carolinas, where they met, were filled with a black folk of primitive type, touched and moulded less by the world about them than any others outside the Black Belt. Their appearance was uncouth, their language funny, but their hearts

were human and their singing stirred men with a mighty power. Thomas Wentworth Higginson hastened to tell of these songs, and Miss McKim and others urged upon the world their rare beauty.[1]

Thomas Wentworth Higginson told his own story of his meeting with black song as the commanding officer of a black regiment in the South Carolina Sea Islands in 1863–64, but the story of "Miss McKim," Lucy McKim, is less well known. It is a story that began at the moment when Port Royal became a door suddenly thrown open to challenging worlds of experience for these newly freed men and women, a world which they in their turn would enrich with their unique treasure of song.

On May 21, 1862, a young woman named Ellen Wright wrote to her brother Frank to tell him the news of her friend Lucy McKim.

> We have all been thrown into comparative consternation, by Lucy's projected trip to Port Royal. She and her father expect to leave these peaceful parts tonight, or tomorrow to sail from New York immediately to the Port. Lucy is going as Asst., and Secretary to her father, who expects to be very busy. She is delighted . . . with the anticipation, & can hardly sleep o' nights for thinking of it—I dare say she will dash into some transcendental scheme of a school or something of missionary aspect, and never be heard of again in civilized circles. They say she will be back in a month.[2]

Within a month Lucy McKim had returned to her mother and to her brother and sister in Philadelphia from Port Royal and from the plantations and slave quarters where she had been living on nearby St. Helena Island, on the coast of South Carolina. She was only nineteen years old, but her short journey would leave its imprint on the rest of her life. What grew from her emotional encounters with the cruelties of slavery in the small, threatened enclave freed by the Union forces only a few months before, and by her discovery of the enduring strength of the slaves' songs she heard there, was the book *Slave Songs of the United States*. On its publication in 1867 it was the first book to acknowledge the achievement of the songs that had emerged from slavery's shadows.

Lucy McKim made the journey on a small coastal steamer sailing from New York with her father, James Miller McKim, who was directing the activities of the Port Royal Relief Committee in Philadelphia. He was the leading figure in the group that had hastily organized the committee five months before. Their purpose was to aid the efforts to feed, educate, and care for the nearly one thousand slaves who had been abandoned on

St. Helena Island when the plantation owners had fled the attack of the Union steam frigates the autumn before. The island was a flat table of dark earth that had been deposited by the drifting currents of rivers emptying into the sea at the end of their passage through South Carolina's inland countryside. It was the low bluffs of St. Helena that lined the northern shore of the broad bay that opened onto Port Royal Sound.

A few weeks earlier other hurriedly organized relief committees in Boston and New York had begun sending teachers and supervisors to the island, but Lucy and her father landed in the midst of the hapless confusions of an uncertain war. They found themselves spending their nights in abandoned mansions on isolated plantations, their days swept by uneasy rumor, with people around them nervously conscious of the threat of Confederate forces encircling them only miles away. No one knew what the situation demanded, since no one had experienced a situation like it before. Lucy was traveling with her father as his assistant and secretary, but he found himself forced to attend one hurriedly organized meeting after another, swaying over rutted dirt roads from one plantation to the next in the makeshift carriages that were all that had been left behind in their owners' desperate flight. His days were spent trying to sort through the demands and complaints that met him on every side. Lucy was left the time to walk into the slaves' quarters, to listen to their stories, and in the darkness at night to sit on rude benches in their wretched cabins and listen to their outpouring of song.

What Lucy McKim experienced in those weeks in the South Carolina plantation slave quarters was the same shattering discovery of slavery's realities as that of many others like her who ventured into the South at this moment. In a letter to her mother, she cried, "How lukewarm we have been! How little we knew!" Her father's mission was to create some kind of order out of the chaotic efforts to provide relief for the people on the islands, to secure supplies of food and clothing, and to organize medical treatment. Through the schools that were opening as rapidly as teachers could be found, groups like her father's relief committee accepted a commitment to help the slaves take the first steps toward a real freedom through education. What she and her father learned, as did so many others making the journey, was that the slaves may have been the South's most valued property, but in many circumstances they were the most harshly treated of all its possessions. These early encounters with the cruel realities of slavery helped strengthen the resolve of these newly arrived volunteers to continue with their work, whatever the difficulties.

Among the thousands of relief workers, missionaries, opportunists, and idealists who were frantically attempting to fill the void left in the South by the collapse of an entire social system, there were many who also heard the slaves' songs and were moved by the songs' power. In their early months other volunteers on St. Helena began to jot down verses of songs in letters they sent home, or in their journals. It was Lucy McKim who would be the first to dream of gathering this treasure of song into a book, though it would not be until the war's end that she would find others who shared her belief in the music's value, and who could bring their own knowledge to aid her in the work. At its publication in 1867 what appeared for the first time in their book were the great "sorrow songs," the spirituals created in slavery.

What Lucy McKim and many others of the visitors to the coastal enclave realized was that the changes they were bringing themselves to the islands would have lingering consequences. Within only a few years the songs and the unique styles of singing them would inevitably change, reflecting the influence of freedom, of the first rudimentary education, and of the Christian fervor of northern missionaries. The life of slavery itself that had produced their songs was seemingly swept away by the changes brought by Reconstruction at the war's end, even though its effects would linger for generations as change came slowly to the South.

◆ ◆ ◆

Lucy McKim was raised in the large Quaker community of Philadelphia, but her father, James Miller McKim, with his studies nearly completed to become a Presbyterian minister, was deflected from his course by a meeting with the eloquent Quaker speaker and social agitator Lucretia Mott. Though he never fully became a Quaker himself, he left the Presbyterian Church. His daughter Lucy, he wrote in an account of his own travels to South Carolina, was "a young lady who was of no religious denomination, but who had been tenderly raised outside of sectarian pales on the outskirts of liberal Quakerism."[3]

Much of Lucy's story followed the familiar American pattern of that time of a sheltered young woman's upbringing in her home, an education that taught domestic skills, and finally marriage as the goal. With her family's more liberal attitudes, music was also allowed to assume a larger role, and she became a skilled and ambitious pianist. For Lucy, and for most of those who were to be her friends, there was also another commitment that left an imprint on their daily lives. Her story is also the story of the men and women in America joined by their passionate conviction that slavery was an evil that must be overcome, whatever the cost. Her father was a committed, tireless abolitionist who dedicated his life to the struggle for emancipation. As the director of the Pennsylvania Anti-Slavery Office he spent long hours every day in his downtown Philadelphia office writing articles and pleas, patiently answering inquiries and soliciting funds to further the work. He openly acknowledged his support of the work of the Underground Railroad, though this was an unlawful act which could lead to imprisonment and heavy fines. Sometimes he brought fugitives from his office where they'd sought help to his home and his family. There the slaves were hidden and provided with food and clothing and a moment of anxious rest until safe transfer to the next station could be arranged.

It is not often understood today how seriously the lives of the abolitionists' children were affected by their parents' commitment to their cause. The country was riven by the passionate convictions of both sides. Their homes could be attacked by mobs at any time. In Philadelphia, not long before Lucy was born, a jeering crowd set fire to a newly built meeting house where the abolitionists had begun to hold meetings, and they were diverted from burning the home of Lucretia Mott and attacking her family only by the impulsive action of a friend who hurried ahead of the mob and misdirected them to give the Motts enough time to escape.

The children of abolitionist families often were subject to harassment in the schoolrooms, and many, like Lucy, were sent away to schools with teaching methods that were considered by most of their neighbors as dangerously radical. Often the abolitionists' children spent much of their adolescence separated from their families. As they entered their teens, Lucy, her sister, and her younger brother were sent to a New Jersey progressive school where boys and girls sat in the same classrooms and the girls were encouraged to speak. It was a point of moral principle for the school's staff that the school's sympathies were abolitionist. There were gymnasium classes so both boys and girls could exercise, and the students of all ages were encouraged to take part in school dramatics, with girls performing on the stage with the boys. None of these activities would have been acceptable to most Americans. The young students who were sent to such schools usually left them with a lifelong devotion to the friendships they had made there. When Lucy's friend Ellen Wright was eighty-one she began writing letters to old school comrades to see if someone could be encouraged to write a history of their school.

Lucretia Mott, her husband, her sisters, and the children in their family shared the idealism of Lucy McKim's family. Her own daughters were

Lucy's age and she grew up almost as a sister, the Mott household as much a home as her own. Lucy's lifelong friend Ellen Wright was the daughter of Lucretia Mott's sister Martha, who was married to a lawyer in Auburn, New York. Martha and her family were close friends and allies of the legendary Harriet Tubman who lived nearby. An ex-slave herself, Tubman risked her life again and again to return to the South to lead escapees to freedom.

Close to all of them who were committed to the abolitionist cause was the family of the nation's most radical and influential abolitionist leader, William Lloyd Garrison. It was Garrison who, on January 1, 1831, proclaimed on the front page of his newly launched newspaper, *The Liberator*:

> I am in earnest—I will not equivocate—I will not excuse—I will not retreat a single inch—AND I WILL BE HEARD!

The closely woven lives of these idealistic families, their dreams and their hopes at this moment of turbulence and crisis in the American journey, were the backdrop for the personal story of Lucy McKim and of those associated with her who helped to preserve the spirituals of slavery. The idealistic editors of *Slave Songs of the United States* were determined, much as William Lloyd Garrison, that these songs should be *heard*. Thanks to the assistance of William Francis Allen and Charles Pickard Ware, who joined her in the work, there remains from the dark shadows of the Civil War and Reconstruction this imperishable legacy of African American song.

The publication of *Slave Songs of the United States* is the one moment at which Lucy McKim emerges from the anonymity of most ordinary lives, but there is another dimension that lends a greater depth to her story. Thanks to her lifelong friendship with Ellen Wright—the young woman who wrote the letter to her brother announcing that Lucy was intending to sail to South Carolina—we have an enduring document of the lives of two American women at this period of the nation's division and struggle. Hundreds of letters were saved of a correspondence that is often disturbingly frank in its descriptions of their first pangs of adolescence, the tumult of their emotions as young women, and the physical pain and risk in their lives as young wives and mothers. Over weeks and months they wrote each other daily, on some days a second letter quickly following the first. In the spring of 1861 the letters reflected the fervor of their immediate response to the outbreak of the Civil War. In a show of emotion they proclaimed their indignation at the young men of their acquaintance who declined to enlist and take part in the fighting—fighting that as women they knew they could never experience themselves. In the letters also abruptly come the wrenching moments when the first deaths of the young men they had sent away with such excitement forced upon them a deeper understanding of the war's bitter realities. The letters in the years that followed fill with the excitements of marriage and motherhood. At the last, the letters reflect a trailing wistfulness as the demands of these new roles threatened to consume anything else they might once have dreamed of becoming. The letters themselves tell much of Lucy's story.

Also in the letters is her impassioned protest against the limitations that were placed on her life as a woman in her society. She understood that it would be marriage, with its tight legal and social bonds, that at some moment lay in her future, but she asked for more freedom, more opportunity *now*. She felt the constraints most keenly in the war, when she was forced to accept the reality that as a woman she could never participate in the decisions or the drama of these decisive years. On January 21, 1863, she stormed in a letter to Ellen:

> Sometimes it seems as if God could not really know how willing we should be for any work, or he would give us some.[4]

And again in the winter of 1863 with her life thrown into despair by the death in battle of a man she had come to love she complained bitterly:

> I have as much influence in the fate of Greece whose history I read, as I have in the fate of America, that I love with a love borne of sorrow, whose good happiness is nearer to my heart than is father or mother or brother or every being under the sun. The whole cry of my soul is that all battles may not be fought without my having fired one shot, that all the pain may not have passed without my having saved one sufferer.[5]

Although Lucy shared the enthusiasms and confusions of any young girl growing up at that time, she was supported by her family in one of her own ambitions. She could spend her mornings in piano practice, and she became a gifted pianist, at a period in American life when few women had the opportunity to reach a professional level, or nearly professional, in the world of classical music. To help with the family's always uncertain finances she and her sister advertised in a local newspaper that they were available to give instruction, and they had been qualified for their work by accepted older musicians. Lucy's pupils were at the beginning confined to young cousins. She was only fifteen, and she would continue teaching and performing in local recitals for the next dozen years. What she brought with her when she journeyed to South Carolina were her musical skills. It was her musical training, her musicality that enabled her to *hear* the richness of the slaves' songs, and it was her musical intuition that lay behind her profound emotional response to their music. Her training had been in the classic European concert tradition, but her musical sensitivities—and her heart—were as open to the singing of the slaves.

Four months after Lucy's return from Port Royal she published what was only the second appearance in the United States of a serious musical setting of a slave song, the plaintive "Poor Rosy, Poor Gal," composing her own piano accompaniment. At the same time, announcing the publication of the song, she wrote the first article to appear in a national music journal, *Dwight's Journal of Music*, published in Boston, describing what she considered to be some of the unique characteristics of African American song. Her spirited article, which she sent to the journal as a letter, was different from other travelers' accounts that had begun to appear at the same moment. Those who also were hearing the slave songs for the first time generally told the story of their dramatic experience and their stirred responses to the wretched condition of the newly freed slaves. In her article Lucy strove to describe the character of the singing she had heard and the musical elements that made it distinctive. What was obvious in her writing was that it was her hard-earned skills as a pianist and musician that had helped her understand what she heard in her weeks on the islands in South Carolina.

In her article she tried to put into words what the songs had taught her. She wrote:

> The wild, sad strains tell, as the sufferers themselves never could, of crushed hopes, keen sorrow, and a dull, daily misery which covered them as hopelessly as the fog from the rice-swamps.[6]

The book that finally reached the public in the turmoil of the postwar years, *Slave Songs of the United States*, failed to interest the editors of some of the nation's leading journals, but it was widely reviewed and its first edition was a popular success, selling out its copies within a few weeks after its publication. At the same moment, however, its publisher merged with two other publishing interests, and the promised second edition of the book did not appear. It was not until four years later that it made its appearance with another publisher. Half a century would pass before it was discovered again in the excited awakening of interest in African

American culture in the Harlem Renaissance. It was republished in 1929 in a facsimile printing of their original edition, and it has been steadily in print in the years since then, often in multiple editions.

There was no thought in 1867 of the three "editors" who had been associated with the book continuing with the work. Each had moved on with their lives. Lucy was the mother of a six-month-old baby, without the financial resources to turn her child over to nannies or servants. One of the men, William Allen, had taken on a new and challenging academic post. The other, Charles Ware, returned to St. Helena Island, resuming his work as a supervisor on one of the island's plantations. Though he continued to collect songs, he found that there were now fewer songs to be heard. The three editors during their stays on St. Helena Island had themselves heard and annotated almost two-thirds of the songs that were included in the book.

In an unsigned review of the book with Lucy as one of its writers they wrote in conclusion, "We shall be disappointed if many of the airs do not become popular."[7] Already within their lifetimes the "airs" in its pages, the great sorrow songs of slavery, all but a handful appearing here for the first time, had taken their place in the world's musical culture. Lucy McKim had dreamed that in these songs, the greatest of them in these pages—"Roll, Jordan, Roll," "Blow Your Trumpet, Gabriel," "The Lonesome Valley," "Lord, Remember Me," "Michael, Row the Boat Ashore," "Many Thousand Go," "Nobody Knows the Trouble I've Had," "Rock a' My Soul in de Bosom of Abraham," and "Climbing Jacob's Ladder"—the bitter story of slavery had been told. The role of these songs in preserving and glorifying the spirit of the people who created and sang them was the fulfillment of her dream.

2

Come Liberty!

Alas! and am I born for this,
 To wear this slavish chain?
Deprived of all created bliss,
 Through hardship, toil, and pain!

How long have I in bondage lain,
 And languished to be free!
Alas! and must I still complain—
 Deprived of liberty.

Oh, Heaven! and is there no relief
 This side the silent grave—
To sooth the pain—to quell the grief
 And anguish of a slave?

Come Liberty, thou cheerful sound,
 Roll through my ravished ears!
Come, let my grief in joys be drowned,
 And drive away my fears.

—George Moses Horton
"On Liberty and Slavery," 1829
(Born into slavery c. 1795, escaped to freedom with Sherman's army, 1865)

For children like Lucy McKim who grow up in a closely knit family, it is their mother and father who are the background against which the adventure of their lives will be played. The years before her parents' marriage and her own childhood—the 1830s and the 1840s—were a period of rapid change and expansion, ferment, disputation, and uncertainty in the

United States. For her father it was a period of challenging demands on his skills and his commitment to his abolitionist principles, but he also felt it as a period of optimism, however strained, and he never questioned his determined faith in the nation's future. Like so many of his countrymen he still lived in the innocence of the nation's recent birth. It was an innocence that voiced itself in an optimistic belief that the future could be guided by a uniquely American idealism.

For idealists like James McKim their lives were a continuous expression of their mood of confidence and hope. They would find some way for their nation to live in peace and harmony, while at the same time growing to fulfill what they saw as its clearly defined manifest destiny. Wherever Lucy's father turned to look around him there was encouragement for these hopes. It was these years that saw the founding of the distinct American social ethos, the beginnings of an American literature, the celebration of the landscape by a new generation of American artists. Slavery was the oppressive shadow that darkened this flush of optimism, but it had hung over the consciousness of the nation since its founding: debated, defended, and attacked. Now McKim was living in a period defined by the conviction shared by many American idealists that the moment had come to end slavery. At the same time there were the first stirrings of the struggle for the rights of women, a cause almost as intensely debated as the question of slavery. It was also a cause that had his support. Lucy's father was a man who exemplified the emergence of this new American idealism, and without need for questioning he understood that his children would share these dreams.

◆ ◆ ◆

James Miller McKim's family had their roots in Scotland. The clan was named either Mac Kim or Mac Kimmie. Many Scots could not continue to live in their country after the defeat of the Scottish armies at Culloden in 1746 and the long years that followed of oppressive English rule. Scotland was left impoverished, and with this fueling their despair a flood of emigration emptied many areas of the land. The middle stop for many Scots on their journey to the British colonies in North America was Northern Ireland, which had a swelling Scottish population, encouraged by the English after the Irish were defeated at the Battle of the Boyne in 1690. The Scots were Protestant, and the tensions between them and their Catholic Irish neighbors in Northern Ireland, where they were brought by British entrepeneurs to take up jobs, have yet to be entirely resolved more than three hundred years later.

A James McKim, who was Lucy's great-grandfather, arrived from Northern Ireland at the small settlement of Carlisle in eastern Pennysl-vania in 1774. Lucy's father, James Miller McKim, was born in Carlisle on November 4, 1810. Carlisle's grammar school, established in 1773, had been given new status as Dickinson College in 1783. McKim attended the col-lege and graduated in 1828, when he was eighteen. Like most Scots, his family were firm Presbyterians, and he chose the ministry as his profes-sion. He continued his studies at the Theological Seminary at Princeton, in nearby New Jersey, and at Andover College in South Portland, Maine. Unlike other students around him, however, McKim was unsure of his calling to the ministry, and even of his religious faith.

In the next few years there would be two people whose influence and example changed the direction of his life. The first was William Lloyd Garrison, an unyielding abolitionist and defender of women's rights from Massachusetts. He was only five years older than McKim, but his life had forced him to mature quickly. Garrison's father had abandoned his family when he was still a boy, and unlike McKim, who was educated in college, Garrison began working early and chose a life as a writer and newspaper editor, openly advocating abolitionist views when he was barely out of his teens. By 1830 he had already been jailed for an article revealing that a Massachusetts businessman was importing and selling slaves, despite the prohibition in the Constitution. The article had appeared in a newspaper he owned jointly with another man, and when his fine was paid by an abolitionist sympathizer, freeing him after seven weeks of confinement, he determined to begin his own publication. The first issue of his newspaper, which he named *The Liberator*, appeared on January 1, 1831, and on its front page it proclaimed his intentions, which immediately became widely quoted as a rallying cry for abolitionist sympathizers.

> I am aware that many object to the severity of my language, but is there not cause for my severity? I will be as harsh as truth, and as uncompromising as justice. On this subject, I do not wish to think, or to speak, or write with moderation! No! No! Tell a man whose house is on fire to give a moderate alarm, tell him moderately rescue his wife from the hands of a ravisher; tell the mother to gradually extricate her babe from the fire into which it has fallen—but urge me not to use moderation in a cause like the present. I am in earnest—I will not equivocate—I will not excuse—I will not retreat a single inch—AND I WILL BE HEARD . . . .

Garrison's writings had a galvanizing effect on McKim, who was quickly drawn to the abolitionist cause. In 1833, at the age of twenty-three, he became the youngest delegate to attend a major antislavery convention held in Philadelphia, where he became aware of the dedicated Quaker abolitionist and feminist agitator Lucretia Mott. It was Mott who became the second person who would change the direction of his life. A handful of women were permitted to attend the convention, but only as "listeners and spectators," and Mott was among them. Anna Davis Hollowell, Mott's daughter, described Mott's first awareness of McKim's presence in her collection *James and Lucretia Mott: Life and Letters*[1]:

> ... when she arose to suggest a change in the final document and used the word "transpose" she writes "I remember one of the younger members turning to see what woman that was there who knew what the word 'transpose' meant...."

McKim was the young man who turned in his seat to see who the woman might be, and they met at the convention shortly afterwards. Both Lucretia and her husband, James Mott, were drawn to McKim's enthusiasm and commitment, and they soon also became aware of the crisis of faith he was undergoing.

Lucretia Mott, who would play a large role in both her father's and Lucy's lives, was for much of her life one of the best-known figures in Philadelphia's activist community, where she was a dominant member of the Pennsylvania Anti-Slavery Society. When Mott addressed the convention of the Female Anti-Slavery Society in Philadelphia, in the audience were African American women and two of Mott's daughters. Although for much of her life she was associated with her activities in Philadelphia, she was born on January 3, 1793, on Nantucket Island in Massachusetts. There were two Quaker meeting houses on the island and her father and mother were part of the small Quaker community. She became a schoolteacher while still a teenager, and when her father moved the family to Philadelphia in 1810, James Mott, another young teacher from the school, followed her, and they were married the next year.

Lucy's father and the Motts would be closely associated in the years that followed, drawn together by the struggle for emancipation. It was in letters she sent to friends that their circle of acquaintances first heard the news of James McKim's engagement to a popular young Quaker woman. In a letter to friends on October 12, 1840, she wrote that she had only recently held a wedding party for McKim and his bride, Sarah Speakman. The woman McKim was to marry was, like Mott, a Quaker, and in her letter Mott told her friends of her early meetings with McKim, whom she familiarly called "Miller," and the effect of herself and her husband on McKim's decision to leave his own church. With the term "right sort" she is referring to a rancorous schism within the Quaker community. She and her husband had become what were termed "Hicksites," followers of the Quaker leader Elias Hicks, who proposed a more liberal and engaged social role for members of the Quaker assemblies. Mott wrote:

> [A friend] is now in the city and is coming here this evening to meet a bridal party, in honor of J. Miller McKim, agent of our Anti-Slavery Society. He has lately married one of the finest Quaker girls of Chester Co., and is well-nigh a Quaker himself—of the right sort, I mean. He came to the city in 1833 to attend the memorable A. S. [Anti-Slavery] Convention, and was one of the youngest signers of the notable document. He was then preparing himself for the pulpit in the Presbyterian Society—the religion of his education. [We] frequently conversed together touching on the doctrines or dogmas of that Society; and on his return home, he read some of Dr. Channing's works, and some goodly Friends' books we furnished him, and the result was an entire change of views. . . . He now rejoices in his spiritual liberty, and I doubt not even you would admit that he is every bit as good, as when groping in the midnight dark of sectarian theology.[2]

Mott herself never swerved from her Quaker beliefs, but she was also committed to liberal understanding in her religious views, and her Quaker faith was never a barrier to friendship with others also committed to the causes of feminism and abolition. As she pointed out in her description of McKim's religious views, he was "well-nigh" a Quaker, although he never joined a Quaker assembly. Despite this difference in their beliefs they continued to work together all of their lives. As one of the members of the antislavery society she was witness to many of the trying events and decisions that McKim faced in his everyday work as the society's agent.

At the time that his engagement to Sarah Speakman had been announced in the Philadelphia newspapers in June 1838, Mott sent the news in a letter to a friend and described the woman who would become Lucy's mother, a Quaker woman from a prosperous farming family who had been given an unusually thorough and liberal education.

> She is 'tasty' in her dress, without much ornament, wears straw and beaver bonnets, is not quite as tall as [another friend] lighter complexion and handsomer, altogether very easy in her manners. Her advantages of education have been good and she has profited by them. Her intellect is well cultivated,

her moral perceptions clear and quick, and her heart unsullied by vice, or even by "the superfluity of naughtiness." In accomplishments she exceeds most young ladies of our Order, plays on the flute, sings sweetly and without waiting to be over-persuaded. When she was here last winter I told James [James Mott] I didn't know how Miller could have such command over his heart when in company with such a girl, little suspecting that at the very time they had made the exchange and each had the other's secretly enfolded, enjoying our jokes and remarks in silent exultation. I was much surprised when he told us, and feel a Mother's affection for them both. She was remarkably open and free with me, coming here, after Miller left Philadelphia, to talk about him and read parts of his letters.[3]

As was expected, Sarah's marriage to McKim meant that his bride would be expelled from her Quaker assembly, but she ignored the edict, and continued to consider herself a Quaker, without insisting that her husband and her children join her in her faith.

After their marriage October 3, 1840, McKim continued to act as the society's publishing agent, despite the poor salary and the difficulties of the work. He was wholly dedicated to the abolitionist cause, and the society continued to be the place where his services could be most useful. Their first child, their daughter Lucy, was born two years later on October 30, 1842. Some years later they took in the daughter of a family relation whose parents had died, and she lived with them as Lucy's foster sister, Annie, who was a year and a half older. The McKims' second child, a son, Charles Follen McKim, was born on August 24, 1847.

◆ ◆ ◆

What was the Philadelphia world that Lucy was born into? When she was still a child the city was described by one of the most quick-eyed and intently curious of all the foreign visitors who came to pass judgment on the American democratic experiment, Fredrika Bremer. She was a well-known Swedish novelist, social activist, and dedicated feminist, who spent some weeks in Philadelphia, where she quickly was drawn into the group around Lucretia Mott and the McKims. Bremer was one of the early creators of the genre of the domestic novel in Sweden, and through widely sold translations her books were a staple for European readers. Her novels were "on the bedside table"—as many women she met told her—everywhere she traveled in America. She was now in her late forties, a small, slight figure whose best features were her eyes, like Lucretia Mott. It was

the letters she wrote home to her sister Agatha that were published as her
classic description of life in this new country, *Homes in the New World*.

When Bremer came to Philadelphia on a coastal steamer from Charleston, she was traveling from South Carolina and Georgia where she had
spent three months, intensely engaged in the slavery question and troubled by the contradictions of her daily contacts with the slaveholders and
with the slaves themselves. Her ship introduced her to the city as it sailed
up the Delaware River to anchor at the city's docks. Her characteristically
lengthy letter to her sister was dated June 23, 1850. Her first reaction to the
northward journey was a vast relief at leaving the heat of the South behind
her. The first day and night aboard were boiling hot, "the air and the sea
totally still, as if the wind were dead,"[4] and she understood that people
could die from the heat. To her relief, as they steamed further north the
temperature dropped.

> The voyage was calm and upon the whole, good. . . . The sea sent us flocks
> of flying-fish as entertainment on the voyage. Pelicans with immense beaks
> floated like our gulls through the air, on search for prey, while a large whale
> stopped on his journey through the ocean, as if to let us witness various
> beautiful waterspouts. The sailing up the River Delaware on Tuesday morn-
> ing was very agreeable to me, although the weather was misty. But the mist
> lifted again and again its heavy draperies, and revealed bright green shores
> of idyllian beauty, with lofty hills, wooden country houses, grazing cattle, and
> a character of landscape wholy unlike that which had been lately familiar to
> me in the South.[5]

The Philadelphia of Bremer's visit was a city of three hundred thousand people that had spread on flat lands on the west bank of the Delaware River. The river served as the boundary between Pennsylvania and
New Jersey, its neighboring state to the east. Philadelphia had early been
eclipsed by the bustle of New York's seven hundred thousand inhabitants,
but visitors were charmed by its parks and its wide streets lined with trees
and grassy walkways. Bremer's determined liberal principles drew her
to Philadelphia's Quakers, and they responded by gathering to meet her,
inviting her into their homes, and driving her everywhere in their carriages to see what Philadelphia could offer. What struck her immediately
when she was taken to see the institutions established for the care of the
poor and the aged was the contrast between the scenes along the quiet
Philadelphia streets and what she had witnessed in the South.

The Quakers—the Friends as they are commonly called—are especially kind to me, take me by the hand, call me Fredrika, and address me with *thou*, or, rather, *thee*, and convey me, in easy carriages, to see all that is remarkable and beautiful, as well in the city as out of it. And what large and excellent institutions there are here for the public good! The heart is enlarged by the contemplation of them, and by the manner in which they are maintained. One can not help being struck here, in a high degree, by the contrast between the Slave States and the Free States; between the state whose principal is selfishness and the state whose principle is human love; between the state where labor is free, and the free are honored. And here, where one sees white women sweeping before the doors, how well kept is every thing, how ornamental, how flourishing within the city as well as in the country! And these public institutions, these flowers of human love—ah! the magnolia blossoms of the primeval forests are devoid of fragrance in comparison with them; they stand as far behind these dwellings, these asylums for the unfortunate and for the old, as the outer court of the Sanctuary did to the holy of holies.[6]

Lucy McKim was eight years old when Bremer visited the city. Her foster sister, Annie, was ten, and their baby brother, Charlie, was three. One day near the end of her visit Bremer was a dinner guest at the Motts' and she remarked on "a beautiful, blossoming troop"[7] of children and grandchildren. The three McKim children, who were so often guests themselves at the Motts', could easily have been part of the troop.

The antislavery cause drew to it committed followers from every level of American life. In the emotional climate of the times, the radical views of McKim and the Motts and the circle around them made it difficult for his wife and children to form a wide circle of acquaintances, but the families had a busy social life, and they were close to the other abolitionists who faced the same imminent problems and dangers. There were continuous visits and voluminous correspondence keeping them in close touch with each other. At the Motts' there were six children, and they were often visited by Lucretia's sister Martha with her children. Martha, with whom Lucretia was very close, had married a lawyer named David Wright, who was a leader in the struggle against slavery, and she had raised seven children, a child with her first husband who had died after two years of marriage and six children with her second husband.

For James McKim's children these close ties meant that they had no sense that they lived in isolation from the rest of society. There is little known about their early schooling, but they probably were tutored at home, which meant they never had to confront the confusions and resentments of other children who might have thought their parents too radical for everyday friendships. It was only to be expected that the children would have as their closest friends other children like themselves in their family's tightly knit circle. On July 6, 1851, Lucy wrote the first letter she is known to have sent to Martha Wright's daughter Ellen in answer to a letter she had received from her. Ellen Wright was ten years old, Lucy was eight.[8]

> I wish you would come to see us some time we have got each of us a wax doll and a little bedstead for them to sleep in and Charley has got a velocipede and a sweet little Pussy Cat and a pretty large yard and a play room and we have some little Toy Chairs and Tables and we have a good many flowers of different kinds. We are going to the country next Saturday I do wish you could be with us we have elegant times racing about. You know you wrote to me how tall you are, well I am four feet and three inches and I will be nine years old the 30th of October Mother says that Pennsylvania exceeds New York in the growth of Children. Tell Frank and Willie they must write to me both of them. I must stop now so goodbye your affectionate friend
>   Lucy McKim

It was the first exchange in a correspondence that would continue for the rest of their lives.

◆ ◆ ◆

Nothing that occurred in Lucy McKim's later life, and nothing she ever said or wrote in her letters, suggests that she had a childhood that was anything other than loving and cherished. As part of the family of a dedicated abolitionist, however, she, her sister, Annie, and her younger brother, Charlie, were never free from the threats of those who were opposed to their father's work. Whatever house they lived in was used as a station in the Underground Railroad, and the children had no way of knowing when a wagon or carriage would bring fugitives, or groups on foot, standing at their door, tired, frightened, hungry, and uncertain about would happen to them next.

The antislavery cause made heavy demands on its workers, though few wavered in their commitment. Lucy and Annie were alone with their mother when their brother was born in 1847. Their father was traveling in England and Scotland, raising money for the antislavery committee. The trip to England was McKim's first journey out of the United States and he learned within a short time that one problem for him on ocean voyages was that he suffered severely from seasickness. The journey emphasized, however, that the movement reached beyond the borders of the United States. With the success of their efforts to end slavery in England and the colonies only a little more than a dozen years behind them, the English antislavery groups were buoyed with the optimism born of their success. There was a renewed determination to give whatever assistance they could to the American abolition committees who shared their idealism and their fervor. The English supporters had sponsored the largest gathering of the abolitionist movement, the World's Anti-Slavery Convention held in London in 1840. Lucretia Mott had been part of a delegation from the Pennsylvania committee, where again to her severe disappointment, both as a Quaker "of the wrong sort" and as a woman, she was refused a delegate's role in the convention.

On McKim's return his life resumed its familiar pattern. He journeyed every day from their small house in Spring Gardens on the outskirts of the city to the antislavery committee's office on Fifth Street in central Philadelphia. The city's horse-drawn coach lines were being steadily expanded, and it was possible to cross the city without having to use the family's horse or being reduced to long walks through the summer's heat and rain or the winter's ice and mud. He had an assistant in his office, a young man named Cyrus Burleigh, and they were often visited by Robert Purvis, one of the most indefatigable and successful agents of the Underground Railroad.

Purvis himself was one-quarter black, which meant that he was considered "Negro" and subject to the restrictions and prejudices that anyone of color faced. Purvis had been born free in Charleston 1810, the second of three sons of a free woman of color who was herself born to a mixed-race couple. Purvis's father was an immigrant from England who became wealthy as a cotton broker. His father moved the family to Philadelphia when Robert was nine, and with his brothers he attended the Clarkson School, which was operated by the Pennsylvania Abolitionist Society. He continued his studies at Amherst College in Massachusetts, where he became associated with William Lloyd Garrison. He assisted Garrison in establishing the American Anti-Slavery Society and was one of the signers of its "Declaration of Sentiment." He returned to Philadelphia and worked closely with Lucy's father. He was president of the Pennsylvania Anti-Slavery Society from 1845 to 1850 and his wife, Harriet, was president of the Philadelphia Female Anti-Slavery Society. Purvis's wealth made it possible for him to operate freely in the efforts to free slaves from captivity. By his own estimate between 1831 and 1861 he assisted in the escape of nine thousand slaves.

The address of the antislavery society was widely known and often a tap on the door meant that escapees were on their way. In May 1849 McKim played a crucial role in one of the most widely publicized escapes of this period. Lucy was seven, Annie was nine, and their brother was little more than a year and a half. Their father received word that a Virginia slave had determined on a plan to have himself closed in a wooden packing box and shipped by express from Richmond to the antislavery society office. To forestall closer questioning the address given was the freight company's depot, rather than the office itself. When a telegram reached McKim telling him that the box was on its way he rushed to the freight depot and arranged for the box to be brought immediately to his office. His quick action saved hours that would have been lost as he waited for notification of the box's arrival and certainly lessened the ordeal of the man closed inside.

Lucretia Mott wrote an excited letter to friends on May 28, 1849, a week after the box's arrival, recounting the events of the day.[9]

> ... I must tell you what an exciting fugitive case we had last week. A citizen of Richmond, Va. called at the office and told Miller McKim and Cyrus Burleigh, that a slave in that city was meditating his escape by being placed in a box, as goods, to be sent by Adam's Express. He was told of the great danger of suffocation, as well as the risk of detection, but was not deterred. After some delays a telegraph at length apprised Miller of his approach. The box was received at the depot, more carefully handled than it had been before, and safely deposited at the A. S. office, when a trembling tap and "All right?" from Miller was responded to by "All right, sir!" from the pent-up man. The lid was removed as quickly as the hoops could be loosened, when he rose with a "Good morning, gentlemen!"—Miller says we can hardly conceive the relief and excitement to find the man alive, and the poor fellow's happiness and gratitude; he sang a song of praise. He is a large man, weighing nearly two hundred pounds, and was encased in a box two feet long, twenty-three inches wide and three feet deep, in a sitting posture! He was provided with a few crackers, and a bladder filled with water, which would make no noise on being turned over, nor yet liable to be broken; he however ate *none*, as it would have made him thirsty, and he needed all the water to bathe his head, after the rough turns over, in which he sometimes rested for miles on his head and shoulders, when it would seem as if the veins would burst. He fanned himself continuously with his hat, and bored

holes for fresh breathing air with a gimlet or small auger furnished him. The cracks of the box had canvas over, to prevent any inspection, and to appear like goods. Doc. Noble says, if he had been consulted, he should have said it would be impossible for the man to be shut up and live twenty-four hours, the time it took to reach here, it was fanning so much, which kept the exhausted air in motion and gave place to fresh. Miller took him home, gave him his breakfast and a bath, and then he was conducted here, where he gave us his history.

For those who had dedicated their lives to the abolitionist cause, the determination of a man like "Box" Brown to achieve his freedom at any cost was a vindication of their work. Instead of hurrying farther north as quickly as possible, Brown was soon a much-sought speaker at antislavery gatherings and his story became so widespread that for a brief period he appeared on the popular stage, describing his journey. An unfortunate result of his public popularity was that authorities in Richmond arrested the man whom Brown named as the helper who had nailed him in the box and sentenced him to a prison term—later commuted—of six years. The noted ex-slave activist Frederick Douglass also complained that Brown's tale of success had made it impossible for any other escapee to attempt using this means.

Considering the risks of Brown's journey, however, it would have been a dangerous feat to emulate, and probably would have been the cause of more deaths than successful escapes. Although it seems clear from letters at the time that only McKim and his assistant Cyrus Burleigh were in the office when the box was delivered, a popular lithograph depicting the moment by artist Samuel Rowse, published in 1860, has added two figures, one of them Robert Purvis.

◆ ◆ ◆

Lucy's father was now over forty. In a photograph taken of the Pennsylvania antislavery committee in 1851 he was the tallest figure in the back row, his face set in a fixed, determined expression. At the same time his eyes seemed to be looking toward something else that was occupying his thoughts. He was a handsome man, his dark hair brushed loosely back over his ears. He was clean shaven, without either a beard or mustache, which was unusual for a man at this time, but which emphasized the strong symmetry of his face. Seated in the row in front of him was Lucretia Mott, her body seemingly diminutive and frail, her hair covered with a

Quaker bonnet, a shawl around her shoulders, and her eyes staring at the camera with the fierce intensity of a bird of prey.

McKim's demanding and all-absorbing duties for the society included maintaining an extensive correspondence with abolitionist groups throughout the northern states and also in England and Scotland, staying in contact with the groups of sympathizers he'd met on his trip three years before, and acting as joint editor of the society's publication, the *Pennsylvania Freeman*. At the same time he had to respond to the steady stream of visitors who made their way to his downtown office, and his daily routines were continuously interrupted by the arrival of runaways. There were also uneasy confrontations with the agents of the slaveholders who were prowling the city's streets, hungry for the large rewards waiting for anyone successfully returning escapees to their owners. Like everyone in his situation McKim was conscious of the fact that in some cities abolitionists' offices had been attacked, and in 1837 the young editor of an abolitionist newspaper, Elijah Lovejoy, had been shot to death in Alton, Illinois, in an exchange of gunfire with a mob sympathetic to the South. Perhaps so that McKim's activities would invite less public scrutiny, he listed his occupation in the 1850 city registry of Philadelphia as "publisher."

◆ ◆ ◆

McKim was so committed to the abolitionist cause that in the spring of 1853 he contemplated leaving his family in Philadelphia to return to England for five or six months to continue proselytizing for emancipation and to raise funds for the abolitionist cause in the United States. Largely due to the determination and persistence of an earlier Quaker leader and member of England's parliament, William Wilberforce, England had renounced slavery in the British Isles in the 1790s. Parliament then voted to end the slave trade in the West Indies in 1807. The Slavery Abolition Act, which freed all the slaves in England's colonies, was passed in 1833, two months after Wilberforce's death. This historic act of emancipation had succeeded in great part through large payments made to slaveholders as compensation for the loss of their property. A similar solution to the American dilemma over slavery was never seriously proposed, though this policy eased the emancipation of the slaves in the District of Columbia in the early 1860s. For many years there was an effort to encourage African Americans, whether they were free or still living in slavery, to return to Africa. Many were offered transportation to the newly founded colony of Liberia, a policy that was favored by several leading politicians, among them a young Abraham Lincoln.

McKim's trip would be done "on his own hook," since his office had no funds to finance it, and he had recently purchased a new home in the small village of Bellefield, outside of Philadelphia. He was certain that his day-to-day expenses would be covered by contributions, but there would be considerable expense involved in beginning his journey. To sum up the arguments for and against the trip he created a remarkable double-sided document listing reasons for and against the trip.[10]

His debate with himself began with his reasons why he shouldn't make the trip, beginning with his unhappiness at leaving his wife, Sarah, for such a long period, and also undergoing long and uncertain ocean voyages. He added, "The children too would surely oppose it."

Then, turning the page, he answered his own objections. "[T]hough it would be a great sacrifice [Sarah] would cheerfully or at least willingly make it if convinced that it would be best for the cause . . . as for the children they would soon dry their tears. Children's grief is short. Both Sarah & they would make it easy for me, if satisfied it was right." Obviously struggling with his conscience he continued with questions he listed on his page:

1. Sarah
2. The cause at home
3. Our new house in Bellefield
4. The dangers of the Seas
5. The difficulties on the other side of the water
6. The cost

In the end it was almost certainly his sense of family responsibilities that outweighed the other considerations, and his plans for the trip were abandoned.

◆ ◆ ◆

In a letter written on July 21, 1855, to Ann Agnes Catharine Byrne, the sister of their Irish maid, Mary Byrne, Lucy, who was now thirteen, described their family life, and her very precocious, detailed account gives a picture of a life that was solid and secure.[11]

The Maples, July 21, 1855
My dear Nanny,
    I suppose you think it very queer in me to write to you, but Mary has told me so much about you I feel quite well acquainted, and I hope you will

write to me. Mary is a sweet little thing, she is not so tall as I am by an inch; she amuses me very much by telling me about the girls at Miss Harney's, *you*, Phibs borough school, and Green Erin in general, of which she seems to be very fond, in fact, I never saw anyone so patriotic—always excepting myself you know. But now as you don't know me, or any of our family, I will have to introduce you—Father and mother, are very nice and remind me of yours, from Molly's description. My sister Annie Kate, not as tall as I am, will be 14 next month, she has red hair, hazel eyes, and freckles, is very merry, and is something like you in disposition I suppose. I call her *Royal Red*. My brother Charles Follen, is slim, fair hair & complexion, blues eyes high forehead, 8 years old and squally, we call him Challoby, Kinkey &c. You see Nannie we are fond of giving fancy names. I call Mary Little Dubby, because she's so fond of Dublin.

Lucy also felt obliged to furnish a description of herself.

Imagine a girl before you of mammoth size, 13 years old (consequently very lymphatic) brown hair, gray eyes, snub nose, 12 chicken pox marks on her forehead, and you'll have—me. . .

The family had another maid named Mary Perinne, who despite being very overweight shared the bed with "Dub," as was common for servants. There was also a German handyman named Christophus Fingerle of whom Mary was not at all fond. Lucy concluded:

I wish you would emigrate to this country. I am sure you would like it, we have the most delicious tomatoes, sweet potatoes and Indian corn, Mary is very fond of them all. . . . Our horse is called "Nicholas, the Czar of Russia," we call him Nick. Nance has gone to town, and Charlie is playing with some of his company, and I have been diversifying the time by drawing your interesting sister's face, and she submits to all my criticisms upon her pointed nose &c. with the utmost equanimity. As I have to get ready to go to my Hibernian drawing master, I will bid you goodbye, and hoping you will write to me, I remain your affectionate friend,
    Lucy McKim
Love to your mother, if she will allow it.

Whatever the stresses and the uncertainties of James McKim's work in the antislavery offices, he didn't communicate them to his daughter, whose letter mirrors a quiet satisfaction with her calm life growing up in her close-knit family.

Lucy McKim Garrison. Photo from 1876–1877? Courtesy Garrison Family Papers, Smith College, Northampton, Massachusetts.

The smaller photo is from the period of her South Carolina journey.

Miss Annie C. McKim and Miss Lucy McKim continue to give lessons on the Piano at their residence, corner of Duy's and Cottage Lanes, and at the houses of pupils in Philadelphia and in and about Germantown.

They have the advantage, as teachers, of four years' experience, having given instruction, part of that time, at Eagleswood Boarding School. They make *thoroughness of groundwork with new beginners* a point of the first importance. Terms $15.00 a quarter.

References :—Prof. B. Carr Cross, Prof. Frederick Molinhauer. George H. Earle, Esq., Hon. Charles Gibbons, William Howell, Esq., and Hon. William Morris Davis.

Germantown, Sept. 23d, 1862.

Lucy and Annie McKim announce their services as instructors of the piano. Courtesy Garrison Family Papers, Smith College, Northampton, Massachusetts.

Photos from her years of marriage, above, c. 1875.

C. 1870.

All the songs make good barcaroles. Whittier "builded better than he knew" when he wrote his "Song of the Negro Boatman." It seemed wonderfully applicable as we were being rowed across Hilton Head Harbor among United States gunboats,—the Wabash and the Vermont towering on either side. I thought the crew *must* strike up

> " And massa tink it day ob doom,
> And we ob jubilee."

Perhaps the *grandest* singing we heard was at the Baptist Church on St. Helena Island, when a congregation of three hundred men and women joined in a hymn—

> " Roll, Jordan, roll. Jordan!
> Roll, Jordan, roll ! "

It swelled forth like a triumphal anthem. That same hymn was sung by thousands of negroes on the 4th. of July last, when they marched in procession under the Stars and Stripes, cheering them for the first time as the " flag of *our* country," A friend writing from there, says that the chorus was indescribably grand,—" that the whole woods and world seemed joining in that rolling sound."

There is much more in this new and curious music, of which it is a temptation to write, but I must remember that it can speak for itself better than any one for it.

Very respectfully, Lucy McKim.

The conclusion of her letter/article for *Dwight's Journal of Music*, November 8, 1862.

The executive committee of the Pennsylvania Anti-Slavery Society, 1851. James McKim, Lucy's father, is the tall man to the right, rear row. Sitting in front of him is Lucretia Mott. To her left is her husband, James Mott; to her right is Robert Purvis.

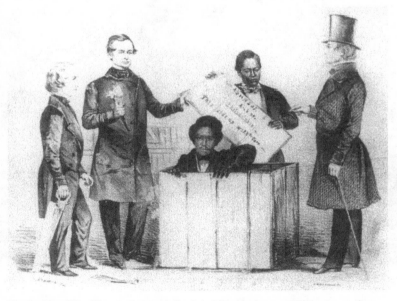

The freeing of "Box" Brown. James McKim is holding the hammer; his assistant, Cyrus Burleigh, holds a saw.

Lucy McKim's mother, Sarah Speakman McKim, c. 1875.

Lucy McKim's father, James Miller McKim, c. 1865.

The Market Square, Germantown, c. 1890. Courtesy Germantown Historical Society, Philadelphia, Pennsylvania.

Eagleswood School, Perth Amboy, New Jersey, in the 1850s.

Ellen Wright Garrison. L. to r.: her sister Eliza, her older brother Frank, Ellen, her sister Marianne. Courtesy Garrison Family Papers, Smith College, Northampton, Massachusetts.

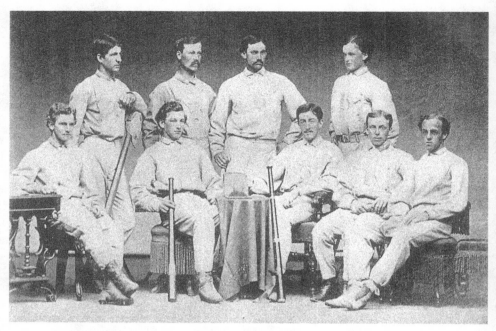

As a member of the Harvard baseball team, 1867, Charlie McKim is at the far right, rear row.

Lucy McKim's brother, Charles (the distinguished architect Charles Follen McKim), c. 1890.

These, certainly, are songs to be desired and regretted. But we do not despair of recovering them and others perhaps equally characteristic for a second edition; and we herewith solicit the kind offices of collectors into whose hands this volume may have fallen, in extending and perfecting our researches. For fully a third of the songs recorded by Col. Higginson we have failed to obtain the music, and they may very well serve as a guide for future investigators. We shall also gratefully acknowledge any errors of fact or of typography that may be brought to our attention, and in general anything that would enhance the value or the interest of this collection. Communications may be addressed to Mr. W. P. Garrison, Office of *The Nation* newspaper, New York City.

NOVEMBER, 1867.

Wendell Garrison's concluding note to *Slave Songs of the United States*, apologizing for songs that were not included.

Wendell Phillips Garrison, photo from early 1860s.

Drawing by William Garrison of his brother Wendell holding William and Ellen's first child. Courtesy Garrison Family Papers, Smith College, Northampton, Massachusetts.

Wendell Garrison in later years.

The family home in Llewellyn Park, West Orange, New Jersey, c. 1920.

3

Schooling of a Different Nature

On fields o'er which the reaper's hand has passed
Lit by the harvest moon and autumn sun,
My thoughts like stubble floating in the wind
And of such fineness as October airs,
There after harvest could I glean my life
A richer harvest reaping without toil,
And weaving gorgeous fancies at my will
In subtler webs than finest summer haze.

—Henry David Thoreau

On June 23, 1856, Theodore Weld wrote a hurried letter to Lucy's father in answer to his question about visiting Eagleswood school at an "exhibition" of his school's offerings in the summer. With his wife, Angelina Grimke, Weld was directing an experimental school on the outskirts of the town of Perth Amboy on New Jersey's Atlantic coast.

> *Eagleswood*, Perth Amboy
> June 23 '56
> My dear friend
> I have just received your note—our exhibition is to be on Tuesday the 1st of July, *not on the 2nd as you suppose*. It will begin at 2 o'clock PM, continue till six—then at 7½ and continue about three hours. Right glad shall we be to welcome you all.
> You refer to our terms for the next year. The necessities of raising our price is to us a *real* affliction—and a great one. When we *agreed* to transfer our school hither, one influential consideration most honestly assigned, but on totally mistaken grounds we could afford to put our prices even lower than at Belleville, thus enabling us to receive pupils of moderate means.

Through great miscalculation and mismanagement at the outset, on the part of those having charge of outlays, we have become saddled with *costly* economies, compelling us either to raise considerably our terms, or to discontinue the school.

Our object is not to *lay up* money by schoolkeeping. The sole *pecuniary end* of our schoolkeeping is make the *ends meet.* Whenever our price effects more than that it will at once be cut down to that point. Besides we mean always to reserve the right and privilege of receiving certain pupils at a lower rate than the "terms" where those cannot be afforded.

This reminds me that you say in your note—"I could have asked for my own sake that your terms had not been quite so high," from which I infer that our terms preclude you from sending any of your children—now my friend this *shall not be so.* It will be to us a real affliction if for such a cause you are forced to keep your children from us, when otherwise you would send them. We will gladly remit to you the "extra charges" for Latin, French, & German and reduce the ordinary charge from $270 to $200. Pray tell us if *that* would bring it within your means.

With most cordial salutations to you all . . .[1]

The arrangement for the school fees that Weld offered to his friend McKim was agreeable, and Lucy entered the school as a boarder at the end of September. Eagleswood might have been unorthodox about many of its ideas, but like almost all American schools during this early period it allowed the children time to finish with harvesting before the fall classes began. Lucy was thirteen, though she would celebrate her fourteenth birthday at the end of October, only four weeks away. With some breaks, the school would be the focus of her life for the next four years; first as a pupil, then as a teacher of music, piano, and whatever subjects needed an extra pair of hands or eyes. The school continually needed teachers for the younger students, and often the instructors were drawn from the school's older students. It was Lucy's abilities as a teacher of music and the piano that made her especially useful to the Welds.

Nothing is known about Lucy's early instruction on the piano, and her parents were not thought of as musical, though her mother had played the flute as a girl and always enjoyed singing. Although many Quakers still regarded music as too worldly, it had become fashionable for virtually all children from the McKims' social background to be given piano lessons. Lucy was clearly one of those unmistakably talented young "scholars," who enthusiastically dedicate themselves to the hours of daily practice that brings them to the level where their music could provide them with a modest employment as a teacher. She had already been strongly influenced by the liberal attitudes of her family, and her years at the Welds' school only encouraged her own consciousness of personal responsibility. For a young woman in the 1850s it was uncommon that any ideas of self-assertion she might have had as a young girl could be sustained and supported through her adolescence in her schooling. The program at Eagleswood, however, was schooling of a different nature.

Lucy's older sister, Annie, was returning to the school for her second year as a student, so Lucy had already an introduction to the people she would meet, and within a few days she was completely settled into the noisy companionship of the other pupils. Another of her classmates who was beginning the September term at Eagleswood was the girl Lucy had begun corresponding with when she was only eight years old, Ellen Wright, the daughter of Lucretia Mott's sister Martha Wright. For Ellen the new term at Eagleswood presented more complications. She had been at Eagleswood as a boarder in the school's opening term under the direction of the Welds in 1854, two years earlier. The previous year she and her brother Willie had both attended classes held in a farmhouse that Weld and his wife had bought in Belleville, New Jersey. It was her happiness with Weld's inspirational teaching that led Ellen to beg to be allowed to attend the new school at Eagleswood, though as her mother made clear, the school's expense was a problem for her family.

When the first term opened Ellen had turned fourteen only a few weeks before. From the first weeks her life at the school was troubled. Part of the problem was her complicated relationship with her mother.[2] There was a stream of letters back and forth between them as her mother attempted to exercise control over her daughter's new life, criticizing her handwriting, responding sarcastically to her daughter's tales of her difficulties, and attempting to discourage her dreams of becoming a pianist. Ellen also seemed to have felt isolated in a way she hadn't in Belleville. Despite the tensions between her and her mother she was suffering from homesickness, and she was beginning to experience the painful episodes of migraine headache which would periodically overwhelm her for the rest of her life.

In the winter Ellen became more and more agitated, and in the early spring she suffered a kind of seizure, so severe that she had to be physically restrained by Anna Mott and Weld himself. Although her mother at first was anxiously sympathetic, trying to find some cause for her daughter's outburst, she soon became critical of what she termed Ellen's "nervous excitement." Ellen pretended to treat the incident lightly but she suffered from headaches and homesickness, and finally Weld kept her out of classes and his wife insisted that she leave her room during class hours and not continue to isolate herself from the other students.

In the summer months following Ellen's collapse, her mother, thoroughly exasperated now, sent her with her older sister, Eliza, to the Clifton Sanitarium, which was a kind of stringent summer health camp not far from their home in Auburn. Relenting a little, as a break in the summer's strict regime her mother took Ellen to a women's rights meeting in Saratoga, thinking perhaps that the example of the accomplished women who were speaking there would encourage her daughter to think more seriously about her life. The speakers included many of the most distinguished women in the movement, including Susan B. Anthony, Ernestine Rose, and Antoinette Brown, but it was one of the male delegates Ellen was drawn to, the young minister Thomas Wentworth Higginson.

In a photo taken about this time Ellen is tall and slim, dark haired, attractive, and with a gaze that showed some sense of amusement and suggestion of challenge. In her letters she was as often concerned with the boys she was attracted to as she was with the more ordinary events of the day, though nothing she did ever went beyond what were considered the boundaries of propriety. Higginson would go on to become one of the best-known figures of American cultural life, but already his handsome looks and his fiery dedication to both the growing women's movement and the abolitionist struggle had drawn people to him everywhere. Ellen related in a letter to a cousin that he asked her to accompany him on his walks back and forth to the meetings, and she tried to find a seat near him during meals.[3] In the fall, when her mother decided not to return her to Eagleswood, Ellen pleaded to be sent instead to a school in Worcester, Massachusetts, to be closer to Higginson, and for several years he would continue to be part of her longing fantasies. She was still only fifteen, and she found her mother's staunch commitment to the women's movement more intimidating than inspiring.

In the autumn she had more opportunity to be close to Lucy. Instead of the school in Massachusetts, in September she was sent to the Sharon Female Academy, in Pennsylvania, fortunately close to Philadelphia. Her mother had probably chosen it because Ellen would be closer to her mother's sister, Lucretia Mott, and the Mott family. Ellen found the school a disappointment after the freer atmosphere of Eagleswood. She didn't like the food, and she objected to the periods of enforced silence and the regulations that kept her out of her room during the day, but she found the schoolwork itself satisfying. More important for her was the opportunity to spend more time with Lucy and other friends in Philadelphia. Included in their group were a number of young men, among them two brothers, Richard and Beverly Chase, and another Philadelphia acquaintance, Ned Hollowell, with whom she persistently flirted. Though she was often precipitous in her emotional swings, with so many family members close by, her mother could relax some of her intent concern with her daughter's well-being.

As she began the new term at Eagleswood in the fall of 1856 Ellen was filled with resolve to act more her age, but also to try to think of herself as the woman she would become—someday. Lucy would be part of this new role she planned to adopt, and the months that had passed since her first difficult year at the school had lessened some of tensions with her mother. She turned sixteen in the summer, determined to try to steer her way through the new school term with less tumult. One of the new habits Ellen set out to acquire as she began the term was to keep a diary, and what she left of its pages gives a fuller account of these first months of her friendship with Lucy, a friendship that would involve them in each other's lives through their marriages and the challenges of beginning their own families. It is impossible now to tell who might have been upset about things that the diary revealed, but at some point scissors were used on many pages, leaving streamers of paper with only parts of paragraphs and sentences surviving. Some pages have been cut out completely. Perhaps there was some pattern in the kinds of sentences that were scissored away—often it was probably only a name that was removed—so it could have been Ellen herself who had later misgivings about some of her adolescent fervors.

The diary was a small notebook with a marbleized paper cover. On the opening page she wrote,[4]

Really Private!!!

then she added in lighter penciled letters,

To *Almost* Everybody!

She had returned to school on September 30, and her first entry began encouragingly, "Everything is improved. I'm as excited as possible." Lucy appeared early. In her entry the next day Ellen wrote, "Luce & I first rate friends," and on the following day she added, "Took walk with Luce—First time."

Walking together was to be one of the ways for Lucy and Ellen to get away from the community life in the school building where all the students had their living quarters. It was on their walks that they could talk, and from the first moment they encountered each other at the school they talked and laughed as though there were nothing else they needed to be concerned with. The land close to the shoreline where the school had been built was sprawling and flat. Most of its area had been cleared for farming and there were paths through much of the extended acreage, though it was already overgrown with a tangled growth of brush and small trees. A walk along a dirt road took them to the school's boat landing on Raritan Bay less than a mile away. The land was windy and hot in the summers, and there were frequent winter storms that swept in off the Atlantic. If the weather was too threatening for long walks they strolled around the small lake that lay in front of the colony's main building. They walked out to see golden sunsets, they stumbled through the night darkness to look at the moon, they fled their room on fresh days and gloomy days, wrapping themselves against the winds and tramping along the paths until their shoes and stockings were soaked and muddy.

◆ ◆ ◆

Both Weld and Lucy's father were conscious that the program and the aims of Weld's school placed it far outside their society's ordinary strictures, but for McKim it was one of the few schools where he could send his children without their having problems with the children of other parents who didn't share their views. Lucretia Mott's granddaughter Anna was returning to the school at the end of September, and among other Philadelphia friends in the classrooms was Hattie Purvis, the daughter of Robert Purvis, whom they all knew through the close-knit abolitionist community.

For Philadelphia's abolitionists Theodore Weld was an old acquaintance who had worked in the city and been a leading figure in the first years of the antislavery movement. What was also of utmost importance to them was that the program and the goals of Weld's school reflected a whole spectrum of the idealism that shaped American intellectual life at this moment. Eagleswood's program had absorbed much of Ralph Waldo Emerson's thinking and his worldview into its hopes for the possibilities of the children. People who were considered to be radical thinkers supported the work of the school, but an anomaly was that one of the persons instrumental in the founding of the utopian colony where the school was located was the cosmopolitan New York newspaper editor Horace Greeley. The Concord writers, Emerson, Thoreau, Hawthorne, and the Alcotts, had already been forced to accept the discouraging failures of first the Brook Farm utopian colony and then the collapse of Bronson Alcott's optimistic venture at nearby Fruitlands. The presence of Eagleswood at least offered some encouraging evidence that their ideas were not entirely ignored, even if the Raritan Union, the idealistic community that had first opened the school, had collapsed only months before.

For most people in the United States in 1856, however, many of the school's principles were not only considered outside any accepted measure of normality; they were a threat to the fabric of American society itself. There was considerable uneasiness over the presence of two of the women closely associated with Eagleswood who were also teaching in the classrooms, Angelina Grimke, who had married Theodore Weld in 1838, and her older sister, Sarah Grimke. The Grimke sisters were born to wealthy slaveholder parents in South Carolina, Sarah in 1792 and Angelina in 1805. It was this early, personal knowledge of the evils of slavery that drew them to the abolitionist cause, and in the early 1830s they moved together to Philadelphia and became members of a Quaker fellowship in the city. When they found they were discouraged from presenting their views to public gatherings because of their sex they reacted by becoming as firmly committed to the new feminist ideals as they were to abolition. In 1837 Sarah published an attack on the morality of slavery, *Epistle to the Clergy of the Southern States*, and she followed it the next year with a passionate defense of women's rights, *Letters on the Equality of the Sexes*. Following Angelina's marriage both women withdrew from much of their public activism, but many of the controversial ideas that Eagleswood embodied had their source in Sarah's writings. Among the students when Lucy attended were the children of the militant feminist leader Elizabeth Cady Stanton.

Since much of the support for the school came from within the Quaker community it was accepted without question that it would openly support abolition. Many of the people involved with the school had also vehemently opposed the US invasion of Mexico and the forcible annexation of more than a third of Mexico's territory only nine years before. What was more of a problem for other parents who were thinking of where to send their children was what they considered to be the school's radical programs. The classes were coeducational, and all students were encouraged to speak out, both boys and girls. There were athletic programs in which the girls also participated. A range of subjects, including music and languages, was taught, and plays were presented with girls taking part in the performances. None of these things were considered to be proper in the eyes of most Americans, and a further disquieting feature was that although the spirit of Quakerism pervaded the activities, there was no strict religious emphasis.

For someone as committed to these principles as Lucy's father, the school was the obvious place for the family to send his daughter, but at the end of Lucy's first year, when he wrote to his brother John, a Presbyterian minister, suggesting that he should also send his son there, John's carefully hedged response suggests some of the ambivalence many parents felt about the school's ideals. In his return letter on July 16, 1857, John admitted that there was no satisfactory school in the Germantown area where he was living that would suit his son Arthur, but he was hesitant about sending Arthur to Eagleswood.

> ... your proposition about Arthur encouraged me to strain a point, & send him to Eaglewood *bye and bye.* I don't know if I can do so *this* year. But I will study it over, and hope to arrange it, so as to get him there next spring. I have no exceptions to make to Weld's "doxy," you know. I take a good deal of latitude myself, not only in my preaching but in my communications with the brethren. Yet I take it to be a matter of consideration [whether] the influence of such teaching as Mr W's would be just the thing *for Arthur.*[5]

The fullest glimpse of the school that autumn when Lucy and Ellen began the new term comes from the letters of a visitor who spent the month of October there. The property that had been purchased by the colony was 673 acres of land spread along the bank of the Raritan River. Although it had been cleared for farming, as Lucy and Ellen found in their walks, much of it had become thickly overgrown with brush and low trees, and there were winding streambeds with steep mud banks. The school's land was situated about a mile and a half on a sandy coastal road southeast from the center of Perth Amboy. Although Eagleswood is still part of Perth Amboy's history, the site where it was situated was taken over for industrial development and today there is no trace of the school.

Eagleswood itself had been only recently reestablished by the Welds, and it had first been sponsored as the school of the Raritan Bay Union. Of all the bravely launched utopian communities during this period Raritan Bay was the only one that had achieved any real economic success. Its operations had grown to include a large communal building, outbuildings, a number of workshops and forges producing a variety of goods.

There was a day care center for the children of the mothers who were working, guest cottages, elaborate grounds that included gardens and orchards with paths and ornamental shrubbery, and an artificial lake that offered a tranquil view in front of the largest building. The lake was used for boating in the summers and in the winter months for harvesting ice.

In a popular lithographic view of the school, strollers are seen on the path circling the lake. A fire in 1854, however, brought an end to the colony's success when their mill and several workshops burned, leaving them with a ten-thousand-dollar loss. The misfortune also forced the colony's own insurance company into bankruptcy. Greeley offered them money to rebuild the colony, but there was no will to begin again and the members of the colony voted to put their surviving assets up for sale on the open market and to disband officially on January 1, 1857. Included in the sale would be most of the property from the original purchase. It was this string of misfortunes that lay behind the tone of Weld's letter to Lucy's father the previous June.

With the sale of the land a reality, the man who was the overall director of the remaining properties and the activities of the school, Marcus Spring, decided the property would be more easily sold if it were divided into lots. This meant it would have to be surveyed. The school found there was no need to go outside of their many groups of supporters to find someone who could serve for the job. Spring and his wife, Rebecca, who both were Quakers, frequently opened their house to Bronson Alcott when he came to spend a few days at the colony. Alcott's suggestion was that Marcus Spring should contact one of his Concord neighbors, Henry David Thoreau. Alcott was aware that Thoreau was a self-taught surveyor who had never done any work outside of Massachusetts, but he insisted his friend was capable of doing the job.

Thoreau arrived at the school on October 25, 1856, only three and a half weeks after Lucy and Ellen had begun their classes. He brought with him, as Spring had asked, not only his measuring instruments but his lectures as well. The Welds welcomed anyone who could offer some mental stimulation to their students. His first letter, to his sister Sophie Elizabeth Thoreau on November 1, opened spontaneously with his surprise at the appearance of the school's main building, which was one of the outstanding features of the original colony. When the property was purchased there were still farm buildings in dilapidated condition left on the land, and the decision was made to rebuild two of them and include them in a much larger structure. They were connected to the new large central building by extended wings. The final building was finished with brick and the inside renovated so that the two farmhouses could be used for cooking and domestic needs. Its final length facing the lake was nearly four hundred feet. The connecting wings were two stories in height and the central building considerably taller. The wings were given over to the students and guests, and the school itself was in the large center building. The structure was said to have cost the unprecedented sum of forty thousand dollars to build. It was named the Phylastery, the common term in utopian communities given to the place where the members of the community could assemble. The Raritan building quickly became one of the noted sights of the area. The school had a stream of visitors, and one of the first people Thoreau met on his arrival at the road that led from the wharf to the school was Elizabeth Peabody, a friend from Massachusetts.

Thoreau's letter opened:

> I arrived here, about 30 miles from N.Y. about 5 p.m Saturday, in company with Miss E. Peabody, who was returning in the same covered wagon from the landing to Eagleswood . . . This is a queer place—There is one large stone building, which cost some $40,000, in which I do not know exactly who or how many lurk—(one or two familiar faces, & now more familiar names have turned up)—a few shops and offices, an old farm house and Mr. Spring's perfectly private residence within twenty rods of the main building. "The City of Perth Amboy" is about as big as Concord and Eagleswood is 1¼ miles SW of it, on the bay side. The central fact here is evidently Mr. Weld's school— recently established—around which various other things revolve. Saturday evening I went to the school room, hall, or what not, to see the children & their teachers & patrons dance. Mr. Weld, a kind looking man with a long, white beard, danced with them, & Mr. Cutler, his assistant . . . Mr. Spring— and others. This Sat. eve dance is a regular thing, & it is thought strange if you don't attend. They take it for granted that you want *society*!
>
> Sunday forenoon I attended a sort of Quaker meeting at the same place— (The Quaker aspect and spirit prevails here—Mrs. Spring says "does thee not"?) where it was expected that the spirit would move me (I having been previously spoken to about it) & it, or something else, did, an inch or so. I said just enough to set them a little by the ears & and make it lively. I had excused myself by saying that I could not adapt myself to a particular audience, for all the speaking & lecturing here has reference to the children, who are not so bright as N. E. children. Imagine them sitting close to the wall all around a hall—with old Quaker looking men and women here and there.[6]

His friend Bronson Alcott protested against Thoreau's description of the Eagleswood student as not so bright, insisting that they were the equal of students he had observed in Concord. In another letter Thoreau also relented a little about his audience's sensibilities. The attendance at the evening entertainments was customary for all of the students, so Lucy and Ellen would have been among the group who came to hear him, seated in the shadows against the wall. Thoreau's second book, *Walden*, had been published the year before, but it had passed without notice for most of the reading public, and for his audience he was simply a somewhat disheveled-looking small, intense figure with a strange beard whom the children would never have heard of. Thoreau noted that he also saw the Grimkes among the crowd.

> There sat Mrs. Weld (Grimke) & her sister, two elderly grayheaded ladies, the former in extreme bloomer costume, which was what you may call remarkable.

The surveying job for which Thoreau had been hired was considerably more extensive and difficult than he expected. He was staying with the Springs in their house, which meant he was living in reasonable comfort, but being Thoreau he felt obliged in his letter to protest over his absence from Concord.

> I have been constantly engaged in surveying Eagleswood—through woods, ravines, marshes & along the shore, dodging the tide—through cat-bur mud & beggar ticks—having no time to look up or think where I am—(it takes 10 or 15 minutes before each meal to pick the beggar ticks out of my clothes—burrs & the rest are left—rents mended at the first convenient opportunity) I shall also be engaged here perhaps much longer. Mr. Spring wants me to help him about setting out an orchard & vineyard—Mr. Birney asks me to survey a small piece for him, & Mr. Alcott who has just come down here for the third Sunday—says that Greeley (I left my name for him) invites & me to go to his home with him next Saturday morning & spend the Sunday.
>
> It seems a twelve-month since I was not here—but I hope to get settled into my den again ere long. The hardest thing to find here is solitude & Concord.

For Lucy, just turned fourteen and away from home for the first time, the new friendship with Ellen and the easy companionship of her sister and other young women at the school became a busy new world that filled her days. Her sister, Annie, was sending the news home to Philadelphia, so Lucy seldom wrote herself. The winter months were unusually cold and like most adolescents away at school, Eagleswood's students spent many nights in each other's beds. They huddled together to keep warm under their bulky coverlets, with a breathless assurance that they were hidden away and could continue whispering long after they were supposed to be asleep. In the bitter cold of this hard winter there was even more temptation to ignore ordinary customs. In one diary entry Ellen wrote of being left helpless with laughter in bed the night before. She is less than clear about what happened, but what she seems to be describing is that Lucy had accidentally stepped into a chamber pot beside the bed as she was searching for a handkerchief she'd dropped in the darkness. It was a winter night and with the fire in the chimney only ashes, the room outside the warm nest of their blankets would have been icy cold. Ellen's diary entry was written on January 24th.

> We'd a great deal of fun last night in bed—I laughed 'til my sides ached! Luce on an exploring expedition after her handkerchief met with an accident not altogether pleasant to her pedal appendages—in fact rather cooling to the same—& there she had to sit in *laid up* [sic] until in spite of laughing, I contrived to light a match. . . .[7]

It is Lucy who appears most often in the pages of the diary, but there were also equally disheveled moments shared with Lucy's sister, Annie, who was also Ellen's cousin, and with the Motts' daughter, Ann, and Hattie Purvis, who were closer to her own age. The winter at the school passed quickly. Much of their days was taken with up with their schoolwork, and a few weeks later it was Lucy who found herself with a serious physical problem and had to break off the term. The exercises at the blackboard, her hours of music, and her efforts to continue her correspondence with her friends and family were finally too much for her eyes, and at the end of March she wrote to her father and mother telling them of her painful dilemma. Her father answered immediately with a letter that might have been sent by any worried parent today whose child has written to tell them about a difficult problem away at school.[8]

> April 3, 1857
> My dear Lucy,
>   This is not *the* letter; but is a note acknowledging the receipt of yours and saying that one draw-back upon the pleasure we had in reading it was the thought of the pain it must have caused you with your weak eyes to have written it. My dear, you must rest your eyes more. Reduce the number of your correspondents to 3, avoid the slate for the rest of the term and take

more exercise in the open air. If you are not careful you may ruin your eyes for ever. I am glad Mr. Weld is taking you in hand in this respect. If your eyes should continue weak and that verified . . . we may find it best to keep you from school and send Charlie in your place.

Affectionately

Ever

Father

Lucy left Eagleswood and returned home. For her first months back with her family she followed a strict regime of care and rest for her eyes. To distract her through the long hours her parents read to her. In a letter to her Irish friend Mary Byrne she described the family readings.

> . . . Do you read novels now? Mother has read me Nicholas Nickleby, & is now reading Dombey & Son. You know I don't read at all & depend entirely on Father & Mother for all enjoyment in that line. While mother was in Norristown [a family visit], father & I spent the evenings reading Plato & playing cards. I never heard any Plato before, & I enjoy it exceedingly. I made a splendid big cake while mother was away, and she acknowledged that it was better than hers. I consider it quite a feat as it was my first one.[9] . . .

Lucy's return to school was delayed in the fall to give her more time to recover, and when her eyes improved she began giving piano lessons. In a letter to her brother, Charlie, who was now ten and had replaced Lucy at Eagleswood, her mother wrote on October 26, 1857:

> "My very dear little son"
> . . . Lucy expects to begin the 1st of Nov. to teach music to a few scholars—I hope she will succeed in her efforts—she is hoping to make enough money to pay for her next year's schooling at Raritan . . . we have the piano in the library & Lucy plays every evening almost to us . . ."[10]

Lucy's teaching was to become an increasingly important part of her life over the coming years. She wrote about the lessons in her letter to Mary Byrne: "I am giving music lessons—perhaps you have heard,—I began on the first of November . . . So far I find it very pleasant." Lucy's first "scholars" were a young cousin and three other girls who were daughters of family friends. Her "music days" took her into Philadelphia where she was obliged to sleep over at another of the family's acquaintances for two nights, Tuesdays and Fridays, since the girls' houses were widely separated. To go from one house to another she wrote that it gave her "33 squares to walk."

◆ ◆ ◆

For many years it would be the world of European classical music that would absorb much of Lucy's interests. In her letters to Ellen she never wrote of hearing the singing of the black dock workers who loaded the ships tied to the Delaware River wharves, and if there were black churches singing what would later be called spirituals their music also went unnoticed. Like anyone who writes a great many letters, however, she sent different news to each of her friends, and she was reminded often by Ellen that she was mostly interested in people and families and in other students she knew. The music that Lucy mentioned in their letters was generally what she was playing and practicing at the moment, and the concerts she described were often classical recitals.

There is no way, however, that Lucy wouldn't have heard the jangling imitations of black song and dance that were an American theater staple and that made their way into most families' parlor entertainments. In the busy gatherings in their homes Lucy and her friends sang and played for each other, and from their letters it is clear that some of what they performed included songs from the minstrel shows. The black-face minstrel troupes were one of the most popular stage entertainments in the United States, and their popularity had spread throughout the world. When he was in his early teens Lucy's brother, Charlie, was already playing the banjo and the bones, the two distinctive instruments of the shows. Much of the comedy was a vicious parody of what was considered to be African American speech and mannerism, but the shows also included sentimental ballads that were intended to be depictions of slave life. Many of the best-known songs were written by the nation's most popular composer, Stephen Foster. Sheet music of Foster's songs like "Old Black Joe" or "Old Folks at Home" revolutionized the music publishing industry, with hundreds of thousands of copies being sold for parlor entertainment. His compositions became such a widely known representation of many Americans' view of slavery that, in an article in the influential music journal *Dwight's Journal*, published in Boston, the question of the article's title, "Who Wrote the Negro Songs?" was answered simply—Stephen Foster.[11]

Lucy's family seems to have had no objections to theater and dances, but the theaters in Philadelphia, perhaps because of its large Quaker population which supported emancipation and welcomed African Americans into their homes, offered only occasional evenings with the traveling minstrel troupes. In the late summer and the autumn of 1857, when she was at home and resting her eyes, the theaters had a variety of entertainment, and more often it was music and dance that would have encouraged her dedication to her piano studies in the European classical repertoire. Opera—generally in excerpts with small casts—was a staple on the city's stages, but it competed with serious drama, and also with widely varied programs of family musical entertainment. In the summer heat the entertainment was less ambitious. In early August the Walnut Street Theater was presenting Nagle's Juvenile Comedians:

Thirty in number, comprising
THE WREN FAMILY
THE BOONE CHILDREN
That beautiful
FAIRY WONDER
Little Julia Christine
And a gallery of lesser lights, forming a perfect
GALAXY OF INNOCENCE

Their performances were described as "a varied, chaste, and high-toned DRAMATIC AND MUSICAL ENTERTAINMENT."[12] The Academy of Music, at Broad and Locust streets, presented a series of Promenade Concerts "honored by *Enthusiasm, Popularity, and Fashion*." There were also Promenade Concerts at Parkinson's Illuminated Gardens, featuring Miss Agnes Sutherland, "the celebrated Scottish nightingale." The concerts included nightly fireworks. Two weeks later the Academy of Music offered the public the Ballet Troupe from the Theater Royale in Turin, Italy, while the Walnut Street Theater offered as competition Nagle's Juvenile Comedians presenting a sketch entitled "The Star Spangled Banner," followed by a burlesque sketch, "*Bombast en Furioso*." At Thomeuf's Varieties, at Fifth and Chestnut, "The coolest place in the city, and the most respectfully attended," there was a nightly "Musical and Terpsichorean Melange." Opera appeared again when the theaters were having less of a struggle with the heat. In the last week of August, Sanford's Opera House, on Eleventh Street above Chestnut, with Sanford's Opera Troupe of sixteen singers and dancers, presented *La Traviata*.

Although Philadephia had a busy professional world of freed blacks, only one of the theaters, Wheatley's Arch Street Theatre, advertised seating for "colored," which suggests that Wheatley's was the only theater offering these seats, since none of the other theaters included them in their notices in the amusement columns of the local newspapers. The prices were noticeably different from what white patrons were expected to pay. The orchestra stalls at Wheatley's for white patrons were 50 cents, Dress Circle (No Extra Charge for Secured Seats) 50 cents; Family Circle and Amphitheatre, 25 cents; Seats in Private Boxes, 75 cents; Whole Private Box, $3; Gallery 13 cents. Seats in the Gallery for Colored Persons were 25 cents and a Private Box in the Gallery for Colored Persons was 38 cents. Although it was a theater in which freed blacks were welcome there was no noticeable catering to what many whites considered black tastes. In August, while Lucy was sometimes in the city visiting friends, Wheatley's was presenting Shakespeare's *Richard III*, and the next month, when she was soon to begin giving her piano lessons and staying over, the stage was given to *Hamlet*.

It wasn't until November that an evening in two Philadelphia theaters featured what was now being termed "Ethiopian" entertainment. Buckley's Serenaders, who were one of the most popular minstrel troupes in the country, appeared at the National Theater on November 16, advertising "Ethiopian Minstrelsy and Dancing." The company was known for their black face parodies of well-known operas, and the night's piece was Bellini's *Sonnambula*. For their appearance the price of seats was set at 25 cents for the entire house, to guarantee a large audience. Also on the program was a musical sketch, "Life on the Mississippi," featuring Miss C. Hiffert as Dinah. To take advantage of the Buckley troupe's popularity the operatic cast at Sanford's Opera House presented their own "Ethiopian Performances." It was described as "Ethiopian Life Illustrated by Sanford's Troupe of Stars—New Dances by the Sanford Children."

◆ ◆ ◆

Lucy was old enough now to take part in many of the activities of the antislavery groups, which all of the abolitionists' children accepted naturally as part of their family responsibilities. For many years the antislavery societies across the North had been holding popular antislavery fairs, which sold abolitionist books and pamphlets and goods made without slave labor to raise money. For the children the fairs were simply lively chances to meet friends they had grown up with and looked forward to seeing every year. In her letter Lucy told Mary Byrne that she had worked at the book table as a sales person and she felt that sales had been very satisfactory, "considering how hard the times are."

Lucy had also begun to accompany her father to some of the meetings and dinners that were part of the intense work life of the antislavery community. Most of the notable figures of the movement, including Wendell Phillips and the Purvises, could be expected to visit the Motts, and often she was among the dinner guests. Lucy was well enough to visit Eagleswood for a noisy, blissful Christmas holiday, joining her brother and sister and seeing many of her friends from the previous year. The visit was also mentioned in her letter to Mary Byrne.

> ... I went on to Eagleswood to spend Christmas and New Year. I had a splendid time, and I was delighted to see them all. Annie & Charlie enjoyed the contents of my trunk almost as much as they did seeing me. I took each of them one of those flour bags filled with cakes ... some home made molasses candy, besides other good things which only children at school can appreciate. However nothing lasted a whole day, everything was divided among the rest, & such a hubbub as they made I never heard.

The next fall, in 1858, Lucy would soon be sixteen and she was finally able to return to Eagleswood, but now as a teacher, so it was possible for her father to send her younger brother, Charlie, to the school at the same time. Her older sister, Annie, was there with her, and she also had teaching duties. On her return Lucy picked up her correspondence with Ellen, writing her a few days after her arrival. Their habit of writing each other almost daily had languished over the many months that Lucy had suffered from the problems with her eyes, and they took up their pens again with some awkwardness. Ellen considered the long silence to be entirely Lucy's fault, while Lucy felt that Ellen had to bear at least some of the blame, but with her usual unwillingness to let herself be annoyed over something for any length of time Lucy proposed simply that they just start again. Her letter also was a high-spirited sign of her pleasure at being back at school – with very little pretense of seriousness.[13]

> Eagleswood Nov. 12th 1858
> So you thought you were a fool for writing to me! Well, we were wont to differ sometimes on certain subjects! Dear Nell neither have you written to me during these long months. Longer to me than to you, who was able to read, write and sew. Yes, here I am again at Eagleswood with only two studies, Latin and Music, and yet so busy that I can hardly get time to turn around. Industry is indigenous to this place! I have ten scholars, take lessons on the violin, practice an hour on the piano, [work with the school's

artistic society], & Eagleswood band, ditto, write compositions & speak, and do a variety of other things too innumerable to mention. This sketch of my daily life may not be interesting to you, and if you please we will resume our intercourse just where we left off, and not count the many stitches that have been dropped in our separate histories. Yet our relations will be somewhat changed, the office of Mentor which I so unworthily filled, I will resign with pleasure. You are now 18, and with the wisdom acquired in the partial retirement of last year you can easily dispense with the mock heroic advice of a girl just launched into the follies and sentimentalities of her sweet sixteenth year! Don't imagine me satirical. I assure you that folly I have renounced long since, now I am only humble.

Having duly considered myself & my personal relations, it now behooves me to inquire after your welfare. How art Ell? Physically robustious, I hope,—intellectually advanced, I suppose,—morally happy, I am sure. How glad I shall be to see you. (There's the bell!) My last recollection of you is as you woke in the morning of July 23rd 1857. Farewell darling, if I had more time I could not say anything else worth your perusal, (I don't mean to convey the idea that what I have written is) so until we meet.

Your affect. friend
Lucy Mc

In the long, full, vital years of their friendship it was the only time they seriously came close to a quarrel. Lucy's own unquenchable joy at her return to Eagleswood was reflected in a hurried note about a music rehearsal with two other students that she added to another of the letters to Ellen a few weeks later.[14]

Russell Bellows, and Annie Solman & I have just been playing a fugue of Bach's. R. on violin, A. on melodia, myself on piano. It is splenderific!.

4

Scattering the seed

Hanging from the beam,
Slowly swaying (such the law)
Gaunt the shadow on the green,
Shenandoah!
The cut is on the crown
(Lo, John Brown)
And the stabs shall heal no more.

Hidden in the cap
Is the anguish none can draw,
So your future veils its face,
Shenandoah!
But the streaming beard is shown
(Weird John Brown)
The meteor of the war.

"The Portent"
—Herman Melville

In the spring and summer of 1859 Eagleswood filled the days for Lucy and her younger brother, Charlie. In the confusing procession of the Wrights and the McKims at the school, Annie, their older sister, was not there for the spring term, nor was Ellen Wright, though Ellen's younger brother, Willie, was. Away from home for the term, Charlie, now eleven years old, was beginning to make himself heard in the family. In answer to a letter from Annie in Philadelphia he produced an earnest account of his membership in one of the school's boat clubs, and his carefully studied note makes it clear that for many students there was a vigorous calendar of daily activities going on outside of the music classes and the tutoring that took up Lucy's days.[1]

> April 10, 1859
> My dear Sister,
>   I received your long and interesting letter the other evening. Father and Mother did not get my letter till Thursday did they? The girls have got their boat at the dock; it is longer than the Argo and narrower. There will be four boat clubs here this summer counting ours. Our uniform is to be red shirts with black trimming . . . Our boat is black with a red stripe around her. We have not got her yet, but we have decided upon the color . . . Lucy read Mother's and Father's letters in school today. Goodbye your affectionate brother
>   Charlie

His closest friend in school was Frank Garrison, the youngest son of the abolitionist leader William Lloyd Garrison. Wherever the abolitionists' children found themselves, the ties of family continued to draw them together. Despite the hot summer, Lucy stayed on at Eagleswood into July, excitedly immersed in rehearsals for a celebration of the school's tenth anniversary, which would be part of the annual "exhibition" of the school's offerings for prospective students and their families. Lucy was rehearsing for a series of stage presentations—one a scene from *Richard III*—as a member of the school's art club, Gamma Sigma. Her letter included detailed descriptions of some of the costumes. She was equally engaged in the rehearsals for an ambitious musical program. Annie was back in the school to take part and they would be performing together. For many of the students the anniversary was a grand event. One of them who was not there, however, was Ellen, and despite all of the hurry and excitement she was missed. Lucy somehow found time to write her a long letter which she started on July 9, but had to break off after a single sentence before she was able to turn to it again the next day.[2]

> Eagleswood, July 9, 1859
> Dear Elle
>   No, I have not excommunicated you from my list, but the force of circumstances has very nearly July 10th. As you see. And so you and Anna [Davis] are not coming to the Anniversary. It is too bad. I can't promise you a great result, but I can testify as to the magnitude of the preparations, & to my (mental) fatigue even more, two weeks before the time. Gamma Sigma, at any rate will be good, the programmes & their promises are charming. . . .

The program Lucy described would have been representative of the ambitious offerings of any school with advanced students at the time, without any references to what some of the spectators would regard as Eaglewood's more disturbing tendencies. There would be an oration, which hadn't yet been furnished to the speaker, but "which report already declares will immortalize its author" and an ode "which is swell, since I've seen it." The recitations would be followed by a "grand dinner" which Lucy had arranged to be served in their parlor. "Room to be decorated in greenery and flowers, members in purple and white."

Lucy continued with an abrupt change of topic. "So much for the Society, now for the concert Programme, which will be given the same day."

It was an ambitious concert, presented by the music teacher at the school, Friedrich Mollenhauer. When Lucy returned for the fall term in 1859 she had begun studying the violin with him, adding the new instrument to her already crowded schedule of classes and piano practice. Mollenhauer was a widely known and highly regarded musician who had been trained in Germany. He had known many of the composers of his day, among them Hummel, Spohr, Mendelssohn, and Schumann, before coming as the member of an orchestra to the United States in 1853. He was determined to show his pupils at their best, and at the same time to present his young son, Emil Mollenhauer, who also was studying the violin. Emil later enjoyed a distinguished career as violinist, pianist, and band arranger and for many years as the leader of the Boston Municipal Band. Frederick himself and his brother were credited with having established the musical conservatory system in the United States, and after leaving Eagleswood he was for many years active as a performer and teacher in New York City. For Lucy to appear in concert with someone of this level makes it clear that both she and her sister were more than competent home musicians.

The lengthy program Mollenhauer had chosen included piano duets, some with Lucy and Annie as the pianists. There were also several technical showpieces for piano solo, among them "Foam of Champagne," played by "L.Mc," which was followed by a solo played by Mollenhauer, "accom. avec piano a me." To conclude the concert Mollenhauer had rehearsed an orchestra of three of the students and himself and his son playing the violins and Lucy and another young woman student playing two pianos. They rehearsed every day after school in Lucy's parlor, and her decided judgment was, "It is jolly."

In a rush to tell Ellen of all of her activities, she included a description of the school's program on the 4th of July, the week before.

... Oh, Lor.' We had a grand time on the 4th, even better than last year. Seven
boats left E. dock at 9 o'clock for the Regatta. But Annie will tell you all about
it—the beautiful costumes & floral decorations—the presentation of flags,
the elegant speeches, the admiring crowd, &c. &c. We came back at 2½ P.M
with faces—well, red flannel looked pale beside my nose. Everybody has been
skinning this last week. Lots of celebrities here among the rest ... visitors
swarm, not only Wednesdays and Saturdays, but daily. ... Everybody is learning to swim & boating has not lost its charms in spite of the heat.

She ended her feverish account of the school's celebration remembering that she wanted to tell Ellen that she'd had an opportunity to become
better acquainted with the music teacher.

... Oh, I mustn't forget to tell you that I spent last Wednesday at Mr. Mollenhauer's. I went down in the morning & came up just in time for supper. You
know he can't write music, & I went down to copy a piece he was composing.
We had a nice little French dinner ... played some, & talked a great deal. Mr.
Mollenhauer is a prodigy! I never talk with him without being astonished
at some new quality—virtue of mind or of heart. Mrs. M. was lovely & the
children an interesting distraction. I am quite enthusiastic about them. Mr. &
Mrs. walked up with me.

Lucy's music and her ambition to become a pianist were becoming
increasingly the focus of her activities, and with the encouragement of
Mollenhauer and her other teachers she would continue to dedicate hours
of her days to the piano. After she left the school Mollenhauer would contact her again to appear with him in further performances.

◆ ◆ ◆

After the excitements of the summer it was considered to be definitely
decided that Lucy would return to Eagleswood to teach her classes for the
fall term. To the surprise of the Welds, however, at the end of the anniversary celebrations and the summer's exhibition she returned to Philadelphia. Ellen, who had visited the school, wrote to her sister Eliza saying that
Mr. Weld had been very anxious she should remain and teach, but Lucy
"considers that her duty lies elsewhere, & will study at home."[3] Nothing in
Lucy's letters to Ellen gives any reason for her decision, but she had been
overburdened with classes and rehearsals at the school, and perhaps she
wanted more time for her own practicing. A more likely reason was that

her father had just purchased a house not far from the center of German-town, in Philadelphia's northwestern suburbs, and their move took even more of her time with the endless packing and sorting. When she wrote to Ellen five months later on February 18, 1860, it was from their new address and she was planning to return to her piano. She told Ellen that she had visited one of Ellen's old teachers, Gustave Blessner, but "he wouldn't give me one lesson a week & as I can't take two, I am going to Ben Cross."[4]

With a new teacher, Lucy could continue her studies, and if she found a few small "scholars" it might be possible for her to earn enough money to return to Eagleswood. During these months she was almost wholly concentrated on her music, although she was aware that there was little chance that she could make playing a career. It was not considered proper for young women of her social background to perform as professionals, and if they could find no other way to continue their playing, the answer for many of them was to become one more of the anonymous army of piano teachers who were part of the everyday American scene, walking with their music folios as they went from one scholar's home to another. They still had their music, but the price they paid was a scant income for guiding the small fingers of children of other women of their own age who had married. Everything Lucy learned in her years of music study, however, from the hours of practice and performing to the arduous hours of music copying, would finally come to be one of her life's important resources.

◆ ◆ ◆

As the weeks passed of the early fall, there was no way Lucy could have known that events outside of her domestic world would change every-thing she expected of her future, and at the same moment would cast its long shadow over the nation's fate. On the morning of October 16, 1859, the militant abolitionist John Brown led his small group of followers in an attack on the federal armory, a storehouse for military weapons, in Harpers Ferry in what was then still western Virginia. Brown had been persuaded by the arguments of one of his men that if their raid on the armory was successful they could distribute the weapons stored there to the crowds of slaves who would surely rush to join them. With the flight of slaves from their plantations to swell his ranks as they marched deeper into the South, the hated institution of slavery itself would collapse. There were one hundred thousand muskets in the armory, and if so many weap-ons were to fall into the hands of his band, it seemed momentarily pos-sible that the plan somehow could succeed.

Brown's men had delayed their attack waiting for a shipment of weapons coming from their northern supporters so that they would have some arms for the slaves whatever the result of their raid. These "pikes," as they were termed, were a thousand long staves fitted with knife blades at their tips, in essence African war spears, paid for by the small, secretive group of Boston activists who were Brown's main financial support. In the months that followed it would be these pikes that would fasten in the public's imagination.

The only part of the plan that succeeded was the attack on the armory. The town was taken unaware. Slipping into the empty streets early in the morning, Brown's men cut the town's telegraph wires, and there was only a watchman guarding the armory itself. With the first exchange of gunfire at the approach of a train to the town, however, the townspeople immediately armed themselves and turned on the attackers. Brown and his group of only eighteen followers were driven into the armory compound. Local farmers hurried to join the men from the town, firing at the armory from the surrounding hills. A force of federal marines reached the scene the next day under the command of Colonel Robert E. Lee. Before Lee's arrival one of Brown's three sons who was with him attempted to negotiate with the townspeople, leaving the armory with a second man under a white flag. In the fevered tide of emotion that had swept through the crowd now surrounding the armory the two men were shot dead before they could speak. Brown witnessed their deaths through gaps in the armory's walls, but he refused to surrender and in a rush the troops broke in the door. In the exchange of fire inside the armory a second son of Brown's was killed at his feet, and Brown himself was clubbed to the ground as he was seized.

It was a foregone conclusion that following a trial Brown and the men who had been captured with him would be hanged, but the raid and his attempt to free the slaves, however poorly planned and ill-advised, aroused a storm of emotion throughout the nation. His act exposed the fragility of the uneasy calm that had been preserved by the long series of evasions and compromises that had kept the two now bitterly divided sections of the country from turning to war to decide the issue of slavery. Brown was convicted of treason, of the murder of five townspeople killed in the attack, and of incitement to rebellion. He was sentenced to death on November 2.

In his final court appearance Brown was permitted to speak, and although later he excused what he felt was the inadequacy of his talk by saying he had not had time to prepare, his words gave a deeper resonance to the poorly conceived raid, the purposes of which still were clouded in confusion and misunderstanding. The reaction in the North to his words was so immediate and his presentation of his cause as obedience to the word of God so profound that ultimately it was widely felt that it was his words that made the war inevitable.[5]

> ... This Court acknowledges ... I suppose, the validity of the law of God. I see a book kissed, which I suppose to be the Bible, or at least the New Testament, which teaches me that all things "whatsoever I would that men should do to me, I should do even so to them." It reaches me, further, to "remember them that are in bonds as bound with them." I endeavored to act upon these instructions. I am yet too young to understand that God is a respecter of persons. I believe that to have interfered as I have done, as I have always freely admitted I have done, on behalf of His despised poor, I did not wrong, but right. Now, if it is necessary that I should forfeit my life for the furtherance of the ends of justice, and mingle my blood further with the blood of my children, and with the blood of millions in this slave country whose rights are disregarded by wicked, cruel, and unjust enactments, I submit, so let it be.

One of the purposes of Brown's trial had been to determine whether there was a conspiracy on the part of northern abolitionists to bring about rebellion in the South. It was clear that Brown had been given financial support by the group of Boston supporters, and that the weapons for the raid had been supplied by people sympathetic with his cause. Though the court failed to produce evidence of a conspiracy, everywhere across the South there was a passionate conviction that the raid was part of a wider effort to bring about slave rebellion. There were mass meetings, militia groups were quickly formed, and there was a dangerous hostility to anyone showing abolitionist sympathies. Newspaper after newspaper published crude drawings of slaves armed with the despised pikes. In the North the mood was one of confusion and uncertainty, since few people believed that the violence of Brown's raid was justified, even though there was widespread opposition to slavery.

James McKim knew of Brown from his earlier role in the bloody battles that had been fought over the issue of slavery in the Kansas territory, and although it is not known if they met he was aware of their shared feelings as abolitionists. McKim himself had never considered armed rebellion as an answer to the problem of slavery, but he was in sympathy with Brown and what he had attempted to do. McKim was not alone. On November 2, the day of Brown's sentencing, a circular appeared in Boston and copies made their way to antislavery offices throughout the country. The copy

Lucy's father received was sent him by Thomas Wentworth Higginson. The circular's intent was to raise money in support of Brown and the men on trial with him. "*Every moment is precious*," it read in part, "and whatever is done must be done now." Signing the document were two prominent Boston supporters of the abolitionist cause, Higginson and Ralph Waldo Emerson.

The situation in western Virginia became increasingly chaotic. Every effort was made to prevent abolitionists from reaching Harpers Ferry or nearby Charles Town, where the trial was being held. A report in the *New York Times* on December 1, 1859, described the tension.[6]

> Today several persons, editors of the Abolition papers published in the North, were evicted from the cars at Harpers Ferry. They had purchased tickets and were very anxious to proceed, but were retained on account of the arrangement entered into between Gov. Wise and the President of the road. They left in the Washington train, declaring they were bound to be in Charles Town to see the execution, and would reach there by the Orange and Alexander road, whereupon the President of that road was informed of the fact.

Heaping further fuel on the already inflammatory situation was the decision on the part of Virginia's governor, Henry A. Wise, to allow Brown to correspond from his cell with members of the press and some of his supporters. A continual stream of stories made their way to newspapers throughout the country, and there was growing sympathy for Brown, who spoke firmly of his personal convictions and of his certainty of the justice of his cause. Particularly heartening for many sympathizers was the increasingly Christian tone of his missives.

In the early days of his imprisonment there was uncertainty over the whereabouts of his wife, Mary A. Brown. She had left their home in northern New York State and was attempting to make her way to her husband's side, but she had broken her journey. On November 5 Higginson urgently sent word to McKim, copying a telegram he had received from George Sennott, a lawyer who was acting for the prisoners. The text of the telegram read[7]:

> Harper's Ferry. To Mrs John Brown or T. W. Higginson.
> Mr. Brown says for God's sake don't let Mrs. Brown come. Send her word by telegraph wherever she is.
>   Geo. Sennott

Higginson expressed his concern at what the message might mean.

> This I cannot yet explain, but I hv. telegraphed Mr. Sennott to write *reasons* by express.

Higginson continued with his note, describing the impression Mrs. Brown made on the people she met on her way, as she hoped, to be with her husband.

> Mrs. Brown was received with great sympathy in Boston & by her simplicity and dignity made cordial friends. She has money enough, at least for the present—but the demands upon us, in that way, are great, & any help to her will be clear gain. Her family whom I hv. just visited, need much help: they are the noblest people on earth.

What McKim could tell Higginson was that Brown's wife had reached Philadelphia and for the time she was remaining with friends, though he neglected to say that the friends she was staying with were McKim and his family. Higginson wrote again on November 9:

> Please give my love to Mrs. Brown, who had best be guided by your advice and by what she hears from Va. as to returning. If she is staying with friends, there is no harm in her remaining for the month, but it is a pity that she should spend her money at hotels—or be a burden on any one.
>
> Please tell her that I wrote two long letters to her children last week and enclosed $25.00 & I shall write again this week.

The morning after his previous letter Higginson hurriedly wrote to McKim with later news. Those who felt some responsibility for Brown and for his action had drawn closely together to aid each other against whatever they faced over the next weeks, and any word was immediately passed from one to the other. Higginson had just received a letter from a Doctor Howe, one of the men with Brown, and it copied a message Brown had sent to both Doctor Howe and to Higginson explaining his reluctance to have his wife travel to Harpers Ferry. Many of the passages had been underlined, some with double underlining.[8]

> If my wife were to come here just now it would *only tend* to distract her mind ten fold [double underlined], & would only add to my affliction; and cannot

possibly do her *any good*. It will also use up the scanty means she has to supply Bread & cheap but comfortable clothing, fuel, etc for herself & children,
through the winter. *Do persuade* her to remain *at home* for a time (at least)
till she can learn further from me. She will receive a thousand times the consolation at home that she can possibly find anywhere here. . . . I ask her to
compose *her mind* & to remain quiet until the last of *this month*: out of pity
to me. I can certainly judge in this matter better than any one else [last three
words double underlined]. My warmest thanks to yourself & all other kind
friends. God bless you all [double underlined]. Please *send this to my afflicted
wife* by first possible conveyance.

    Your friend in truth.

    John Brown

Higginson added a note:

> This is a most beautiful and affectionate letter, and though it may be hard for
> her to bear this delay, it must be comforting to know how tenderly he thinks
> of her.

Lucy, at Eagleswood, certainly knew of the situation, but there was no correspondence between her and Ellen referring to the mood in the house
during these tense days. Like all abolitionist children she had early learned
that there were many things that were not to be spoken of, which probably explains her silence. For a few days McKim considered sending Mrs.
Brown to Eagleswood, where the school's sympathetic teachers could offer
her their own comfort, but finally the decision was made for her to remain
in Philadelphia with McKim and his wife, Sarah, with both daughters and
young Charlie staying at the school.

Higginson wrote again on November 12:

> In consigning Mrs. Brown to your care I of course hoped that she would be
> guided by your judgement; although of course neither you nor I can claim
> any authority over her. It may be well enough for her to go for a few days to
> Eagleswood (for the more friends she makes the better)—but certainly Phila-
> delphia is the best place for her to remain. There she will be sure of friends &
> good advice, & will also be in the best position for communicating with her
> husband & her friends.

Hoping to reassure Brown that his wife was well, on November 25
McKim sent him a solicitious account of her sojourn in Philadelphia.

Dear John Brown,

It will comfort you to know that your wife has borne this part of her trial with becoming fortitude. Her behavior is the admiration of all who have opportunities of observing her. She is calm without insensibility, tender without weakness, sorrowful but not as one without hope. Her hope however is not that you will be pardoned or reprieved, or your sentence commuted, but that the brief moment of your life on earth will be so spent as that its influence, added to that of your example & preaching up to this time will not only accrue to benefit, but precipitate the *triumph* of the great cause which you have so long had at heart.

She is still an inmate at my house, though is intending as I before wrote you to spend a day or two with Mrs. Mott. Yesterday she accompanied me (it was Thanksgiving Day) to the church of the Rev. Furness; and was greatly refreshed & comforted. The prayers, the hymns, the sermon were all just what she could have desired. As we were coming out it was discovered accidently that she was present, and large numbers came around her with their eyes overflowing with sympathy to shake her by the hand and say "God bless you."

She reads of course with avidity every thing that has been [written] concerning you . . . Your letter to Mr. Vail gave her the greatest pleasure, but your allusion in it to your "two noble boys" quite broke her down . . . .

Others were also concerned for Mrs. Brown, among them the most prominent of the abolitionist activists, William Lloyd Garrison, who was close to the McKims and contacted him about her whereabouts. McKim answered Garrison on November 25, telling him, "Mrs. Brown has been at my house all this week. The more we see of her the more we like her."

◆ ◆ ◆

The days were filled with rumors wildly circulating in the South about perceived plots to free Brown and to incite the long-feared slave rebellion. In the North the sympathy for Brown grew as the newspapers everywhere circulated letters and tales passed on from people who had spoken to him in his cell. Another difficulty emerged for Lucy's father and the people close to Mrs. Brown. It was now obvious that the disposal of Brown's body was a sensitive and troubling issue. If it were to be claimed by radical abolitionists there was the risk that Brown's remains would be exhibited publicly, and Brown would be hailed by crowds drawn to spectacle as a martyr to his cause. If, on the other hand, it were to come into the hands of pro-slavery groups there was the likelihood that the body would be mutilated and possibly even burned, which would only serve to intensify the sympathies of the North. The newspapers were already spreading rumors that Brown's remaining son might journey to Charles Town to claim the body, which he denied.

In Philadelphia McKim helped Mrs. Brown compose a letter to Governor Wise, and it was sent on November 21, ten days before the hanging. In the letter she appealed to what they had perceived of Wise's lenient attitude toward his prisoner.[9]

> I am made bold to address you by my trust in your feelings as a man & by reports that have come to me of the respectful words you have spoken of my husband now under sentence of death in your State.
>
> I ask for myself & my children that when all shall be over, the mortal remains of my husband & his sons may be delivered to me for decent & tender internment among their kindred.
>
> I do not ask for his life, dear as it is to us, and right honorable as I know him to be. I am perfectly aware that, if public considerations cannot avert his doom, private feelings, however agonized, will not be allowed the slightest weight.
>
> In the letters which I have received from him there is not a word expressing a desire that I should ask for his life. But he tells me that if, after he is no more, I think it fit to come to Virginia "to gather up the bones of my beloved sons" & my "husband" it will be well.
>
> I ask, Sir, for the exertion of your authority and personal influence in furthering this most earnest desire.
>
> Little as it is that I ask, if you will grant my request, your humanity in this particular shall have the sincerest thanks of his afflicted wife and children.
>
> Mary A. Brown

The copy of the letter in the McKim papers is in his handwriting. On November 29 he was able to inform Brown that Governor Wise had granted her request. At the same time he wrote to Brown to confirm that funds Brown had sent for his wife's care had arrived and been given to her, adding, "Your letters are her greatest solace."

◆ ◆ ◆

In his messages to his wife Brown had always made it clear that it was his intention that she should join him in the last days of his imprisonment, and she began making preparations to travel to Harpers Ferry to be with him before the execution. The situation in Harpers Ferry was now a maelstrom of suspicion, rumors, anger, and intense anticipation. Everyone around Mrs. Brown realized that it was not a situation she should have to face alone, and it was immediately decided that Lucy's father should travel with her, and see to the details of her stay. It was quickly obvious that Mrs. Brown would need a woman to be with her as well, and Lucy's mother, Sarah, joined her husband.

The small party traveled by train through Baltimore, and in Harpers Ferry they found the mood of the people even more tense than they had anticipated. In the family's memories of their days there McKim told them on his return that they were fired upon in the streets.[10] She was allowed to have a final supper with Brown in his cell, but when she was not permitted to spend the night with him, Brown, for the only moment in his ordeal, showed emotional distress.

Brown's last statement, written on the morning of December 2, hours before his hanging, was a harsh foreboding of the violence he now could see awaited the nation.

> I, John Brown, am now quite certain that the crime of this guilty land will never be purged away but with blood.

The hanging, coming after so many weeks of emotional turmoil, traumatized the nation. In the North bells were rung in honor of Brown's death as a martyr to the antislavery cause and the newspapers were filled with articles discussing the events at Harpers Ferry and the sentencing of Brown and his men. In Concord the town's selectmen decided that the town would not show honor to Brown, but Thoreau rang the bell of the church himself, defying—as he had often done before—the wishes of the town's more conservative people. For the South every act honoring Brown was further evidence of the North's implacable hatred of what they considered was a way of life acknowledged and justified in the nation's Constitution, and there were cries for secession, which would become increasingly shrill in the coming months. Perhaps the most emotional statement honoring Brown's act was made later by the ex-slave and fervent abolitionist Frederick Douglass:

> His zeal in the cause of my race was far greater than mine—it was as the burning sun to my taper light—mine was bounded by time, his stretched away to the boundless shores of eternity. I could live for the slave, but he could die for him.[11]

Brown was led from the prison under tight guard with no possibility for anyone to approach him. A drawing published in a popular New York illustrated journal shows the gallows in the center of an empty parade ground with the troops stationed at a distance away, leaving the ground open around the gallows.[12] Brown had refused to have a minister with him, dismissing any who were offered as tainted by their implicit acceptance of slavery.

Twelve days after his hanging the inflammatory poem "Brown of Ossawatomie" by the fiery Quaker abolitionist and popular poet John Greenleaf Whittier made its first appearance in print. Overnight it was spread throughout the nation by the local newspapers that were published in every community. The title referred to Brown's attempt with a small force to defend the town of Osawatomie in Kansas from an attack by a much larger pro-slavery force attempting to invade the territory from Missouri. The poem appeared at a time when there were no copyright restrictions on the local newspapers that reached virtually every American household and within days the poem came to serve as a definition of the nation's emotions over the traumatic events. The most often quoted stanzas described Brown being led to the gallows, but stopping to kiss a small child held up to him by a slave mother.

John Brown of Ossawatomie spake on his dying day:
"I will not have to shrive my soul a priest in Slavery's pay
But let some poor slave mother whom I have striven to set free,
With her children from the gallows-stair put up a prayer for me!"

John Brown of Ossawatomie, they led him out to die;
And lo! a poor slave mother with her little child pressed nigh.
Then the bold, blue eyes grew tender and the old harsh face grew mild
As he stooped between the jeering ranks and kissed the negro's child.

The shadows of his stormy life that moment fell apart
And they who blamed the deed forgave the loving heart;
That kiss from all the guilty means redeemed the good intent,
And round the grisly fighter's hair the martyr's aureole bent!

The appearance of Whittier's poem served to give its countless readers an emotional image that justified whatever Brown and his small band might have done. Although there was no meeting of Brown and a slave mother as he was led under tight military guard to his death, the poem and the celebrated painting by Thomas Hovenden of the scene became an indelible part of the lore that surrounds the events. Illustrations of

Brown's embrace of the slave child based on Hovenden's painting have appeared in countless forms since that time. For many who were swept up in the drama of the events there was an absolute certainty that if Brown had not been surrounded by troops he could have been approached by a slave mother and he would have kissed an offered child. It took only a moment of emotional need to substitute "it could have happened" with "that *is* what happened."

◆ ◆ ◆

The newspaper notices of the journey of Mrs. Brown and the McKims away from Harpers Ferry with Brown's body were brief and without comment. It was almost as though there had been so much emotion that for the moment there was nothing left to express. Sarah McKim left them at Baltimore and returned to Philadelphia, while her husband continued on with Mrs. Brown to North Elba, the village in northern New York State where the family burial plot lay. There would continue to be an outpouring of support for her by the antislavery activists and money raised for the family by subscription and by the sales of writing offered in Brown's defense. On February 12, 1861, Mrs. Brown wrote again to Lucy's father[13]:

> Mr. McKim, Dear Friend.
>   Your kind and welcome letter of Dec. 2 was received in due time and I can not tell you how glad I was to hear from you once more, although I have neglected to answer it sooner ... I would express again my sincere gratitude to you for going with me to Baltimore and then to Harper's Ferry and returning home with me at that time in my affliction. I hope me or my family never forget.

The other members of the group who had been captured with Brown were also hanged, but the executions took place over the next four months. Two of the men, Aaron Stevens and Albert Hazlett, were not hanged until March 16, and they were befriended by people from Eagleswood during their imprisonment. It was arranged for their bodies to be turned over to the school, and the night before his hanging Hazlett wrote to Rebecca Spring. "Your letter gave me great comfort to know that my body would be taken from this land of chains ..."[14] Following their execution a woman from the school who had been with them in the final weeks returned with their bodies, and the two men were buried in a quiet ceremony in the school's small cemetery. Brown's prophecy that slavery would only be abolished "with blood" hung over the nation. The seeds of mistrust and suspicion between the two societies, the slaveholders of the South and the freemen of the North, had been scattered everywhere there were newspapers or the telegraph, and now fueled with the emotions raised by Brown and his hanging the seeds would ripen to harvest.

◆ ◆ ◆

In the months that followed, the country was rocked by the turbulence that followed Brown's execution. The months of his imprisonment and the bitter debate that raged in the nation's newspapers had exposed the hypocrisies of the uneasy compromises that had kept the country united. The South couldn't forget what his plan represented, and in the southern press there were continued angry references to the thousand pikes that Brown intended to use to arm the slaves. For women like Lucy and Ellen there was also the reality that whatever they might feel about the wrangling debates, they would never be allowed to participate in any of the decisions that would result. They could only continue their lives with as much calm as they could muster.

In the winter of 1860 Lucy visited Eagleswood for a rehearsal of the art club's extravagant production, *The Rival Queens and The Lady of the Bedchamber*. She wrote to Ellen on February 18 to give her the minute details of costuming and the boisterous rehearsals. Her letter opened with a description of the trip from her home to the school, and it is a richly detailed glimpse of her winter journey through Philadelphia's dark, silent streets, and the jubilant chaos that awaited her.

> Hilltop Feb 18th 1860
> Dear Eleanor,
> Father handed me your letter the evening previous to my departure for Eagleswood. You know that I had put off going for a week on acc't of a letter rec'd from Annie telling me that they were sick and wouldn't be ready at the time originally appointed. So a week ago yesterday morn I set off; and, taking it for granted that you are in your usual indulgent humor, I mean to give you a description of the whole thing from the starting point. You recollect how frightfully windy it was that day—well, I had the full benefit of it from 4½ A.M. to 12 M. I had staid all night at Gibbons's, so as to be on time for the 6 o'clock boat the next morning. Half an hour before the time I set out alone for Walnut Street wharf. The city did look magnificent. At the Exchange I positively had to set down my valise & take a good look. It was

three hours before dawn and the moon was shining brilliantly. The side
on which I walked lay in deep shadow, while the opposite was illuminated.
Not a soul was stirring, which seemed so queer down in those streets usually so crowded and bustling. Do you remember the shape of Dock street
[she included a small sketch]? Well, it looked like Bagdad (vide Arabian
nights entertainment). Dirt luckily doesn't show in moonlight, & the architecture of some of those buildings is really fine. But the wind roared as if
Aeolus' *Wind Depot.* (it's well to Americanize where you can) was about
two squares up Walnut. My skirts danced the worst kinds of tarantellas, &
my feet would willingly have joined in an Irish jig, had not (fortunately)
[they'd been] weighted a little this side of 20 stone. But if I don't hurry, I
shall never get to Eagleswood. We reached Perth Amboy without any trouble, other than delays caused by fallen trees, ice in the river &c. &c.... Now
please skip over a few hours; imagine me duly arrived, & seated in the Hall
of Gamma Sigma, where eight or ten Persians in various stages of undress,
are reclining or standing about; some making gold goblets out of gilt foil,
others practicing stabbing, others planning gorgeous turbans out of very
limited material. A Queen is sewing a muslin train in a state of desperation
& an old woman is quavering her sorrow over her disobedient children.
When the old woman stops the Conqueror of the World squirms on a narrow sofy [sic] in the agonies of slow poison, or tries how gracefully he can
kill an old man his tried friend with a little wooden stick called by courtesy
a javelin....[15]

Perhaps Ellen, who was two years older than Lucy, felt herself a little
beyond the high spirits of a rehearsal for a school pageant, but she often
dreamed of emulating Lucy's determination to become a pianist. On May
14, 1860, she wrote to Lucy to tell her of a more complicated moment with
a music teacher named Robert Neustadt, but ended with her more usual
spirited account of the immediate excitements of a visit to friends.

My dearest Luce,
 ... Let's say something about Bob Neustadt, Yesterday afternoon was there
at 4, stayed to tea, and himself waited upon me home at 9. If I didn't have a
treat in music—He played, & I played: and when he left me at Mr. Gibbon's
door, he said—If you will allow me to kiss you Miss Ellie! and he *did* kiss
me—Was it because I loved his music? ...
 I stayed two nights at Gibbons—slept one night with Sallie, & once with
Julie—they are *splendid,* and Mrs. Gibbons gave me a most cordial invitation
to come again at any time.[16]

In Philadelphia Lucy spent the spring teaching her small pupils, practicing her own classical repertoire, and continuing her personal studies of history and German. Though she had turned nineteen and was considered a mature woman by the measure of the times, there was nothing to suggest that her life would take a different path. She was old enough to be married, but in her letters she made no mention of a pressing suitor in the background. However, though it was something she chose not to confide to Ellen, there was now someone in her life. She and a young man she had known for much of her life, Richard Chase, another of the Philadelphia group who had been at Eagleswood, met often at the informal gatherings of Eagleswood friends. They found themselves sharing the first moments of talk and confidence that both realized would be considered an "understanding." It was the first step toward what could become an engagement.

Richard Chase's name is mentioned in the correspondence between Lucy and Ellen, since Ellen also knew him and considered him one of her friends. She was aware that he and his younger brother, Beverly, were an indispensible part of the gathering of young men and women from Eagleswood who stayed close after they'd returned to Philadelphia. They met often and joined in singing, often to Lucy's piano playing, and in small feasts and laughter and energetic excursions. Chase was admired not only for his slim handsomeness, but for his good spirits and sympathetic personality. For Lucy it was his sensitivity and his intelligence that drew her to him, though she still thought of herself as too young to marry, or even to acknowledge an open "attachment." Ellen was attracted by his tender eyes.

Knowing nothing of this, Ellen wrote Lucy of her own decided reaction to the news that another close friend from Eagleswood, Lucretia Mott's daughter Anna, had been married in the spring. Ellen was experiencing one of her usual contrary moods, and she roundly denounced the thought that she might ever decide to commit herself to anyone. Instead, her letter expressed her current hope that they both might continue to consider themselves as beyond thoughts of marriage, and still she longed for a career in music.

May 18, 1860

... Please don't be married as Anna has done—Isn't it heavenly not to be *particularly* interested in only very very sorry—Let us be engaged to each other and go on the Spenlow & Jorkins principle, until the right time comes—for we can have such elegant times together, & if nobody cares for us & we care for nobody, let us have a Hall—or even a barn chamber, & let us be literary and *so* accomplished. Ah jolly! Can we not go to Europe—(?) land? that is my Paradise—if they do only wash once in three months. If I can't *make* music I can love it, & you can make it, with those easy gliding, capering fingers.

After I am dead Luce, I think I shall *surely* be a musician. Perhaps a wind that sighs through the pines—will you listen.[17]

The Spenlow and Jorkins that Ellen refers to in the letter were partners in a proctor's firm described in Dickens's very popular novel *David Copperfield*. David was a young apprentice in their office. Their "principle" was that when Spenlow was pressed to agree to something he didn't like he would say something on the order of "I certainly could agree, but Mr. Jorkins, I'm afraid, will say no." It wasn't much of a strategy, but both Ellen and Lucy had matured into fresh and engagingly attractive young women, and she felt it was now time for them to muster their defenses.

Lucy continued her studies with Ben Cross into the spring. On a June afternoon she came into the city to see a parade of the Japanese Embassy, and she wrote Ellen that "first we are going to Cross's where I play a glorious trio by Beethoven, with Ct. and son, for piano, violin and violin cello." Besides her lessons, she related, she was teaching five pupils of her own, "enough to take me into town twice a week and keep me there all night, took French lessons, and studied a little Latin & History by myself." She ended with a complaint over one of the banes of her everyday existence, housekeeping, "the most necessary & most hateful . . . . the worst result of Eve's offence, the very core of her fatal apple."[18]

Despite the rising winds of uncertainty and the fears and anxieties that were sweeping over the country, Lucy and Ellen found themselves absorbed in their continuously shifting roles as young women. What occupied them through these troubling months were more simply the problems of growing up.

5

Beat! beat! drums!

Beat! beat! drums!—blow! bugles! blow!
Through the windows—through doors—burst like a ruthless force,
Into the solemn church, and scatter the congregation,
Into the school where the scholar is studying;
Leave not the bridegroom quiet—no happiness must he have now with his bride,
Nor the peaceful farmers any peace, ploughing his field or gathering his grain,
So fierce you whirr and pound your drums—so shrill you bugles blow.

Beat! beat! drums!—blow! bugles! blow!
Over the traffic of cities—over the rumble of wheels in the streets;
Are beds prepared for sleepers at night in the houses? no sleepers must sleep in these beds,
No bargainers' bargains by day—no brokers or speculator—would they continue?
Would the talkers be talking? would the singer attempt to sing?
Would the lawyer rise in court to state his case before the judge?
Then rattle quicker, heavier drums—you bugles wilder blow, . . .

—Walt Whitman

It is possible today to stand in the center of Germantown, a neighborhood of northwest Philadelphia that still retains much of its past, to walk in its Market Square and feel that you're seeing how it might have looked when Lucy and her family moved to Germantown in 1860. Along the narrow, uneven sidewalks that enclose the square, three- and four-story houses from the Colonial era still sit in stern solidity. Some have carefully tended facades of wood, brick, and stones, uneven under old paint, with rectangular outlines of small-paned windows and ornate carved wooden door lintels. In the small block of land left open in the center of the square a cluster of trees and a planting of flowers brighten a small park. The park's level ground was created out of the land's awkward slope, since the square is on the side, rather than the summit of the hills that rise from the plain where Philadelphia is spread below. To feel that you have come to this earlier time, however, you have to stand with your back to the center of the park, since in its center is one of the most elaborate and handsome of the monuments erected in small cities and towns across the nation to honor the dead of the Civil War.

To emphasize its importance the monument is girdled in thick iron chains supported by stone pillars at the corners, and its figure of a Union soldier is set atop a globe and a stone tower that lifts above the dark stone bulk of the base. In the base of the memorial is a stone chamber with a list of the names of the men of Germantown who perished in the war. Even after the nearly century and a half that its ornate carving, its lone figure of a soldier capping it, and its polished marble pillars have adorned the center of the square, it still seems somehow new, as if the war it commemorates remains a living reminder of the small community's story.

Along the uphill side of Market Square is Germantown Avenue. It is a long avenue that labors in lapping curves up the long slope from Philadelphia itself. So much has been built along the avenue over the years that as it rises toward Market Square it is hardly different from the other Philadelphia neighborhoods it passes through. What was once known simply as Germantown now includes the districts of Chestnut Hills and Mount Airy. In size the houses around Market Square seem inconsequential in scale, certainly not mansions, but they are a comfortable reminder of the wealth of many of these new communities when the country was still young. These were the homes of the town's gentry, and in the obvious attention to their construction and the precisely decorated windows and doorways they are continuing reminders of the people who lived in them, the merchants or owners of small manufactures, who first built on these hills.

The McKims' new home was on the crest of a hill at a distance from Germantown's center. The house was called Hilltop, and it was in a modest area several blocks to the east of the square, at the edge of the next township. Despite the move, their life went on without change, quickly returning to its steady rhythms after the anxieties of Mrs. Brown's weeks with the family. Lucy's father continued his work at the antislavery offices in downtown Philadelphia, riding the horse cars up and down the slope to the city. Nearly fifteen years before they moved to Hilltop the horse car line had opened between Ninth and Green streets, close to his office and Germantown's Market Square. After a few months the horses were replaced with a steam-driven engine. The horses had taken forty-five minutes to make their six-mile journey up the slope; the steam engine needed only twenty-eight minutes.

For Lucy the steam line was as much a part of her everyday life as it was for her father. She rode the cars on her twice-weekly journeys into central Philadelphia to the homes of her young piano scholars. To reach the square Lucy had to walk nearly a mile from their house on its hilltop, along a path that led her down into a shallow valley, and then rose again before it came closer to the square. On her walk she would have passed a scattering of small frame houses, many of them still surviving today, though Hilltop was demolished many years ago to make room for a large red brick dormitory at LaSalle University, which rests on the site. The hilly path leading toward Market Square is now a paved sidewalk, but the hillside she passed in her walks is still a rough patch of trees and brush, probably just as it was when she walked along it many years ago.

◆ ◆ ◆

In the months that followed the trauma of John Brown's raid and his execution, the nation struggled with a confused consideration of its conscience and its uncertain aims in an effort to elect a new president in the coming fall. The emotions that had been steadily building through the last decades had been stretched to an almost unbearable tension by Brown's act. Many felt they must respond personally to what was happening. When Ellen found herself in yet another school in the fall she hung a portrait of Brown in her room, in the hope that she could upset the placid mood of the new corridor where she had been placed. Others, as they felt the tensions of the rising storm, sought comfort in recalling for each other that this crisis had been part of the national situation for decades. Perhaps there was no reason to believe that this time it would be more serious than the by-now-familiar threat. The leading presidential candidate for the new Republican Party was a little-known figure for Philadelphians, an Illinois lawyer named Abraham Lincoln, who was campaigning "from his porch," as was the conventional style of the period, declining to travel or make speeches. His party's platform for the November election had intentionally avoided any provocative allusions to slavery or controversial issues like the Fugitive Slave Law. Though the party had been built on a foundation of antislavery oratory, they had presented a moderate platform intended to assure the South that no threat to their special institution was impending.

Lucy's life was still concentrated on her musical studies, which were devoted to the classical European piano repertoire, but there was a reminder during the summer of the other musical traditions that were part of the world around her—music that came closer to roots of African American culture than the minstrel show ballads or banjo strumming she certainly was familiar with. In August 1860 the family received a letter directed to her from her uncle, her father's brother, Reverend John McKim, who had expressed his doubts about sending his son to Eagleswood some years before. He lived in southern Delaware in the small community of Georgetown, which had drawn many families of freed African Americans to work on its docks. Perhaps intrigued by her dedication to music, he sent her his transcription of the song "very much admired and sung by our colored people about here." The song itself that he sent has not been found, but in his letter he wrote[1]:

As to the *Music*, I have done the best I could to reduce it to notes—but I fear I have not expressed the melody truly— ... Perhaps by *fancying* the rich tones which a colored congregation can throw into their musical performances, and the various embellishment of *appogiaturas & after notes* they are so fond of—especially of making a decided *fall* on the last note of the air—Lucy can render the piece as we have it here—every day & all night long.

Whatever her response was to the music her uncle sent her, the letter was saved.

◆ ◆ ◆

Lucy returned to Eagleswood on September 29, and on November 14, she sent a high-spirited letter to Ellen. It sparkled with all of her pleasure in word play and imaginative stretches, even if the letter also described a major disappointment she had experienced in the first weeks back.[2]

Eagleswood Nov. 14, 1860
My dear abused Ellen!
Please don't call me an "audacious young animal," & I'll never do it again. Offended me? Little fool? Just as if you hadn't done that long ago—if it were a possible thing. . . . I'm proof against offence! Well, what is the reason that I didn't write then? Why I'll tell you. Let me see, here is your last letter, lying as it has done for an age, on the very top of the unanswered pile, and the date is

Sept. 21st. From that point until the 29th when I started for the abode of—who
were the critters who presided over Hurry, Bustle, Work, Virtue, Qui vive-ity,
Steady Progression, Unswerving footsteps, Fixed aims, &c &c? never mind, I
mean in short Eagleswood. I was so busy preparing the outfit for the writer of a
sufficiently powerful nature to survive the contortions of the gymnasium & the
unknown terrors of the laundry. . . . Heavens! What an undermining it is of my
Religious Plan (everybody here has one o' them, did you know?) & reflect that
my salvation is the laziness & other wickedness of relaxation that I occasionally indulge in. If I kept conscientiously up to my intentions—ideals I mean, I
should be wrinkled by the time the next Anniversary comes.

Mr. Weld called me into his office one day at the opening of the term &
almost inverted me, as you might say, with surprise by telling me that it was a
possible thing that you would be here this year at school! I immediately flew
round, & made preparation for you to room with me, just you and I all by
ourselves in the dearest little room with heat and lights, & bookshelves & lots
o' nice things, when Willie [Ellen's brother William] told me that it was fully
decided that you were to go to Lenox. The Deities were grinding me uncer-
emoniously hard just then or I should have written to you immediately, &
poured out several vials of wrath upon your head. All to be said now is, "may
it be for the best!"

By no means ever forget three years ago! I wouldn't spare it from my
memory for anything. It was exquisite, idyllic. The darker side does for shad-
ing, & makes the brighter events stand out. Mr. Weld spoke beautifully of it
that same day in his office, & you would almost have judged the pain to be
worth bearing that brought such sweet balm with it!

Ellen had been sent by her harassed mother to Mrs. Sedgewick's Young
Ladies School in Lenox, Massachusetts. Mrs. Sedgewick was married to
the brother of a famous novelist of the day, Catherine Maria Sedgewick.
The school was some distance from Ellen's home in central New York
State, but it was closer than the journey to Eagleswood. Most of the students were comfortably suited to the familiar routine of the Sedgewick
school, but Ellen, used to the freedom and stimulation of Mr. Weld and his
school program at Eagleswood, was dissatisfied and restless. Also she was
twenty, and she was almost too old for what was essentially a girl's school.[3]
In her journal Ellen wrote that it wasn't "half as delightful to study" as she
expected. "There is so much committing to do, and lessons to *recite* are
such a bother . . . Catch me at school again—no, no, dear." Adding to the
problem, even though the Sedgewicks were known antislavery sympathizers, Ellen missed the fervor that had filled the atmosphere of her home

since her childhood. She couldn't think of the settled Mrs. Sedgewick as an abolitionist, and the woman seemed as uninterested in the rights of woman. At least Ellen's disappointment led her to think more positively of her years growing up when she was continually at odds with her mother. She began regarding herself a radical, with a touch of pride at being one of what she now termed "reformers."

At the same time, however, Ellen was conscious that she hadn't the necessary qualities to follow her mother into the group of charismatic activists whose circle also included her mother's sister, Lucretia Mott, and her associates. Ellen was crushed to find that women even younger than she were already addressing large groups and they were spoken of in admiring tones. As Ellen realized that any dreams she had of becoming a pianist were also beyond her reach, she became increasingly discouraged. She concluded in her journal:

> I don't care for anything now—hardly feel Enthusiastic now. It seems much pleasanter, & is so much more to my taste, to sit down quietly & read, or hear wise people talk, or listen to music, than to do *anything*.

In a despairing note in her journal about the role her mother had assumed in the women's movement, Ellen concluded, "Young people are entering the field, while yet I lag behind, & see no opening in my Forest of Difficulties."[4]

◆ ◆ ◆

Both Lucy and Ellen had matured into attractive young women, dark haired, with clear eyes and forthright expressions. Anyone looking at them would have assumed that they were as confident and assured as their appearance suggested, but they found themselves now, Lucy at eighteen and Ellen at twenty, still without any clear aim or direction in their lives. Lucy at least could see a future for herself as a piano teacher, and she continued to practice for hours at home. Her journeys into Philadelphia to give instruction to her piano scholars took part of every week, with whatever hours left over given to her study of languages and history. Ellen had already been attracted to several of the young men at school, and sometimes in her letters, unaware of Lucy's attachment with Richard Chase, she would urge her to be more responsive herself.

For Ellen the easy exchange of friendships and flirtations became more complicated when she found herself the object of an adoring affection from Richard Chase's younger brother, Beverly, always known as Bev, who was also younger than Ellen. She was annoyed that the age difference seemed to be less of a difficulty for him than it was for her. For this moment, however, Lucy and Ellen still were insisting that they would find better lives on their own terms if they didn't commit themselves to anyone so quickly. But as the summer passed, the tensions dividing the nation became even more sharply etched.

For the moment it could have seemed that nothing really had changed. Lucy was at Eagleswood, teaching music and feeling nostalgic at the advanced age of eighteen. On November 14 she wrote to Ellen, "School isn't much this year, except as I make it . . ." At the school, however, Lucy had matured into a useful and well-regarded member of the small teaching staff. During the Christmas recess her brother, Charlie, became ill, and she remained at Hilltop to aid her mother in Charlie's sickroom. Then apprehensive that she might bring an infection back to the school, instead of returning immediately to Eagleswood, she remained away for a few days longer until Charlie was better. Her father sent a letter to the school explaining her absence and Louisa Grimke responded with a half-teasing, affectionate note.[5]

> December 28, 1860
> Dear Miller,
> Your letter is handed to me to answer. How came dear Lucy to forget the *grand* concern at Eagleswood & and indulge her sisterly feelings by visiting the infested chamber? However nature will out so we forgive her. But inasmuch as she has done the deed I believe the sentence of banishment from this charming place must be passed on to her, only we wish it to be as short as prudence may suggest, & to atone for the lengthened holiday we expect her to return doubly bright & amiable.
> LM. Grimke

Although Lucy's life at Eagleswood that winter was passing in the familiar routine of schedules and lessons, a few weeks before Louisa Grimke sent her note to Lucy's father the presidential election had been decided, and Lincoln had emerged as the winner. The radicals in the South had made threats of secession before, but this time they acted. Lincoln himself might have made conciliatory remarks directed toward the South before the election campaign began, but despite the promises of their election platform his party stood for principles that the South found abhorrent. On December 24 in the small coastal town of Beaufort, South Carolina, an aroused group committed to the right to hold slaves issued the lengthily titled "Declaration of the Immediate Causes which May Induce and Justify the secession of South Carolina from the Federal Union." The document set out in detail the reasons why it was their conviction that a sovereign state was entirely within its Constitutional rights if it chose to leave the union. Exercising the terms outlined in the declaration, South Carolina formally seceded from the United States. The other states of the historical South—Mississippi, Florida, Alabama, Georgia, Louisiana, Texas, North Carolina, and Tennessee—rushed to follow suit, and the Secessionists, as they termed themselves, claimed control of Maryland, Kentucky, Missouri, and the territories west of Texas as well. The nation was effectively split in two. For many in the South, Brown's raid and the North's reaction had stiffened their resolve. The proud state of Virginia suddenly found itself divided, as Unionists in the west of the state seceded on their own terms and entered the Union as the new state of West Virginia.

Through the winter months the two sides frantically prepared for the war that now seemed inevitable, each waiting for the other to make a decisive move. Everywhere in the country there was now little time for talk about anything else. Lucretia Mott wrote her sister on January 15, 1861, about a visit to the McKims.

We took tea lately at Miller's. There was not much variety in our subjects of conversation for the political outlook is all absorbing. Secession, civil war, compromises. Do you think the Republicans will, after all, make unworthy compromises?[6]

Whatever would be the result of the South's declaration, Lucy still could write to Ellen on February 1, 1861, of a round of playing and performing.[7]

I have just recovered from a two week's illness . . . Mr. Mollenhauer gave a concert at Amboy right in the midst of it, at which I promised him to play. So I bounded out of bed, went down in a carriage to the hall (at 2 o'c. p. m.) practiced on the magnificent new Steinway, and poked around . . . until 7 o'clock, when the concert began. Had a good deal to do so took a cup of strong coffee and *went* it. Never felt so lightheaded in my life, and never played so well.

The concert took place on January 19 at a concert locale named The Wigwam, and featured the playing, not only of Friedrich Mollenhauer, but of his brother Edward and his nephew, a prodigy of ten, both of whom came from New York for the occasion. The *Perth Amboy Journal* for January 5 and 19 predicted a large enthusiastic audience, but neglected to list the program. No review of the concert appeared among the columns of political dispatches, so it is possible only to guess at what Lucy played or what the audience's response could have been.

◆ ◆ ◆

On April 12, 1861, the months of uncertainty came to an end. A newly organized southern force shelled the Union garrison at Fort Sumter in Charleston Harbor. Three days later Lincoln declared a naval blockade of southern ports and the war had begun.

Within hours after the decisive step was taken the country awoke to a dizzying storm of emotions. After so many decades of debate and recrimination, accusations, and spirited proclamations the issue of slavery would finally be resolved. There was no one on either side, North or South, who doubted that their armies would win the war. They were as equally convinced that the issue would all be decided in a few weeks. With an audible shout of relief, there was a rush of people hurrying to play their own role in the drama. In Germantown's Market Square a poster appeared advising any interested persons where they could enlist for service. In the fervor of these first months there was no hint that as the war went on it would ultimately be necessary for both sides to begin compelling men to join the fighting. In the tide of emotion in these first weeks any local person with some means could form a company and quickly fill it with volunteers to attach to an army unit. With a tone of certainty that the war would quickly be over, the poster announced[8]:

Citizens of Germantown!
TO ARMS!
THREE MONTHS SERVICE!

A ROLL IS NOW OPENED AT
George Hardy's and Syl Wunder's
HOTELS,
FOR THE PURPOSE OF ORANIZING A COMPANY AT ONCE.
NOW IS THE TIME, OR NEVER!!
Capt. J. Reeside White

Germantown's men and women responded to the rhetoric. One of the first companies was already commissioned into the army on April 23. By the war's end more than two thousand of the small city's seven thousand inhabitants had served as soldiers, sailors, doctors, or nurses. So many volunteered from a single street, Haines Street, that they were given the name the "Haines Street 100."[9]

Although the first rush to volunteer was enthusiastic and its fervor was sustained for the first months of the war, it also posed a difficult choice for some of the most dedicated abolitionists. Many were Quakers, with a firm conviction that slavery was a moral evil, but as Quakers they were as firmly committed to nonviolence. The issue was never resolved, and in some families the split became difficult to heal. Of William Lloyd Garrison's four sons only one, the oldest, George, who had presented many problems for the family, served in the army. In the enthusiasm of the first months Ellen and Lucy were passionately insistent that everyone must volunteer.

As arguments grew over the role each individual should play in the conflict, a vocabulary was created to clarify the differing convictions. Anyone who opposed the secession of the South from the Union by armed force was a "resistor." Anyone who out of religious convictions or sympathy for the southern cause would not use force to end the rebellion was a "nonresistor." There was also a third term. Those who were opposed to the nonresistors and their willingness to accept the division of the nation were termed "anti-nonresistors." Lucy and Ellen counted themselves as passionate resistors, though Lucy shared with many Quakers the belief that if the war was not to be fought over emancipation it was little more than mass murder, and it would only have to be fought again sometime in the future.

Ellen also expressed some misgivings. At the moment the war broke out she was in Philadelphia with her father, while Lucy was away teaching at Eagleswood. Ellen wrote to her brother Willy, who was at home in Auburn, "The Martial sound of drums inspires me, the warlike tramp of many feet." She continued with her enthusiastic response to the many among the men who were hurrying to enlist and her admiration of the women who were giving so much time to sewing uniforms, but she added, "*Everybody* here is enlisting for the War & it seems very very sad."[10] Her letter expressed her concern that her father, who was also a confirmed resistor, might decide to join the New York cavalry on their return.

When Willy enlisted later in the year Ellen described his excitement in a letter to Lucy, an excitement he shared with thousands of young men like him in both the North and the South. He took to "the art of War," she wrote, "with a might most meritorious. His sword is much more dear to him than ever his piano was & and he looks upon his sash with tender affection." Even their mother was drawn into the enthusiasm, telling him "to die before he helped to return a slave to slavery."[11]

◆ ◆ ◆

In the first months of the war, despite a series of disastrous defeats by the Union armies, some southern territories were occupied and northerners found their way into the newly freed areas to perform myriad services. For many of them their journeys into the South were a voyage of discovery to another continent, another planet, exotic and alien. For the first time they saw slaves—not just as vague figures they had imagined from what they read in the newspaper or from crude drawings they had seen in illustrated journals. None of these travelers were prepared for the nearly unbridgeable gap they found, physically and emotionally, between the two worlds—free and slave. For many of them it proved impossible to grasp the psychological effects that centuries of living in slavery had made on those who had suffered it. The newly freed slaves trailed after the troops, forming their own ragged camps beside the Union tents, desperate to cling to whatever support they could find. At times the struggling columns of the desperate followers were longer than the ranks of the marching men. The firm expectation had been that the war would end in a few weeks—months at the most—but no one had thought about what would happen to the swelling numbers who were dependent now on some new society that had still to be created.

It was in these chaotic months that for the first time there was a growing consciousness of slave song, and ultimately this interest would reach Lucy. Before the war occasional travelers in the South had brought back stories of banjos and drums and slave dances, and it was this music that had been appropriated by white entertainers for their wildly popular black-face minstrel shows. What these travelers hadn't realized was that beside the spirited jigs and comic ballads they heard there was also another world of music with stronger roots in the slave world. The visitors weren't aware that the solemn hymns of the plantation chapels and the surging prayers of the great camp meeting assemblies had been absorbed by the slaves who had been allowed to attend. The slaves in their turn had freely used the melodies and biblical verses to create their own impassioned sacred songs.

Already by the fall of 1861 accounts of the spiritual songs of the slaves began to appear in the northern press, and Lucy's father through his work in the antislavery press quickly learned of the new discoveries. One of the first reports was a letter to a New York newspaper from a man who had been given permission to travel to Fort Monroe on the coast of Virginia. It had been occupied by Union forces shortly after hostilities had broken out and was already crowded with slaves fleeing the surrounding countryside. For lack of a better term the newly freed men and women had been designated as "contraband." There was a legal dilemma hanging over the federal forces as to the status of the refugees, since they were technically still the property of their owners. One of the Union officers who was responsible for the ever-increasing numbers came to the decision that since as slaves they could be considered illegal property aiding the South in its rebellion, they could be classified as contraband. The term quickly became widespread. The letter was sent by someone who signed only his initials and has never been identified.[12]

> **CONTRABAND SINGING—**
> It is one of the most striking incidents of this war to listen to the singing of the groups of colored people in Fortress Monroe, who gather at their resorts after nightfall . . . I passed around the Fortress chapel and adjacent yard, where most of the "contraband" tents are spread. There were hundreds of men of all ages scattered around. In one tent they were singing in order, one man leading, as extemporaneous chorister, while some ten or twelve others joined in the chorus. The hymn was long and plaintive, as usual, and the air was one of the sweetest minors I ever listened to. . .

The letter continued with one verse of the hymn.

> *Shout along, children! Shout along, children!*
> *Hear the dying lamb!*
> *Oh! take your nets and follow me*
> *For I died for you upon the tree!*
> *Shout along, children! Shout along, children!*
> *Hear the dying lamb!*

And the writer concluded:

> There was no confusion, no uproar, no discord—all was as tender and harmonious as the symphony of an organ . . .

The letter was signed C. W. D.—NY

The letter was first published in a New York newspaper, the *New York Commercial Advertiser*, then reprinted in the prestigious Boston music journal *Dwight's Journal of Music* in the issue of September 7, 1861, where Lucy could have read it, since she followed Dwight's columns of the country's musical news.

Another newcomer to be moved by the spiritual hymns of the freedmen was Reverend Lewis C. Lockwood, who was employed by the Young Men's Christian Association, and was sent by the American Missionary Association to see the conditions that the freedmen faced in their improvised camps in the newly freed territory around Fort Monroe. He arrived at Monroe on September 3, 1861, and experienced the singing for the first time on the night of his arrival. His account was included in his report to the Missionary Association.

> Last evening . . . on the piazza of the hotel, I overheard music, and directed
> my footsteps thither, and in a long building, just outside the entrance of the
> Fortress, I found a number of colored people assembled for a prayer meet-
> ing. The brother who led in the concluding prayer had a sing-song manner,
> but his sentiments and expressions were very scriptural and impressive . . . I
> told my mission in few words and the message was received with deep, half-
> uttered expressions of gladness and gratitude. They assured me that this was
> what they had been praying for; and now that "The good Lord" had answered
> their prayers, they felt assured that some great thing was in store for them
> and their people. There are some peculiarities in their prayer meetings. Their
> responses are not boisterous; but in the gentle, chanted style. . . . The themes
> are generally devotional; but they have a prime deliverance melody, that runs
> in this style:
>
> *Go down to Egypt—Tell Pharoah*
> *This saith my servant, Moses—*
> *   Let my people go.*

As archivist Dena Epstein noted in her description of Lockwood's account, this was "the first published account of what we know as the great spiritual 'Go Down, Moses.'"[13]

◆ ◆ ◆

Lucy would also certainly have read of the slave spirituals in a letter that appeared in the *National Anti-Slavery Standard* a few weeks later. The *Standard* was a fixture of virtually every abolitionist household, and her father wrote for it as the paper's Philadelphia correspondent. The letter, reprinted from its initial appearance in the *New York Tribune*, appeared on November 30, 1861, with a short introductory paragraph. The appearance of the new letter was also important because some hints of the song's background were included. It makes clear that it was only on his later return to Fort Monroe that Lockwood understood the importance of what he had heard and made an effort to transcribe the full text and melody.[14]

THE CONTRABANDS' FREEDOM HYMN

The following curious hymn comes to us from the Secretary of the Young Men's Christian Association, who received it from the Missionary among the contrabands at Fortress Monroe. It will be seen that there is evidence in this hymn that the slaves in a considerable part of Virginia, at least, had a superstitious faith in being freed some time in the future. The air to which the hymn is sung is in the minor key, and very plaintive.

To the Editor of the N. Y. Tribune:

SIR: I this evening received the accompanying song from the Rev. L. C. Lockwood, recently employed by the New York Men's Christian Association in its army work, and at present laboring under the auspices of the American Missionary Association, among the slaves at Fortress Monroe.

Mr. Lockwood publicly referred to this song during his late visit to this city, and upon his return to the Fortress took down *verbatim* from the dictation of Carl Hollosay, and other contrabands.

It is said to have been sung for at least fifteen or twenty years in Virginia and Maryland, and perhaps in all the slave States, though stealthily, for fear of the lash; and is now sung openly under the protection of our government and in the enjoyment of Mr. Lockwood's ministry.

The verses surely were not born from a love of bondage, and show that in a portion, if not in all of the South, the slaves are familiar with the history of the past, and are looking forward hopefully toward the future.

Yours respectfully,

New York, Dec. 1861.   Harwood Vernon

In the chorus and three verses of the text that were appended to the letter it is obvious that Lockwood has drawn on his knowledge of the biblical texts that were the source of the song's imagery, and he has corrected the slaves' own vernacular expression. The version sent to the newspaper included twenty verses.

LET MY PEOPLE GO
A Song of the "Contrabands"

When Israel was in Egypt's Land,
    O let my people go!
Oppressed so hard they could not stand
    O let my people go!

    CHORUS—O go down, Moses,
        Away down in Egypt's land,
    And tell King Pharaoh
        To let my people go!

Thus saith the Lord bold Moses said
    O let my people go!
If not I'll smite your first born dead
    O let my people go!

No more shall they in bondage toil,
    O let my people go!
Let them come out with Egypt's spoil,
    O let my people go!

The sheet music for the song itself was published on December 14, 1861, with an arrangement by a musician named Thomas Baker, and this time eleven verses were presented, with much of their text derived from standard hymnal material of the period instead of transcriptions from slaves' singing itself. The arrangement had as little relationship to the singing of the slaves as the formalized text. Baker chose to arrange the melody in 6/8 meter, although virtually all slave songs transcribed later were annotated as in either 4/4 or 2/4 meter. Baker's setting lent the song the feeling of a formal slow march, which would have been a familiar meter to most listeners from their own church anthems. His harmonization also conformed to European models, and the setting of the melody itself was in the customary form of a solo voice singing the verses, with a vocal quartet answering with the choruses. Its importance as a historical document is that it was the first complete spiritual to be published, and considering the time and the circumstances of its publication, the style of the arrangement can be easily understood. The unexpected message of Lockwood's transcription for those who purchased a twenty-five-cent copy was the discovery that there was some element in the culture of the slaves that must be valued. The publication notice in *The American Missionair* suggested, "It would be worth hearing if sung by a hundred or two . . . It is a sweet melody."

If Lucy had read of "Let My People Go"—and almost certainly she had—it was still the European concert piano repertoire that she spent several hours every day practicing. In an undated letter fragment to Ellen, probably from October 1861—at the same time as the first contraband song was attracting some attention—she wrote of hearing the news of another disaster to the Union forces when she was at a symphony concert. It was the music of Schumann that was being performed in the concert hall that filled her thoughts and strengthened her in the resolve that the war should go on.[15]

> Wasn't it horrible? I hadn't heard a word of it until Annie told me in the Germania [concert]. Just then they began to play Schumann's wonderful 'Beiden Grenadiere' and every one of those grand *inevitable* descending chords struck a fresh resolve from my heart never, *never*, **never**, to pray for anything but War until we smote them . . .

In these same weeks a small victory by the Union navy in a coastal town of South Carolina would bring Lucy close to this music of the slaves in a way she could never have expected. It would serve to give a direction and a purpose to her life. When she wrote to Ellen two days before the year's end, however, Lucy had no anticipation of the changes that awaited. What she expressed was a conflicted sense that the war was changing them, changing everyone, and that it was affecting her in ways she couldn't fully comprehend. The mention of "John Bull" probably refers to problems over trade with England as a result of the naval blockade of the South, and the new collections by popular American poet Henry Wadsworth Longfellow were popular gift items. "Wm. Jameson" may refer to a book by abolitionist writer Robert William Jameson. The husband of her close friend Ann, formerly Davis, was now serving in the Union Army, which Lucy describes as having the effect of "military regulations" on her friend. Certainly most important for her was that Dick Chase joined the others who came to the house to help with the celebration and that they would meet again when everyone gathered a week later to celebrate the New Year.

Lucy wrote on December 29, 1861[16]:

Wednesday was Christmas, which we spent quietly. Santa Claus was stingy this year, or else scared by John Bull at any rate he only left us Longfellow & Wm. Jameson in blue & gold, some candy and a few little knick-knacks. But who cares? Not I, I'm sure. There are better things than Christmas presents when one's nineteen. I finished *Monte Cristo* which Bev brought out to me. That child is evidently wise. He knows my weak points, & so brings me books, & buys sugar-plums when we go to lectures. He, Dick & Laura spent the evening. What a jolly time we had! Ann, who has unbent wonderfully under military regulations, laid herself out to be fascinating. Laura more than ever *appreciative*, smiled blandly on her cousin's sallies. Dick bloomed on the sofa, Bev conversant opposite. We were all in a close cluster around a piano stool holding a basket of candies. Would that you had been present! & would that you were going to be when that same party meets again on New Year's Eve. Ma chere, how can she [Providence?] abuse [us with?] daily events! But there's where Providence puts it, why shouldn't we? In the midst of life we are in death! Never truer than this hoary bloody '61. What has the New Year for us, I wonder? How much can we enduvre? Can you answer for yourself, Elle? The papers say the city was never gayer than at present. There is something frightening in the wonderful recuperative power of this people. Mercy! We shall dance at funerals next year, & flirt across corpses.[17]

The men who marched away from the Germantown's Market Square in one of the regiments hurriedly trained in those first weeks of the war were known by the name "Bucktails," and one of them described his own feelings in a ballad poem of his war experiences. At the same moment that Lucy and Ellen were writing each other emotional letters of their dreams of joining in the struggle, Private Patrick Mulhatten was turning his feelings into rough but fervent verse. His was the nation's voice in these excited early months of the war.[18]

> *We are the Pennsylvania boys, from Germantown we came*
>   *We have a noble captain, and Jones it is his name.*
>   *We came to meet our Country's foes—to them we ne'er would yield;*
>   *We were bound to gain some victory or die on the battle field.*

> *We started from Nicetown; right well I remember the day;*
>   *Some bid their friends a last farewell and started on our way.*
>   *We marched to Philadelphia and thinking all was right*
>   *Till we got aboard the Harrisburg cars which took us to the fight.*

From there we went to Cliffburne on the old Maryland side,
  Where rolls the mild Potomac in all her former pride.
  But on that lovely hill-side we had not long to stay.
  For the brave old General Hooker soon ordered us away . . .

When this cruel war will cease and peace return once more,
  We will bid adieu to Dixie's land to seek our northern shore.
  And may our sweethearts of the north to our soldiers generous be,
  For we left our homes and firesides to fight for Liberty.

from "Ballad of the Bucktails"
Private Patrick Mulhatten

6

De Northmen, dey's got massa now

De Northmen, dey's got massa now.
    Hallelujah.
O Massa a rebel, we row him to prison.
    Hallelujah.
Massa no whip us any more.
    Hallelujah.
We have no massa now, we free.
    Hallelujah.
We have the Yankees, who no run away.
    Hallelujah.
O! all our massas run away.
    Hallelujah.
O! massa going to prison now.
    Hallelujah.

Verses sung by slave rowers as they rowed their master to imprisonment by Union soldiers following the capture of Port Royal, South Carolina, November 7, 1861[1]

For the northern press, hungry for any positive news, November 7, 1861, was a welcome opportunity to print banner headlines proclaiming a victory. For the Confederacy it was another discouraging sign that the southern victory, though certain, still lay in the distance. For the slaves on the islands around the broad bay at Port Royal in South Carolina, it would always be known as a day of jubilee, "the day of the gun-shoot at Bay Point." The day was warm and bright, a sunshine-filled Sunday morning. The waters of the vast bay lay empty, the usual light haze clouding the horizon, the ocean as flat and bright as a glass mirror. Then a line of newly built naval vessels powered by steam engines and trailing clouds of smoke emerged from the north, rounding the headland into the channel. The battle for Port Royal had begun.

So much that had happened to the Union forces mired in the coastal plains of Virginia in these first months of the war had been defined by gaping errors of command and failures to grasp the enormity of the struggle. Each fumbled engagement seemed inevitably to become yet another in the appalling string of disasters. On the sea, however, the odds were weighted on the Union side. The blockade of southern ports by the US Navy was one of the few things that had succeeded for the Union, and the new steam vessels that were at the head of the line of ships churning into the bay had the immeasurable advantage over what vessels the South had for a navy in this early period of the war; they weren't dependent on winds or tides. The new ships, however, brought with them their own problems. It was necessary for them to take on coal if they were to spend the months they were needed on patrol. The government had only two coaling stations on the East Coast, with a virtually insurmountable distance between them—Hampton Roads in Virginia, and Key West, Florida, both of which had been seized early in the war. The patrolling ships used up much of their fresh coal loads returning to their blockading stations.

If it had been considered possible to seize one of the larger port cities along the southern coast, the empty bay would not have been the destination. On the coast to the north, less than sixty miles away, lay Charleston, but it was now protected by the fortifications that had been part of its defenses when it was still a Union city. South of Port Royal, half the distance away was Savannah, and its fortifications were considered to be as difficult to attack as Charleston's. Port Royal Sound, as the bay was formally named, was large, and it was a protected anchorage, but unlike the harbors of the two larger cities, the land around the bay had not attracted large numbers of settlers. On its shores there were only scattered wharves at isolated landings and the town of Beaufort, with two thousand people, many of whom used its quiet streets as a vacation resort from the crowds of the other cities. The sound was three miles wide, and it could accommodate the large numbers of blockading vessels that would help to prevent the South from inviting any intervention from a European power, tempted by the riches of southern cotton to assist the South in the war.

The ships steaming into the bay at Port Royal were prepared to be fired on. It was as obvious to the Confederate government as it was to the Union navy that the bay would be a logical point for the northern fleet to attempt to secure an anchorage. The discussion in Washington had gone on for months, and despite attempts at secrecy it was clear that some point along the coast would be attacked, and Port Royal was the most likely site. The land around the bay was flat and featureless, shaped by broad islands of mud deposited over the centuries by the streams that emptied into the Atlantic. Their soil was rich and deep with a leavening of sand, and it needed only to be cleared of its brush and trees and the land plowed to create an array of cotton plantations that lined the islands' meandering dirt roads. The cotton planters and their families owned the islands, and to do the work in the fields they maintained a force of thousands of slaves. The numbers vary from eight to fifteen thousand in conflicting accounts, but at least ten thousand workers were out in the fields on November 7. Although it was a Sunday, usually their one day of rest, the day came in the middle of the cotton harvest, and there was no break in the work. The largest of the islands, St. Helena, lay to the north of the bay's mouth, with a mile of open water across the channel dividing it from the line of low bluffs that marked Hilton Head, and it was on St. Helena that the largest numbers of slaves were quartered in crude huts.

The plantation owners around the bay had belatedly realized that an attack was probably imminent. In the little time they had as they awaited the northern attack their slaves had managed to erect three low-walled mud forts and they had placed behind the walls as many artillery pieces as they could muster from the surrounding countryside. Handling the guns were their sons and neighbors, who had been given hurried, rudimentary training. Early in the morning the planters gathered on the porch of one of the St. Helena plantations with a view over the bay to watch their defenders destroy the northern fleet. Many of the slaves had noticed their masters leave hurriedly in the early morning, and at the first booming sound of the guns they deserted the fields and hurried to the plantation houses. Most of them understood immediately what the sound meant.

For once nearly everything about the plans for the attack had been effectively handled, and a massive fleet had been assembled of fourteen warships, twenty-six supply vessels, and twenty-five transports with twelve thousand troops. The flotilla was under the command of Commodore Francis Dupont, an experienced veteran of the blockade operations during the Mexican War, and he prepared his ships and crews for the attempt with considerable skill. He attacked in a classic maneuver. He ordered his strongest ships to pass the forts in a line, his own ship, the *Wabash*, leading the procession. They were to fire continuous broadsides as they sailed past the fortifications. Then since as "steamers" they could maneuver in the broad waters of the sound, they were to turn, and with their line intact pass the forts at closer range continuing their fire. They passed first along St. Helena, out of range of the forts on Hilton Head, firing into the single fort on the low bluff. Then after their turn they passed close to the two forts on the Hilton Head side, approaching them from the rear. The moving ships presented difficult targets for the inexperienced gunners. By sailing past the forts and then turning back on them, Dupont's trained batteries could concentrate on the fortifications' poorly defended rear walls. In four hours the fleet repeated its maneuver three times. The flags over the forts were lowered, the few remaining guns silenced, and Dupont's troop transports followed the warships into the harbor. Then, after sending small parties ashore to secure the landings, Dupont anchored his fleet and began what he thought would be simple negotiations to assure the safe passage of civilians in the towns inside the harbor mouth, but the confusion continued after the attack for several days, and left Beaufort to its fate.

◆ ◆ ◆

In these first moments, the planters and their families, most of them born into slaveholding families in a society driven by slavery, could not make themselves understand the vehemence of the slaves' desire for freedom. Now anticipating that the fleet would continue on to Beaufort, the men rushed back to their plantations, alerting any of the planters who still hadn't gotten news of the disaster that they had to leave and save whatever they could. The slaves had already understood the situation, and they fled as precipitously into the islands' swamps and brushy thickets. The planters struggled frantically to load wagons and carriages with what they could save of their personal possessions and to drive their slaves to the ferries crossing the inlets surrounding the islands. At the same time Beaufort's residents, momentarily expecting a landing by the Union forces, rushed to leave the city. By the end of the afternoon every white person from the town and the islands had fled.

In the panic of the first hours planters used every kind of threat and inducement to persuade their slaves to follow them, but the slaves also knew that the forts had fallen. Over the next days and nights, as Dupont and his flotilla waited at anchor, the masters used small boats to slip back to their plantations, vainly trying again to gather the slaves for flight. They were men who had always considered themselves as rich, as members of a privileged ruling class, but their riches were the land and its slaves, and now they understood that at the same moment both land and slaves had been lost. Some planters in their desperation attempted to beat the slaves into submission, but the slaves already knew about beatings and another beating couldn't affect their stubborn refusals. In their fury some of the planters drew forth particularly troublesome slaves and shot them, holding out their deaths as an example to the others. The slaves only retreated further into the swamps and forests. A few house servants were indecisive and showed signs of following their masters, but most soon returned to join the hideaways.

In her classic study of the events at Port Royal, *Rehearsal for Reconstruction*, Willie Lee Rose related the story of one slave's adventures on that day.

> The conflict of the day was recalled vividly after nearly three-quarters of a century by Sam Mitchell, who had then been a young slave of John Chaplin, living on Ladies Island. It was typical of scenes enacted on nearly every plantation. Sam's master, who had been in Beaufort, tore into the yard in his carriage and ordered out the flatboats that would carry his family to Charleston. The boat had eight oars, and the master wanted young Sam's father, the plantation's carpenter, to man one of the oars. When Sam's mother heard of this, she shot out to her husband in the Gullah vernacular, as her son recalled, "You ain't gonna row no boat to Charleston, you go out dat back door and keep keep a-going."[2]

In retaliation—and certainly in a furious response to the cruelties they had endured—the slaves from the plantations descended on the deserted streets of Beaufort. They brought wagons and emptied the houses of anything that struck their fancy, from the elaborate furnishings to stores of wine. What they didn't take they destroyed, and they fouled the rooms and the walls and what was left of the carpets. When Dupont finally moved his fleet into the harbor close to the town he found it a shambles.

When one of the owners was apprehended by the Union forces as he returned to try to save more of his property, he insisted to the officers who had seized him that his slaves would never turn against him. As he sat in the boat being rowed across to imprisonment at Hilton Head, he listened to the slaves at the oars singing a jeering boat song, "O massa we row him to prison, hallelujah." When the boat reached Hilton Head and he was taken ashore, he ruefully confessed to the men leading him off that he knew now he'd been mistaken.

◆ ◆ ◆

Port Royal and its bay would remain in federal hands until the end of the war, though it continued to be isolated and surrounded by Confederate military units. It efficiently performed its functions as a coaling station for the blockade vessels, and it also forced the Confederacy to keep a significant force in South Carolina to prevent any attempt to push out from the port toward either Charleston or Savannah. Port Royal, however, would also have a significance that no one could have anticipated. The southerners' self-justifications over the moral issues of slavery had led many owners to expect some show of loyalty, at least from their personal slaves, and on some plantations there were house servants who remained throughout the war. Without hesitation, however, virtually every slave who could break free fled to the Union armies. In the first months the northern armies hadn't considered the possibility that they would find themselves struggling to care for the large numbers of slaves who streamed toward their columns.

At Port Royal, Dupont and his forces to their dismay found themselves responsible for the care of nearly ten thousand men, women, and children. With the collapse of the plantations the slaves huddled helplessly in their quarters, without work or food, and for the first time in their lives, without directions. In the first days following the occupation by Dupont's troops, the soldiers had seized whatever they could find to eat in the plantation storerooms. For the northern abolitionists the Port Royal slaves immediately presented a crucial problem, but it was also clear that they presented a significant opportunity. Despite the early disappointments with the Union armies there was still the firm conviction in the North that the course of the war would change to their advantage, and soon the number of freed slaves would number in the millions. Whatever was achieved with aid to the newly freed slaves at Port Royal could provide a template of what might be possible to prepare all of the slaves for life as free men and women in a new society. Abolitionists who had assisted runaways in the North had learned at least that the slaves were desperate to be taught to read and write, to receive some kind of elementary education, and they were determined to prove to anyone doubting the ability of the slaves to learn that with education the slaves could take their fit place in America's society. More immediate, however, was the need to find some way to feed the slaves and find work for them to do. The reality was that they needed everything that could be provided for them.

The Port Royal Experiment, as it came to be called, evolved over the next eighteen months, and it was to become, as Willie Lee Rose termed it, "a rehearsal for reconstruction." In a letter to Ellen, Lucy McKim had written that she understood the story of her life would be "and they were married and lived happily ever after," but she lamented that she wanted to live for herself first. Port Royal would give her the opportunity.

◆ ◆ ◆

For the North the mood of the autumn momentarily lifted with the news of the Port Royal success, and Ellen could write Lucy with an amused tolerance for her brother Willie's eagerness to be part of the excitement.[3] As she continued her letter, however, she also made it clear that she had no patience with the other side of the debate in abolitionist circles, those who because of their pacifist beliefs were willing to let the South leave the Union with slavery still undisturbed. Ironically, although William Lloyd Garrison had been one of the most strident and committed among the abolitionists, he was a "nonresistor" as they were termed. He and Lucy's father were close friends, and they chose not to bring the issue up between themselves, but even in Garrison's family there was no agreement. Two of his sons, William and Wendell, were committed nonresistors, while their older brother, George, the Garrisons' first son, would serve in the Union army for the last two years of the war. In the fall of 1861 William was twenty-three, Wendell twenty-one. They had begun traveling to abolitionist meetings as Wendell addressed the listeners in an effort to justify their position. Both were tall and gangling, Wendell with the beginnings of a beard. The Garrison family had never been economically comfortable, dependent as it was on their father's income from his newspaper *The Liberator* and his occasional lectures. His sons were used to spending summers "adventuring," which meant, since they couldn't afford to ride trains or take coaches, they did a great deal of walking.

The two Garrison men visited Philadelphia in early November, and whatever disagreements there were between the two families, they had all been close since they were children, and Lucy became their guide to the city. Though it was fall and the days were chilly, they walked everywhere, talking endlessly. The emotional subject of Wendell's nonresistor lectures doesn't seem ever to have been raised. Ellen, after commenting in her letter on the amount of walking Lucy described to her, continued with her own spirited defense of the resistor's point of view, pointing to their friend Ned Hallowell as an example of someone who had enlisted.[4]

I never knew a person so gifted with ambulatory powers—seems to me when the Garrisons were with you, you did nothing but walk—I wouldn't *look* at a non-resistor. What do they suppose is going to become of our firesides—Isn't Ned a fine grave fellow, for all his lounging about? What do you think of my disguising myself & and accepting an office under Mr. Higginson—will you bear me out on it? We might make excellent warriors. Won't there be a jubilee when the slaves are emancipated? I look forward to that ...

Ellen's mother and father were close friends and supporters of the work of Harriet Tubman, one of the most highly regarded figures in the efforts to free the slaves. Tubman was a neighbor of the Wrights in Auburn, New York, and in the years that she was part of the Underground Railroad she often led fugitives to the small town, where they were fed and given a chance to rest, then sent on north to Canada. In her letter Ellen made it clear that her own support was unwavering for the abolitionists' work, even if what it mostly involved was sewing.

... There are several fugitives about here that Harriet Tubman got away. Among their babies, & our babies, & the soldiers, we are sewing ourselves into inch bits—every morning I teach Eliza's children the rudiments of Christian civilization. Milly takes kindly to the science, but Flory has to be gently decoyed into the mazes, & then as carefully assisted out. I confess a feeling of black despair when after I have laboriously striven for a week to place before her uncontradictory proof that 3+2=5 she triumphantly asserts at the end of that time that 3+2 are 14. ...

Whatever their differences, the abolitionists responded quickly to the situation in Port Royal, and for once the government hurried to add its support. The missionary societies in the North hastily began to collect money and supplies. A representative for the government, Edward L. Pierce, from Boston, was sent to Beaufort to determine on a plan of action to help alleviate the difficulties the military officers in the area faced. At the same time as Pierce journeyed to the islands, Reverend Mansfield French was sent by the American Missionary Association in New York to prepare their role in the future months. Relief committees were quickly formed in New York and Boston, and in Philadelphia Lucy's father was at the head of a group who convened the first meeting as the Philadelphia Port Royal Relief Committee on February 15. 1862.

McKim, through his network of wealthy supporters of the antislavery office, was successful in gathering money and materials to send to the island and within a few weeks more than five thousand dollars had been collected. Sympathizers had also contributed large amounts of clothing. A newly organized Educational Commission in Boston and the National

Freedmen's Relief Association in New York were already recruiting volunteers for the islands. In March the steamer *Arago* brought a group of nine teachers from Boston who were housed in one of the deserted mansions in Beaufort, and they were soon joined by a group from New York.

McKim had determined that there should be a representative from Philadelphia to accompany any shipment of materials to South Carolina, and the decision was made to send a woman with medical training, who could assist in caring for the sick and injured among the slaves and also advise the Philadelphia committee as to their next step. The woman chosen was one of their group who shared their commitment to the abolitionist principles. Her name was Laura Towne. She was born in Pittsburgh in 1825 and she was thirty-seven when she was asked to make the journey. Neither the members of the committee nor Towne herself had any idea that she would become the central figure in the long drama of the Port Royal Experiment.

Towne was suggested as a nurse because she had studied homeopathic medicine at the Women's Medical College in Philadelphia, but she had also trained as a teacher and for several years had been teaching in charity schools in the Philadelphia area. She had been an early convert to abolitionism and she was determined in her support. Unlike most of the volunteers who were sent to Port Royal she came from a wealthy family and had a small inheritance which gave her a degree of independence. She took no salary for her years of work on St. Helena. She was small and slight, always carefully dressed in the voluminous dark dresses of the period, her hair drawn straight back and gathered on her neck. She was not a beauty, but her face was strong and decided, with a candid, observant glance and a firm mouth. When she decided to make the journey she was emotionally committed to a younger woman named Ellen Murray who returned her feelings, and also was a teacher. Their dream was that Murray could join her in the work at Port Royal.

Towne was sent early in April with the funds that had been collected, arriving on the steamer *Oriental*, which also had as passengers several new arrivals for the Boston group. She landed at Port Royal on April 15. The goods that had been gathered were sent separately and arrived on April 25. The shipment included bacon, smoked fish, molasses, salt, clothing, boots, shoes, sewing materials, brushes, soap, hats, caps, and bonnets. Willie Lee Rose wrote:

> The prankish soldiers handling the large amounts of freight sent by the
> Philadelphia Committee and assigned to "Miss Laura Towne" could not have

been further from the mark when they sketched the imaginary consignees on the numerous boxes, showing a large, rawboned female of frightful expression astride a keg of molasses. Laura Towne could enjoy the humor of this, but about her abolitionism she tolerated no levity.[5]

As more people came into contact with groups of freed slaves, discussions of slave music became more common in the press, and in March 1862 Lucy's father's antislavery office offered for sale copies of the musical arrangement of "Let My People Go," which Reverend Lockwood had heard and transcribed at Fort Monroe the previous autumn. There was considerable interest in the everyday music of the "contrabands" who were following the union armies, though most of the artists doing the sketches were drawn to the ex-slaves' comic dancing and their performances of songs already known from the minstrel stages. In illustrations of camp life a black camp follower was often depicted playing a banjo or performing a jig for the entertainment of laughing troops.

In May, James McKim traveled to Washington on business of the antislavery office and there experienced the emotional effect of slaves' singing. His detailed account appeared in the *National Anti-Slavery Standard* on May 26, 1862, as "Philadelphia Correspondence." He was standing in a group in his hotel lobby when he heard someone say, "There they are," "There are more of them," "More contrabands," etc., and he hurried to the door and saw a group of newly freed slaves, "contrabands," passing on the street, guarded by a file of soldiers. He estimated that there were more than twenty in the group, both men and women of all ages.[6]

The men had packs over their shoulders, and several of the women had babies in their arms. They were all travel-worn and dusty. I took advantage of a pause on their movement to ask one of the party some questions, such as where they had come from and how they got off, but I was stopped by one of the guards, who said their orders were strict to allow no one to ask them any questions. This was well, as among strangers it was impossible to tell friend from foe. . . .

The government had appropriated a large building not far from the Capitol and it was serving as a "contraband quarters" for the escapees, who in official documents were described as "self-emancipated." The quarters also served as a school and that evening he went with several others to see the school in session. Two teachers had been employed for the instruction and McKim judged they were "well qualified for their duty."

When we entered we found the room crammed with scholars of all ages and every variety of complexion, and a teacher with a pointer giving them lessons from a poster on the wall. He would explain, and ask them questions which they would answer collectively. They seemed both eager and apt to learn. . .

After a period of instruction the teacher laid down the pointer and called for a pause.

Already in these first months of contact between the "self-emancipated" and those who were responsible for their care, the slaves had learned that visitors were moved by their singing. That the freed slaves and the missionaries and abolitionists shared Christian beliefs was one of the meager stock of things they could communicate to each other.

"That will do for the present. We'll rest awhile now," said the teacher. "In the meantime, let us have some singing. What shall we have?" Someone answered, but her words—it was a woman—were inaudible. "Very well, 'Go Down, Moses' let it be. Who'll start it?" Someone began in a low tone, and soon the whole school swelled the chorus . . .

For McKim, and probably for all the spectators gathered in the room, it was their first experience of the distinct, rich musicality and the expressive emotions of slave song. No one in these first months of their meetings with the men and women they had struggled to bring to freedom for so long would ever forget this moment.

It was a touching scene. The moistened eyes and swallowing throats of the spectators showed that none were unmoved. An opportunity was now given to the visitors to make remarks to the school, by way of encouragement and exhortation, which you may be sure we were ready to avail ourselves of. . . . Mr. Woods, "government agent appointed to look after the 'contrabands'" warned them to beware of slave-catchers, who he said were prowling about and had already succeeded in carrying off some of their number. "Keep within bounds," he said; "don't go out into the streets, trust no white man you don't know to be a friend."

McKim ended his correspondence with three stanzas of the singing, as he had transcribed them. The verses are similar to those that were heard by others in Virginia a few months before, and it is clearly the same song.

O go down, Moses
Away down in Egypt's land
And tell King Pharoah
To let my people go.

"Thus saith the lord, bold Moses said
O let my people go;
O let my people go.

"No more shall they in bondage toil,
O let my people go;
Let them come out of Egypt's peril,
O let my people go," etc.

In Port Royal, Laura Towne had begun to make plans for the work she intended to do and how she would manage to live. Already she was finding more that pleased her in her new life in South Carolina than she had expected. She had kept a diary since she was a girl, and she began writing again as the days passed. She landed on April 15, and on April 17 she recorded some of her early impressions in a lengthy entry, already noting the slave songs she was hearing.[7]

April 17, 1862
At Mrs. John Forbes', formerly Mr. Tripp's house, a modern built new building with expansive sea wall and other improvements. The wind blows freshly nearly all day and the tide rises over sandy, grassy flats on three sides of the house. These sands are full of fiddler-crab holes, and are at low tide the resort of negro children with tubs on their heads, crabbing. Soldiers, fisherman, and stragglers also come here, and we see not a little life. Boats frequently pass by, the negro rowers singing their refrains. One very pretty one this morning Moses told me was—

"The bells done rang
An' we goin' home
The bells in heaven are ringing."

Every now and then they shout and change the monotony by several very quick notes, or three or four long drawn-out notes. One man sings a few words and the chorus breaks in, sometimes with a shout or interjectional

"Oh yes, ma'am," at every five or six bars. Another song was, "We're bound to go"—to heaven, I suppose . . .

Beaufort was filled with soldiers, and Laura Towne was uneasy with their manner and at their open dismissal of the volunteers who were arriving in the steamers from the North to take part in the experiment. She found Beaufort itself still beautiful, though the damage to the houses was an unpleasant reminder of the violence that had swept the town's streets only a few months before. Her diary entry continued:

> . . . The walk through the town was so painful, not only from the desertion and desolation, but more than that from the crowd of soldiery lounging, idling, growing desperate for amusement and occupation, till they resort to brutality for entertainment. I saw a soldier beating a horse so that I think it possible he killed him. Others galloped past us in a most reckless, unconscionable manner; others stared and looked unfriendly; others gave us a civil military salute and a look as if they saw something from home gladly. . .
>
> The streets are lovely in all that nature does for them. The shade trees are fine, the wild flowers luxuriant, and the mocking-birds perfectly enchanting. They are so numerous and noisy that it is almost like being in a canary bird fancier's.

In these first days she was presented with so much that often gave her a different glimpse of aspects of the slaves' situation she had never fully understood. One of the house servants where she was staying took her to see her mother, and the lives of the two women as pampered maids for the plantation owners' wives and daughters were bound more closely to the everyday life of their masters' homes than Towne could have expected, though the women had chosen not to follow the families in their flight.

> Yesterday Caroline took us [Towne and two companions] to her mother's house. They were expecting us and were neatly dressed, and elegantly furnished indeed was their room. It had straw matting and a mahogany bureau, besides other things that said plainly "massa's" house had contributed to the splendor, probably after the hasty retreat of "massa's" family. . . . They begged us to stay, for it "seemed like they couldn't be happy widout white ladies 'roun.'" They hoped it would be healthy so we could stay, but they thought it would not be so, because the city is not cleaned as it used to be. They would have gone with their masters, both of them, but they had relations whom they did not want to be parted from "except by death" who were not going.

One of them had gone at first, but ran away and found her way back "by de direction of de Lord." ...

On her arrival Towne was taken to visit the schools that had already been set up in Beaufort by the teachers who had arrived the month before. She found very few pupils because the Union general commanding the area had ordered the black women and children to go back to the plantations. In Hilton Head, the town on the other side of the harbor, there had been trouble with slaves who had mingled too freely with the soldiers, and the concern of everyone working in the islands was to prevent another outbreak of violence like the slaves' attack on the mansions of Beaufort. Her most emotional passages in the diary entry affirm her commitment to the work she had undertaken and also make clear how much Ellen Murray, who was still in New York waiting for permission to make the journey, was necessary to her.

I have felt all along that nothing could excuse me for leaving home, and work undone there, but doing more and better work here. Nothing can make amends to my friends for all the anxiety I shall cause them, for the publicity of a not pleasant kind I shall bring upon them, but really doing here what no one else could do as well. So I have set myself a hard task. I shall want Ellen's help. We shall be strong together. I shall be weak apart.

Messages streamed back to Philadelphia from the steamers and the warships sailing up and down the coast, and McKim realized that before he proceeded to dispatch more money and new supplies of goods to Laura Towne's care he needed to have a clearer idea of her situation. At a meeting of the Port Royal Committee it was decided that one of their members should journey to South Carolina to talk with Towne and the military authorities who were overseeing the operation. McKim was the obvious choice. The decision was also made that the situation was so complex and uncertain that for him to be able to see and learn as much as possible in a short visit he would need an assistant. Without hesitation he selected his daughter Lucy. She would join him on the journey as his secretary.

Ellen quickly heard of the plan from Lucy, and on May 21, 1862 she sent a breathless letter to her brother Frank.[8]

We have all been thrown into comparative consternation, by Lucy's projected trip to Port Royal. She and her father expect to leave these peaceful parts tonight, or tomorrow night, to sail from New York immediately to the

Port. Lucy is going as Asst., and Secretary to her father and can hardly sleep o'nights for thinking of it—I dare say she will dash into some transcendental scheme of a school or something of missionary aspect and never be heard of again in civilized circles. They say they will be back in a month.

The departure for Port Royal, however, was delayed and Lucy became increasingly impatient. On May 28 she fulminated in a letter to Ellen, "As to Port Royal! O' demnition! I still live, but shant long, if this delay continues."[9]

At that moment it might have seemed to Lucy that the days and time itself had come to a standstill.

William Francis Allen. William Allen worked as a supervisor on St. Helena Island in 1863–1864 and was an active song collector. Lucy Garrison's pregnancy during the final months of the book's preparation meant that much of the work fell to Allen, and his lengthy introduction was an important addition to the resulting collection. He had a brilliant career as professor of history and ancient languages at the University of Wisconsin and published a series of successful textbooks on Latin grammar. Courtesy Wisconsin Historical Society, WHi–58369.

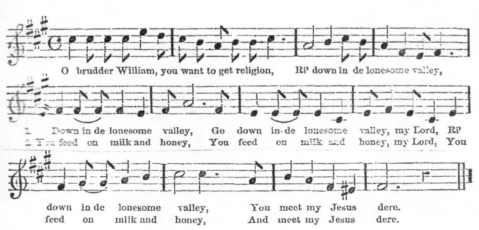

The music and words of the spiritual "Lonesome Valley" that Allen taught himself to sing from this notation in the journal *The Continental Monthly* before his arrival on St. Helena.

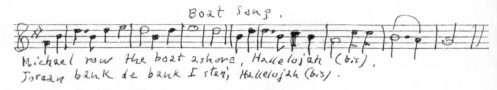

Allen's notation for the now well-known "Michael, Row the Boat Ashore."

Allen's hand-drawn map of the roads leading to Beaufort from the island's plantations.

Musical notations of spirituals collected by Allen on St. Helena.

In her pioneering research into the story of *Slave Songs of the United States* Dena Epstein found these copies of songs Charles Ware had collected that were not included in the book. To preserve them he pasted them into his own copy.

Charles Pickard Ware. Of the three editors of the collection it was Ware who spent the most time on the island as superintendent of a cotton plantation, and he contributed the largest number of songs. After the book's publication he returned to St. Helena and continued to collect songs, but found there were now fewer songs for him to notate.

SLAVE SONGS

OF THE

UNITED STATES.

New York:
A. SIMPSON & CO.,
1867.

The book's title page from 1867, the already famed spiritual that opened the collection, and the announcement in *The Nation* of the planned second edition.

SLAVE SONGS OF THE UNITED STATES.

I.

1. ROLL, JORDAN, ROLL.

1. My brudder* sit tin' on de tree of life, An' he yearde when Jor-dan roll; Roll, Jor-dan, Roll, Jor-dan, Roll, Jor-dan, roll! O march de an-gel march, O march de an-gel march; O my soul a-rise in Heaven, Lord, For to yearde when Jor-dan roll.

2 Little chil'en, learn to fear de Lord,
And let your days be long;
  Roll, Jordan, &c.

3 O, let no false nor spiteful word
Be found upon your tongue;
  Roll, Jordan, &c.

* Parson Fuller, Deacon Henshaw, Brudder Mosey, Massa Linkum, &c.

[This spiritual probably extends from South Carolina to Florida, and is one of the best known and noblest of the songs.]

Laura Towne and students, 1862.

Ellen Murray and students, 1862.

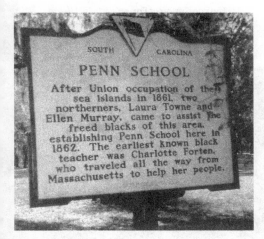

SOUTH CAROLINA

PENN SCHOOL

After Union occupation of the sea islands in 1861, two northerners, Laura Towne and Ellen Murray, came to assist the freed blacks of this area, establishing Penn School here in 1862. The earliest known black teacher was Charlotte Forten, who traveled all the way from Massachusetts to help her people.

The founders of Penn School.

Laura Towne in later years.

Daily the long-oppressed people of these islands are demonstrating their capacity for improvement in learning and labor. What they have accomplished in one short year exceeds our utmost expectations. Still the sky is dark; but through the darkness we can discern a brighter future. We cannot but feel that the day of final and entire deliverance, so long and often so hopelessly prayed for, has at length begun to dawn upon this much-enduring race. An old freedman said to me one day, " De Lord make me suffer long time, Miss. 'Peared like we nebber was gwine to git troo. But now we's free. He bring us all out right at las'." In their darkest hours they have clung to Him. and we know He will not forsake them.

While writing these pages I am once more nearing Port Royal. The Fortunate Isles of Freedom are before me. I shall again tread the flower-skirted wood-paths of St. Helena, and the sombre pines and bearded oaks shall whisper in the sea-wind their grave welcome. I shall dwell again among " mine own people." I shall gather my scholars about me, and see smiles of greeting break over their dusk faces. My heart sings a song of thanksgiving, at the thought that even I am permitted to do something for a long-abused race, and aid in promoting a higher, holier, and happier life on the Sea Islands.

Charlotte Forten joined Towne and Murray a few months after the founding of their school. She was one of a handful of African American women who made the dangerous journey to the South to aid in the welfare work.

The conclusion of Forten's article "Life on the Sea Islands," published in the *Atlantic Monthly*, May–June, 1864

The Brick Church on St. Helena where Forten began working as a teacher. Photo by Ann Charters.

Prominent Abolitionists

Thomas Wentworth Higginson, c. 1870.

William Lloyd Garrison, c. 1870.

Robert Purvis, c. 1850.

The Fisk Jubilee Singers. A promotion photo signed by each member of the troupe.

JUBILEE SONGS:

COMPLETE.

AS SUNG BY THE

JUBILEE SINGERS,

OF FISK UNIVERSITY,

(NASHVILLE, TENN.)

UNDER THE AUSPICES OF THE AMERICAN MISSIONARY ASSOCIATION.

PRICE 25 CENTS.

NEW YORK:
Published by BIGLOW & MAIN, 425 Broome St.
CHICAGO: 736 Wabash Av.

Title page of the first selection of Theodore Seward's musical
arrangements for the spirituals performed by the Fisk singers, 1872.

7

How little we knew!

At Port Royal

At last our grating keels outside,
Our good boats forward swing
And while we ride the land-locked tide,
Our negroes row and sing . . .

The land is wild with fear and hate,
The rout runs mad and fast;
From hand to hand, from gate to gate,
The flaming brand is passed.

The living glow falls strong across
Dark faces broad with smiles;
Not theirs the terror, hate and loss
That fire yon blazing piles.

With oar-strokes timing to their song
They weave in simple lays
The pathos of remembered wrong
The hope of better days—

The Song of the Negro Boatmen

Oh, praise an' tanks! De Lord he come
To set de people free;
An' massa tink it day of doom,
An' we ob jubilee,

De Lord dat heap de Red Sea waves
He jus' as strong as' den.
He say de word, we las' night slaves,
To-day, de Lord's freemen.

De yams will grow, de cotton blow,
We hab de rice an' corn:
Oh, nebber you fear, nebber you hear
De driver blow his horn!

—John Greenleaf Whittier, 1861

Whittier's poem on the fall of Port Royal was published only a few days after the attack and it had wide circulation in the abolitionist press. To his verses he appended a "Song" as he supposed would be sung by the rowers who were transporting the first abolitionist travelers journeying to the South. For many who made the journey their expectation was they would also hear the boatmen singing.

To Lucy's intense disappointment she and her father didn't leave the night that Ellen wrote to her brother. Little in those early days of the war went as planned, and she waited at Hilltop for some news. On June 1 Ellen wrote a hurried note to Beverly Chase in Philadelphia[1]:

> June 1
> Lucy sent me a sweet note Thursday morning, which was cordial to me in the hot cars. How I do miss that young woman! I wrote to her today, & shall have to repeat a great deal in this, but you will never be the wiser—
> I feel sorry for you to lose her if she really goes to Port Royal & my sympathies will be enlisted in either case for she longs to go and prove herself of some use to the world, and each disappointment in starting is a pang to her ...

Two weeks later on June 15 Ellen felt obliged to maintain the pretense that Bev also had tender feelings for Lucy, and she soon would be leaving Philadelphia behind.[2]

> I wish for your sake that Lucy wants to hurry back. I'm only afraid that Mr. McKim will leave her there, as she will no doubt find much contraband work to do that she has longed for ...

Her letter, however, crossed with Lucy's excited news in a letter sent the same day[3]:

Hilltop, June 1, 1862.
Dear Ellen,

The *Arago* actually does sail for Port Royal tomorrow afternoon, and we have been busy as bees all day getting ready to leave here tomorrow morning in the 8 o'clock train for N. Y. What larx! Ain't it? The way one happened to know it, was by father's going himself to N. Y., to find out the cause of the delay. As it proved one might have gone on the *Ericsson*, or any other vessel that has already sailed if the folks there only had known, & we shouldn't have got off now if there hadn't been a little Phila. energy at work! But I won't care, as it's settled at last. That is happiness enough . . . .

On St. Helena Island, Laura Towne was waiting as impatiently. Ellen Murray, the woman to whom she was attached, was now on her way to join her there, as they had dreamed, and her situation was as uncertain as Lucy's as she waited in the North. Murray was being sent by the Boston Port Royal Committee to the island as a teacher. In her journal for May 11 Towne wrote:

Ellen has not yet come and I am so afraid the Boston Committee will not send her, because they will not accept Mr. Pierce's pass now that he thinks of leaving, or because their funds are out. I expected her fully a month ago.[4]

As Lucy waited in Germantown for her father, who had gone on to New York to see what could be done to get them on their way, Laura turned to her diary on May 23 to consider some of the uncertainties surrounding her in Port Royal. The daily threat of a Confederate effort to recapture the island hung over every decision she had to make. Two of the blockage ships patrolling the harbor were crippled, and the ring of Confederate troops surrounding them continued to press their slender defenses with raiding parties. For many of the people across the island it was almost a certainty that this small enclave in the midst of the hostile South soon would fall. In her diary Towne wrote of her apprehensions and of the continual wrangle over the organization of the relief operation on the island, but it is Ellen who is most present in her thoughts.[5]

It is storming most furiously, and I fear Ellen is out in it. It worries me and yet I feel faith that she will come to me. It seems impossible, though, all coming seems stopped. The new war, excitement at the North, the calling-out of the militia, the battles, etc, have made it almost impossible that this place can command much notice. The *Oriental* is wrecked; the *Atlantic* up for repairs, and communication difficult. That wretch, T., who refused Mr. McKim and

Ellen a passage on their permit from Barney and pass from Mr. Pierce, has it in his power to do such mischief and cause such delay and vexation as will make it almost impossible for Ellen to come. She has already had one expensive journey to New York for nothing. Poor Ellen! her trials are far harder than mine—she has borne much more.

As their steamer neared Port Royal six days later, Lucy and her father were completely unaware that only two days before their arrival there had been a feverish panic over rumors of a Confederate attack in Beaufort. Word was hurriedly sent to Laura Towne on Saturday morning, June 7, telling her that she should be ready to leave the island at any moment. The Union troops who were protecting them had been reduced as units were shifted for a planned assault on Charleston some sixty miles to the north. For nearly two weeks Towne and the others on the island had realized with some apprehension that they were unprotected. The night before there had been an attempt by a Confederate party to pass the pickets stationed at Port Royal Ferry. It was defended by black troops who challenged the approaching flatboat. In the darkness a voice of a slave called out from the boat, "Don't shoot, massa!" Then fifty men stood up in the boat and emptied their rifles into the guard, killing four of them. In the darkness the survivors of the fusillade fled into Port Royal.

There had been much ridicule by the soldiers stationed in Beaufort of the young and inexperienced "supervisors," most of them university students. They had been sent at the same time as the missionaries and teachers to try to manage the plantations and somehow to supervise the planting of the spring cotton crop. Most of them had no experience for what they were undertaking, but the owners and their overseers had fled and there was no one else the relief committees could turn to. A further problem was that the slaves begged to be allowed to plant food for themselves in the fields, not having any faith in cotton to keep them from hunger in the coming winter.

In their defense Towne wrote in her diary of the response of the young supervisors when they were faced with the threat of the southern attack.[6]

This morning all the ladies, cotton agents, and civilians, except our men, embarked on the *Ottowa* and went down to Hilton Head ... Our men of the Commission have been bold enough. Little Taylor has shouldered his gun and he this morning went to within four miles of the enemies' lines. Ashley acted as a guide to the scouts and others have gone readily to the aid of the soldiery.

Her supervisor, Edward Pierce, related that the regular soldiers "were swearing at the 'nigger lovers'"—as they coarsely described the civilian workers of Towne's commission—for running away at the first danger, but Towne maintained that they hadn't lost their courage. "Not a man has gone—not one."

In their panic the people who had begun returning to Beaufort fled again after it was rumored that the Navy was ordering gunboats into the harbor to remove all of the commissary stores. The town would then be abandoned and the newly freed slaves would be left alone to face the rage of their returning owners. Towne went so far as to prepare her own possessions ready for flight, and she continued in her diary:

> We packed our trunks to-day, according to Mr. Hooper's orders, and we can run at any time, but leaving much behind us. I cannot bear the thought of going while the poor people must stay—Aunt Bess, whose leg is so bad; and some of the babies who are ill now—they will suffer so in the wood and marshes if they have to fly. While we were packing this morning, Susannah, then Rina came and asked anxiously about our going. I told them all we knew—that we might have to go off, but would not if we could help it; that our soldiers had all gone off to take Charleston and that Sesech might come down to attack us, and then the gentlemen would insist on our going.[7]

Lucy's days on the ship, at least as much as we know from the glimpses we have of her journey, were as idyllic as Towne's days on the island were frantic. In a fragment from an undated letter that Ellen copied for Beverly Chase, Lucy presents a joyous description of her mood on their voyage.

> We played cards a little, talk an infinitude and sang all the rest of the time. Capt. Gerrish of the 6th Conn. had quite a fine tenor voice, and Field and Cooley good baritones. We four made a pretty tolerable quartet, and everybody else joined in the Choruses. Mr. Severance played the flute.[8]

Lucy's father wrote more fully of the voyage in a brief letter to his wife the day after their arrival at Port Royal. In the confusion of the situation it was necessary to take advantage of any vessels leaving the port to get letters out.

Pope's Plantation St. Helena Island

June 9, 1862

My dearest wife

I have the opportunity of dropping you a line; nothing more however. Mr. Prince leaves unexpectedly—in a few moments for the North. The ship in which he had taken passage leaves sooner than he was expecting them to leave. So I hurry to say a few words.

We reached this place at noon yesterday; having arrived at Port Royal Saturday night. We had a long, and with the exception of sea sickness, a pleasant journey . . . I suffered greatly, as I always do at sea from Monday afternoon till Saturday when we cast anchor. I took in nourishment and my own alleviation increased Lucy's enjoyment. She was a little ill, but notwithstanding she enjoyed the voyage, the company, the incidents, even her occasional [sapphic] emotions with the cruelest relish. We came to off the bay at Hilton Head before afternoon. We put into the harbor in the midst of a violent thunder storm about dark. The heat during the day was extreme; but the [storm?] cooled the air, and a good night's sleep, and some breakfast this morning— the first I had been able to eat—put me all right again . . .

McKim also included a description of the trip across the bay from Hilton Head to St. Helena. The trip had been arduous, but it had been such a stirring experience that he found it was beyond his powers of description when he tried to describe it in his letter to his wife.

How we reached here I shan't try to describe—our row across the bay; the negroes' boat—sings—so musical so touching. . . .[9]

Lucy wrote briefly to her mother at the same time, and in her letter she avowed that her experience, even within her first few days, had only strengthened her conviction that slavery must come to an end.[10]

St. Helena Island
9 June 1862
Dear Mother,

The letter, which I had half written to thee, is in my trunk, which has not yet been taken from the *Arago*. I am sorry that that this can be nothing more than a pencil note, for Mr. Pierce has only this moment arrived to take the *Massachusetts* for the North, so there is not time for anything more. Stopping to write anyhow is a very hard thing, there is so much to be seen & heard every minute. The voyage was enchanting, although Father was seasick enough, & suffered more from it he said, than when he crossed the Atlantic. . . . Everything so far has been beyond my most sanguine expectations, Father, I think can say that too, though perhaps I had better let him speak for

himself as I refer now particularly to the good time I have had since I left.
It has been splendid. I can't bear to think of coming back yet. The climate is
delicious, air cool & soft. For the contrabands—but that word suggests such
volumes that I can't tell you anything now. Yes! The pro-slavery folks were
right when they said, Go South, Abolitionists, if you want to have your views
changed on the subject of slavery. Mine have been most profoundly. Thence
forth "Garrisonism" shall express to me but the positive (not the superlative,
I mean) of Anti-Slavery. How lukewarm we have been! How little we knew!

With Lucy and her father in their small party was Ellen Murray. In her
diary later in the day Towne described her own emotions when she heard
of the party's arrival.[11]

> Sunday, June 8, 1862
> Before church we all, superintendents and the few ladies, stood under the
> oaks and talked of our dangers, and then Mr. Horton led us in to service.
> After service we talked long again, till the coming rain made our party from
> the Oaks hasten home, Parks and others going to the Episcopal church to try
> the organ. Mr. Pierce had gone to Hilton Head, as a steamer was expected. I
> had reached home before the rain and was lying down, when Rina rushed
> into my room with a haste and a noise so strange to her, calling out. "Miss
> Murray has come!" I got up suddenly, but felt so faint I had to lie down again.
> Jerry and his boat's crew had arrived with her trunk, but she did not come for
> an hour.

Towne took the time to calm herself so as not to gratify her supervisor, Pierce, who stayed close to her during the wait at the Pope Plantation
house. She was aware that he hoped to see some evidence of her attachment to Ellen when the carriage brought its soaked passengers to the
plantation house.

> The men had told Mr. Pierce that they would row up sooner than he could
> ride up to tell the news, but he did not believe them, and galloped all the
> way from Land's End to be the first to make the announcement to me. He
> came in about a quarter of an hour after they did, and as I was then upstairs,
> heard from Nelly the arrival of the men. When I came down he greeted me
> with, "So you fainted at the news?" "No," I said, "not at the news, but I have
> not been well for a week and was startled by Rina, and getting up suddenly
> made me faint." He was determined to see a scene if possible, but when Ellen
> came and I stood on the porch as she came up the stairs from the carriage,

we shook hands very quietly and walked into the parlor in the ordinary manner of acquaintances. It was not until we were upstairs that we cut any capers
of joy. She had been detained by the rain, the whole party stopping in the
Episcopal Church where they played on the organ and sang, Mr. McKim and
Lucy being highly delighted at the ride, the romantic church, and the meeting
with some of the superintendents.[12]

Lucy was finally able to spend some hours on June 12 to write to both
her mother and to Ellen. The letters are virtually fair copies of each other
and there is no way of knowing which was written first, though the letter
to her mother contains more details as she excitedly described the events
of her first few days on St. Helena. She had heard the singing of the slaves
for the first tme, and as she excitedly told her mother, "I have also copied
down a number of the wild sad songs of the negroes—tunes & words
both."[13]

St. Helena Island, June 12
Dear Mother,
    While over at Beaufort this afternoon we heard that the *Arago* is to sail
tomorrow at 2 o'clock P. M., so I occupy myself with the others in writing
a line to send by her. Father left me at Dr. Peck's (in Beaufort) after dinner
on Tuesday last, to go with Mr. French to Hilton Head again, & after that to
Stone—one of the islands. Yesterday instead of returning as he had expected
to do, he sent me a note saying that we wouldn't go back on the *Arago*, as
there was more to be seen and done than he had known of. Most likely he
will return to "The Oaks" tomorrow. ("The Oaks" is the name of the Pope
Plantation, where Miss Towne is.) So we await the next steamer. I only hope it
will be a long time sailing.
    I am keeping a diary as I must tell you everything when I get home
instead of writing it now, as there is so little time. I have also copied down a
number of the wild sad songs of the negroes—tunes & words both. Almost
everybody is going back on the *Arago*, not from any general reason I believe,
unless it is a groundless fear of sesech from "The Main," as they call South
Carolina proper. The weather could not be finer. So far it has not been as
warm as we had it just before leaving home. After nine o'clock A. M. there
is always a fine sea breeze. I hardly know how to write without beginning at
some point & describing on regularly; so I guess I'll start from Hilton Head,
as we left it Sunday morning last. While waiting for the row boat to get ready
we stood on the deck of the *Ericsson*, then unloading at the wharf, & watched
the scene. Nobody could have guessed it to be Sunday. Contrabands pushing

round barrels & boxes, officers riding up & down the dock, a line of baggage wagons continually on the move, & everywhere men, men, men—soldiers chiefly. Quite noticeable among the latter were some of the 1st. Reg't. of S. Carolina volunteers, fine looking blacks, dressed precisely as our other soldiers. When we bade adieu to our *Arago* friends, Mrs. Cooley, Captain Gadsden & the rest, it really seemed as if we had known them a very long time. Five contrabands, viz. old Joe, Jerry, Gabriel, Pompey & John Cole rowed us to Land's End, singing all the way. Whittier's "negro boatmen" was "bebuilded better than he knew," & as for Sanford's, it's more like the creation than they are themselves! Land's End is on St. Helena. There we got shore, the darkeys carrying the gentlemen on their backs & pulling us up in the boat. At a little distance from shore was an old plantation house, where our friend Mr. Eustis & his son, who had taken refuge there the night before, on hearing of the arrival of the Rebels. A few Conn. soldiers were with him. After some chat Mr. Pierce started off on homeward, & we in the most distressed secesh equipage, with a pair [of] enormous Gov't. Rosinantes, and an "intelligent" contraband of Mr. Eustice's named Chance to drive us. There were ten miles to go to reach "The Oaks." The first part of the way was through young cotton fields, blackberry wildernesses, but soon we entered the "Pine Barren," a smooth broad white road through a real tropical forest. Miss Murray & I were exclamations from that point forward. Just wait till I get home to go off over live oaks, magnolias, hanging moss, & superb foliage. All of a sudden it began to pour like one stream & me almost wholly wet by the time we arrived at a small Paradise in the shape of a deserted church surrounded by oaks. There we alighted, & found some other storm [stained] folks who proved to be Mr. Philbrick, a son of Mr. Weld's friend, his wife who is a sister of Rufus Windsor's, Miss Ware, daughter of May and Henry Ware, Charles Sumner, Kitty friend's friend that I was to meet, Mr. Horton the Baptist minister, several young gentlemen, Garnett, Parke, &c. &c. A most delightful half hour was passed there talking & playing on the organ, which strange to say had not been destroyed. I never touched an organ before, queer experience to have there for the first time, wasn't it? We sang "Dennis"! Presently the storm was over, & we drove on again, passing another very beautifully situated church, the negro church—Miss Towne was standing on the lower verandah as we drove up, & her welcome was most cordial. Miss Nelly Hansen, & Mr. Edward Hooper, two very young folks from Mass. (that is about 22) were introduced. I know them very well now, & think them "tip top", as [?] would say. After a little brushing up we lunched off of cucumbers, hominy, blackberries, figs, tea coffee & cocoa, & hard biscuits. Now I must stop particularizing, for it is so late; everybody has gone to bed save Mr.

Hooper & myself. We have visited four islands, H. Head, P. Royal, St. H's. &
Ladies', ever so many plantations, negroes are as thick as flies everywhere, &
as black, I have hardly seen one mulatto, been to two "shouts," & one "praise,"
went over the ship "Onward" blockading, been introduced to profusions of
milliingtary [*sic*], have seen of Seymour Severance a good deal, expect Commodore Dupont here to dinner, dined twice at Dr. Peaks, ride on horse back
yesterday, am bringing up four mocking birds, am looking daily for Genl.
Saxton; don't want to go home, got a shark, mistletoe bough, palmetto in various shapes, variety of leaves &c. as trophies. Most of all though, we are with
the negroes. I cannot tell you how intense I am. I have jottings of their talk to
tell you when I get back, *if* I come! Now good night. Best love to all.
   Excuse this hurried bit of a letter. We are both ...

(She continues writing across the opening lines of the letter's opening
page.)

We live in the greatest estate, two cooks, two waiters, three coachmen, always
a footman, never touch our rooms &c. How would you like to drive with
Chance in front, & Cupid behind? Besides these there are Plenty, January,
Orchard, Dido, Scyla, Venus, & c. & c. They smile & grin all day long I never
saw such a set! Susannah the cook says it can't last—it's too much happiness!
But what cruelty there's been on this plantation! One woman whose back
is covered with welts like wens, gave birth to three different children whose
limbs were found broken—eyes knocked out. You can guess how. There is
a bent tree in the back yard that Aunt Phillis says could tell a tale! It feels
smooth & human to the touch.
   Now adieu. Ever affy—Lucy

   The term she used, "Rosinantes," was a reference to Don Quixote's rawboned, tottering horse of that name. In her copy of the letter to Ellen she
identified Rufus Windsot as "an old Eagleswooder," someone else they
knew who had been at the school. In Ellen's letters to their friends, keeping them informed about Lucy's journey, it is clear that her feelings were
mixed. She was at once pleased and excited that Lucy was having a time
that was so satisfying for her, and at the same time she was envious that she
hadn't found any adventure like it for herself. She couldn't resist writing
comments on the letter, as though she and Lucy were having another of
their intense conversations. When Lucy wrote of the two twenty-two-year-
olds from Boston as "very young," Ellen added a half-mocking rebuke: "(I
think Miss Lucy's own age is 19—she wants veneration in speaking of [her

elders]?)." After Lucy wrote that she was bringing up four mockingbirds Ellen added: "(one can't say wot larks! E. W.)." The oarsmen in the boat with their parcels and baggage had rowed them across the sound from Hilton Head to the indentation in the shoreline known as Land's End. The plantation road across the island ended there, and though it was not any particular place on the island it was probably called Land's End simply because it was here that the road ended.

◆ ◆ ◆

Today there is a wooden pier at Land's End, but when the boat carrying Lucy and her father and their party were rowed across from Hilton Head there was no pier for assisting their landing. When the boat drew close to the beach the rowers leaped into the water, and as Lucy related, they carried the men on their backs over the last stretch of water and deposited them on the rough stones and gravel of the narrow beach. Then the boat was pulled up on shore with the women still in it, clinging to its sides, and the rowers helped them step out onto the land. Across the bay behind them Hilton Head was a low, flat stretch of earth with no dimensions to the north or south.

The party would have scrambled up the low bluff, about fifteen feet above the beach, and walked to the carriage waiting for them on the high ground. The road that Lucy described still crosses the island, and for the first hundred yards, before it joins a modern paved road, it is still a rough dirt track. It is lined with young pines, and darkened by the shadows of the outstretched branches of the oaks that had covered so much of the island before it was cleared for planting. The branches are heavy with the gray mist of Spanish moss, trailing loosely in the almost continuous breeze off the ocean. For the first stretches of the paved road it takes short turns through land still left to wilderness and dense with brush. Then the road straightens, obviously following old plantation boundaries. For three or four miles it passes unwaveringly through the fenced fields that Lucy noted were then a lush wilderness, but now are green with grasses mowed for animal fodder in the summers.

At a turn in the road there is a crumbling ruin of a building about the size of a small barn, but with the unmistakable rectangular dimensions of a church. The roof is long gone, and at the end of the open space where the altar once stood the wall is open to the elements, with the patch of grass outside the ruined walls crowding toward the opening. Probably the altar was once framed there by a wood enclosure and the wood had rotted away. The heavy remaining walls, slowly eroding with the years of rain and sun, are a thick masonry made of mussel shells bound together with mortar and covered with plaster. Two brick pillars still frame the opening that was once the door. The ruin is the Episcopal Church where Lucy and the people from the wagon fled to get out of the rain and where Lucy played an organ for the first time.

Today none of the buildings of the Pope Plantation itself have survived, but on the land at the edge of the road Pope had the slaves erect a large brick church, and it still stands among the darkness of the massive oaks that perhaps were already rooted there when the church was built. Beside the church is a small cemetery, one small area enclosed with a rusting iron fence, with the large, carved headstones marking the graves of three women of the family who had died only a few years before the plantation was abandoned. A less elaborate cemetery plot close by could contain the remains of the house servants.

What was the plantation is now the historical site of the Penn School and Cultural Center, with its museum across the road from the church. It was this school that Laura Towne and Ellen Murray founded in the turbulent months of 1862. In the museum an exhibition relates the story of their role in the school, with James McKim's name there in association, with two photos, one of Laura sitting and reading to a group of children, the other of Ellen surrounded with her own small group of children. The open grounds of the school are still marked by the presence of the great oaks, their long sweeping branches reaching out as if they yearned to touch the oaks separated from them across the bare ground, the branch ends and the twigs gray with the wind-stirred thickness of the moss. As a jaunty contrast, palmettos with their ragged crowns of leafy fronds are scattered across the open spaces, their skinny trunks punctuating the sober spread of the oaks.

◆ ◆ ◆

The long trip had been exhausting, but there was a praise meeting in the slave quarters and everyone went in the darkness to hear the singing. McKim and Pierce sat up into the night in the downstairs parlor, talking about the problems and the prospects of the workers who were gathering on the island while the women sat around them silently listening. When the house finally was quiet, Ellen and Laura slept on mattresses on the floor in a room upstairs, while Lucy and Nelly Windsor slept in the two beds left in the room.

The house where Lucy had found a bed for the night had been the home of Daniel Pope, the owner of the plantation, the land, the buildings, and the slaves living in the quarters behind the main house. At the fall of Port Royal he had abruptly fled with his family, exhorting some of his slaves to follow him. Of the few who remained long enough to listen to his speech, none showed any interest in joining him. The other plantation slaves were already hiding out of sight of the house in the brushy swamp. With the house lying abandoned there had been damage in the slaves' outburst of plundering, but most of the house's furnishings had been seized by one of the government agents on the island, who had been instructed to seize all rebel property, which he decided also included the furnishings in the plantation houses. The later arrivals who were to supervise the new planting and organize the schools and some kind of health care found themselves given empty rooms, begging battered chairs from the government's storehouse of seized goods, and making do with the few beds and tables that had been left.

◆ ◆ ◆

In her days at the plantation Lucy quickly learned that their house was the center of the island's activities as people streamed in and out of the parlor and the verandah. In her diary Laura Towne noted the daily activities of the new party. Sunday night, June 8, there was a prayer meeting in a house on the plantation grounds; the next night they went together to a shout, the first that Lucy or her father had ever experienced, which, Towne noted, "Mr. McKim was inclined to think was a remnant of African worship."[14] The next day, Tuesday, June 10, Lucy, Laura, Ellen, and Nelly Winsor rode to the Mary Jenkins plantation, "where the children screamed and ran to hide at the sight of white faces." The women had brought with them looking glasses and salt, with other provisions to distribute, not aware that after what the slaves had suffered in the last days of their captivity, when they had been subject to raids and attacks on the slave men still on the plantations, any white face could be yet another threat.

So much of the time in the two months since Towne had come to the island had been a tangle of misunderstandings, sudden frights, confusions, wary uncertainties, and despairs that when she wrote a letter to a friend on June 13 she seemed surprised herself at how her mood had changed. Ellen had arrived, and at the same time the cotton agent, who had been consigned half of the house, had moved and left the whole house to her and the other teachers.

You don't know how comfortable and even elegant our apartments are, now that we have all the furniture the cotton agent had in his half of the house. There are no other such accommodations in this region, and we shall be foolish to go away for anything but health.[15]

Anyone coming to the islands from the northern states was cautioned strenuously by friends about the summers, when the southern air was thought to breed disease. Towne considered the warning, but she continued:

If there should be any likelihood of sickness, we can remove easily to the watering-place of the islands, St. Helenaville, about six miles from here, and then we can ride over twice a week or so to see our people. But I do not see why this place cannot be a good enough location to stay in all summer. As for the late alarm about "Sesech" coming, everybody is ashamed of it, and all try to prove that they were not frightened at such an unlikelihood. It is an impossibility now, as gunboats are stationed on all sides . . .

She was annoyed that a letter she had written earlier had been printed in its entirety, but she was also aware that many of the people were writing about what they were experiencing. Lucy, she notes, was recording her own impresssions of the island.

If my present leisure continues, I shall perhaps write for the Tribune an occasional letter, but Mr. McKim is taking notes, and will tell everything, I fancy. Lucy is a very nice girl and she is busy collecting facts, etc. Mr. French, too, is writing a book, and so there will be an overstock of information, I think.

In a letter to Beverly Chase, Ellen Wright told him of the war spirit that was gripping the people she knew, then added cheerfully that Lucy's trip was going well.

13th (I guess) June
Our young men here are quite enthusiastic over the call for more troops, & several of them are deciding to enlist, notwithstanding the good business and the dear friends they leave behind them. How unpleasant it feels to be a woman, and so obliged to stay at home, but we can write letters to keep up their spirits & nurse them when they are sick. . . .
Lucy, angelic she! does write me such dear old letters about her trip. You have probably heard it all by word of mouth.[16]

James McKim was hurried from one part of the island to another, listening and attempting to make some judgments on everything he was told about the problems and the expectations of the people already on St. Helena. As he sat through seemingly unending meetings with the military commanders and the civilian staff, he became increasingly unsure of what his plans should be. There was much for him to accomplish on the island, but the committee in Philadelphia had at least as much use there in the city for his skills. On June 13 he wrote to his wife that he might stay on in Port Royal:

> ... Lucy does not know of my purpose to stay, but she will be delighted to hear of it for her heart is wholly in the work, and she is as happy as she can be. I left her in [?] at Pope's Island "at home."[17]

After mailing his letter he followed one of the men staying on the island on an "excursion" to have some better idea about how secure they were from a military threat, and the next day Laura Towne added an anguished note to her diary.

> Mr. McKim has returned from his excursion with Mr. French and he is so impressed by our dangerous situation, regarding the enemy and the climate, that he urges us to go home at once. Ellen and I are determined not to go and I think our determination will prevail over his fears, so that he will not order us home, as he has the power, I suppose. We are troubled about this. The military cram every newcomer with fears.[18]

As in confirmation of his misgivings the next night there was a Confederate raid on Hutchinson's Island. Some of the people on the island were seized, and, in an exchange of fire, men from the island were wounded. General Hunter, who had the military command of their area, ordered the other people on exposed islands to be removed to Beaufort. The next day, Monday the 16th, Lucy, Ellen, and Laura went on a visit to four nearby plantations, but the men in the party, concerned for their safety, rode on horseback beside their carriage, dismounting to walk ahead to determine if there were any danger when they came to damaged bridges or shallow fords across the rivers.

By now it was clear to Lucy's father that they should return, but it was just as clear that Laura and Ellen would stay. Ellen held the first class of what would become the Penn School in the back room of the house with nine adult "scholars." There was such interest in her class and the enrollments grew so quickly that she realized she would soon have to move her classes out of the Brick Church. She and Laura were never to leave St. Helena except for short visits to their families. Their lives together continued there for forty years, never wavering in their commitment to bring learning to the people of the island.

◆ ◆ ◆

On June 23 there was a formal review of the black regiment in their camp by General Hunter, and he took the McKims, Laura, and Ellen with him as guests. On their return Laura saw Lucy and her father off for their return voyage. There had been fighting only a day before at the island of Edisto, halfway to Charleston and a crucial staging place for any of the attacks planned on the city. There had been no decisive victory for either side, and the stalemate on the coastal islands would continue for three more years until 1865, when General William T. Sherman, his army having ravaged north Georgia, burnt Atlanta, and destroyed much of Savannah, turned north toward Charleston. Towne noted that the steamer that was to take the McKims back to Philadelphia was loaded with the wounded from the Edisto fighting.

As Lucy had promised, after her return she wrote a long letter to Ellen Wright about what she had seen and heard, though there was no time for her letter until they were back in the house in Germantown. She ended it with the promise to continue.

> Hilltop July 3rd 1862
> Dear Ellen,
> Here I am, back again, brown as a chestnut, perpetually hungry, & not in the least dead of malaria! To be sure I did indulge in a few measles, but otherwise never as better all the time I was away. And did I have a splendid, glorious, splenderific, magnificent, nice time? My dear, those are feeble adjectives . . . I enjoyed myself so much, that in recollection there is even a halo around the sea-sickness & an ecstatic thrill in every flea-bite! . . . one can slowly realize that one lives in a cage, until accident sets you flying outside. . . . I will go on from our first luncheon at "The Oaks." The rest of that afternoon was spent in visiting the "Yard," which down there refers particularly to the enclosure containing all the outhouses—i. e. stables, corn house, cotton house, chicken house, cabins of house servants, etc. & the Quarters—or "Nigger-houses." These were built in two long rows, facing each other, with a row of beautiful trees, "Pride of China," down the center. Behind every cabin was

a garden patch, containing a few vegetables, groundnuts & always a fig-tree. This appears to be the plan of almost all the "quarters" I saw.

There was a general opening of doors as we made our appearance at the entrance of the "street," as they call it, & we shook hands as if we have been candidates for Congress. Miss Murray was introduced as "Miss Ellen," the nice young lady who was to stay & teach them, & myself as "Miss Lucy, who sent the clothes, & molasses, & bacon to them!" (N.B. "Some have greatness thrust upon them.") "Sweet Jesus! Cant–be, cant-be! Dear Lord! Just look at her! O! Missis! De tings *too* good, *too* good!" etc etc. The party of children at our heels soon divided, some following me & some Miss Murray, & the boldest holding on to our skirts gently. We could hear, "O, you get out, you Dido. Dis yer *my* missus!" "Keep off, Elsie, Keep to y'oun missus!" Their huts are inconceivably small & filthy. With but few exceptions, the occupants lie on the floor, in bundles of rags, that have been reduced to one common dirt color. Under their beds they keep their corn, which get full of weevils, & what with these & fleas & mosquitoes & other vermin, they are kept constantly on the scratch. But I didn't mean to enter on a description of things that you will probably see printed—After our tour, during which I couldn't make up my mind whether I wanted most to laugh or to cry, we sat down in the parlor . . . About eight o'clock we were called out to dinner; bill of fare (I forget what we had that particular meal) generally fricasseed chickens—the sole kind of fresh meat available—some splendid fish, mullen or whiting, hashed crabs, beets or peas, or squashes—twice green corn—always rice & govt. biscuit. Then dinner was removed, & supper, consisting of tea or coffee, waffles, cornbread, wafers, clauber cakes, hot biscuit, cucumbers & figs, carried in. We did not always have clauber cake, but always the others. Wasn't that "roughing it"? The cooking was all done in an outhouse & carried in. A woman & a boy waited on us. The boy kept off the flies with an oleander bough. After dinner we went down to the "praise," which was held in the biggest & cleanest cabin—Aunt Phillis's. Boards were laid across for seats, & an end of a tallow candle stuck in a black bottle stood on a shelf in a corner & gave the only light. The little place was quite crowded, but room was made for us. The services were nearly over when we entered, there remained only two interminable hymns & a prayer. For the prayer we all knelt down &—well, I just cried, all through it. A prayer so simple, touching, & eloquent—I never heard. The preacher was an old black man whose work was to supply the table with fish, figs & vegetables. He was husband to one of the cooks, who has had 21 children—not an uncommon case, they said. But I must stop now. "To be continued." . . .[19]

As an afterthought Lucy added—above the opening of the letter—a short paragraph on the first page.

> I went to bed that eventful day, as if I'd lived a year since morning. The *Arago* was like an old memory. And that was a sample of the following days; each contained a month's interest. So you see I am in such a hurry to give you all the *facts* that I skip the *impressions*, which a wise narrator never would do.

Her promise was repeated in a note two weeks later.

> Hilltop. 18th July 1862
> Dear Ellen
> ... Not a word yet of Port Royal, you say. This is why. I am about writing out my adventures, & you shall have the benefit of a perusal when it is done; which I think would be better, as you see I have so much to say about other things that it would make my letter entirely too long to write ... [20]

If Lucy went on in those hot summer months to write her promised chronicle, it has never been found.

8

Poor Rosy, Poor Gal

Poor Rosy, Poor Gal
Poor Rosy, Poor Gal
Poor Rosy, Poor Gal
    Heab'n shall-a be my home
    Before I spend one day in hell,
        Heab'n shall-a be my home
    I sing and pray my soul away
        Heab'n shall-a be my home
    Poor Rosy, Poor Gal, etc.

Got hard trial in my way!
Hard trial in my way,
Hard trial in my way.
    Heab'n shall-a be my home
    O! when I talk I talk wid God.
        Heab'n shall-a be my home
    O! when I talk I talk wid God.
        Heab'n shall-a be my home
    Poor Rosy, poor Gal!
    Poor Rosy, poor Gal!
    Poor Rosy, Poor Gal!
        Heab'n shall-a be my home.

Songs of the Freedmen of Port Royal
"Collected and Arranged by Miss Lucy McKim"
Philadelphia, 1862

The summer heat that Lucy had expected in South Carolina lay in wait for them when she and her father returned to Hilltop. Though the house was on the crest of the hill they never felt the sea breezes that had cleared the air under the oaks around the Pope Plantation house on St. Helena's Island. They missed the torment of the mosquitoes that plagued the island later in the summer, but Philadelphia on their return was hot, sticky, heavy, and numbing. On the hottest days Lucy sometimes didn't come downstairs for breakfast. As long as she stayed in her room she didn't have to dress. Just putting on a light summer dress would also mean putting on all the other garments she had to wear under it.

Her journey to South Carolina had given Lucy a glimpse of a kind of life that was beyond her dreams, and on her return she began the summer in a rush of anticipation. On July 3, 1862, two weeks after their return, she wrote to Ellen in an effusive outburst:

> Life opens so grandly in 1862, Elle, even if we 'only stand & wait' that I cannot wish to write *finis* to my history yet and of course the end of the story always is: So they were married & lived peacefully & happily ever after. Oh, I'm so thankful I'm not married or engaged. There is too much to see, to hear, do & feel first.[1]

Ellen's reply on July 7 was a return to her usual banter, but it ended on a tone of annoyance. She clearly was still envious of Lucy's adventure.

> It is a comfort to feel that you are safely home again, after this strange experience & the greatest comfort of all is to know that one at least of your dreams has been realized—it is such a horrid bother to feel so tied to mortality, a base law of space as it were. So that you never can carry out any plans. But I've got a Steinway, so off with your caps boys! Only I might as well be a chair or a sofa pillow or any other article of furniture for all I can play upon it. But let us be joyful—diminution!—I was afraid that you would find it not quite so delightful going as you anticipated (young people's ideas sometimes being extravagant)—I rejoice that you enjoyed it so, but now I suppose you will be subject to fits of anxiety to return . . .[2]

She also responded to Lucy's declaration that she was so thankful she wasn't "married or engaged" by reminding her that their Eagleswood friend, Dick (Richard Chase), had already made it clear, at least to Ellen, that he felt himself attached to Lucy. Ellen had no idea that Lucy had responded to his feelings, since they had said nothing openly of their growing affection.

Now Luce, don't let Dick slide . . . If you would only be very patient you know, you may be glad someday . . . He is provoking of course, being a male person.

Then she continued testily:

With all your minutiae you are a trifle unsatisfactory, you don't say enough about people. Why didn't you say how Miss Murray looks, and whether you knew her well enough to like her, & you speak of your "set". I didn't know you had any *set* except Mr. & Mrs. McKim. Was Mr. Frank Conley sent down by the Port R. Soc. too, that he belongs to you? Now do describe these folks so that I can have them in my mind's eye. How shouldn't I like to be sitting in one corner of your comfortable sofa now—oh no—of course not.

Lucy was less effusive in her letters to Ellen about the men around them, and she chose not to tell her that although there had been no formal declaration between her and Dick Chase, it was clear to each of them that they had an understanding. She only wanted more time. He laughed and joked in their meetings with friends, but he was also sensitive to her wishes, and they had known each other so long that they were certain of each other's trust. Not even his brother, Beverly, spoke of their attachment, though he must have known about it, and it drew him closer to Lucy. Whatever Ellen thought about Beverly's infatuation with her, he was unwavering in his devotion.

Lucy was already working on arrangements of a number of the songs she had collected in Port Royal. The arrangements would be for voice and piano accompaniment, intended for musical evenings with friends. At the same time she found hours for her own piano practice and the piano lessons for her young scholars. In the mornings she joined other women at one of the hospitals that had been opened for the wounded in Germantown "picking lint" for bandages, and sewing flannel undershirts and carpet slippers. There was a break in July when one of the blockade ships she and her father had been invited to board in Port Royal, the *Wabash*, returned to the Philadelphia Navy Yard for repairs. She and her sister, Annie, were invited by friends and the young officers of the crew to spend a day being shown around the vessel, one of the newly commissioned showpieces of the fleet. The visit with the ship's very hospitable officers only strengthened Lucy's already intense stirrings of patriotic fervor. She wrote to Ellen, still in the tide of her feelings, and upset—as the entire North was—over the failure of the Union armies in the summer's fighting on the roads to Richmond.

It's too hot to go down for callers, & besides I'm not dressed,—entirely. The weather here is shockingly hot & close.... Elle, Anne & I have had a steady influx of patriotism since the Richmond battles, & we are not going to countenance young men who stay at home for purely selfish motives. Seriously, the indifference of some people makes me indignant. I don't want to talk spread-eagle, but every day it comes to me with greater force,—we *must* conquer. Why are the men so sluggish? Well—"since I can't be a man with wishing I will die a woman with grieving." I mean to get at Bev,—Dick couldn't be more useful than he is now at his gunboats—& fire him with "dulce et decorum est pro patria mori" or if not "mori," at least "pugnare."[3]

She was softening the Latin phrase meaning "sweet and beautiful it is to die for your country" by substituting the word "pugnare," which translated as "fighting for your country." She was sure that Dick was now doing enough by working in a Philadelphia foundry that was outfitting gunboats for the Union Navy. She ended the letter with a laconic aside. Ellen had already begun to suffer from severe migraine headaches, and Lucy was aware that writing letters could bring on an attack.

Don't write when you have a headache, but any how write soon. And don't be blue. I am too much, notwithstanding the nonsense I've scribbled.

♦ ♦ ♦

The abolitionists of Philadelphia were engaged in the search for teachers and supervisors to send to Port Royal, and Lucy's father was responsible for much of the fund-raising and finding of teachers who would be suitable for the school on the island. He spent hours in his downtown antislavery society office. To satisfy the gnawing hunger for information about everything on the island, he supervised a stream of meetings, gatherings, and discussions in the city. In the evenings people crowded into each other's parlors, or gathered in the churches and small meeting halls. Lucy's own contribution to the meetings now was the songs she had heard on the island and taught herself to sing. Among the gatherings where she sang them was a meeting held in the Motts' parlor. In a letter on August 17 Mrs. Mott wrote to a friend of Lucy's singing and playing. She spoke of the songs as "the Port Royal hymns which were very touching and some of them sad."[4] Lucy taught some of the songs to her sister, Annie, and by the end of the summer they were performing them together.

Lucy was still intent on learning more of the slaves' songs. Within weeks of her return from the South she was already writing friends who might be able to send her more examples. One letter went to Laura Towne, on St. Helena's Island. Towne answered in a note she sent to Lucy's father on August 2, as part of their continuous correspondence over the difficulties with the school there. She asked McKim to tell Lucy "she'd be very glad to help her with songs, but that she was no musician, and could take down only the words."[5] She had learned from Lucy's letter or from her father that Lucy had now finished arrangements for six of the songs for voice and piano accompaniment, and she mentioned them when she wrote again to McKim on September 24, enclosing some examples she had gathered of slave songs and saying that she would be happy to send more. "If the six she has undertaken are successful, in these hard times, she will surely want more 'by & by.'"

There is no question that Lucy would have continued to be absorbed in the music she had heard, and her dream of making a collection would have been realized. Whatever she intended to do with the songs, however, and whatever she wrote in her letters to Ellen, the war always intruded.

◆ ◆ ◆

The young men from Germantown who had hurried to enlist spent their first few weeks as new soldiers drilling in one of the nearby parade grounds, and crowds came to watch. These were sons of neighbors or friends Lucy had known in school. On bright summer days the bands and the marching music were an irresistible show. In a letter to Ellen she described one of her Sunday afternoon visits to a parade ground with her sister, Annie, a visitor, and some friends, only to have their pleasure dampened by the latest news from the war, which continued with no sign of a pause or any measurable success all through the summer.

> Will Bispham [a friend] made a flying visit of twelve hours to us last Sunday. . . . Mrs. Gibbons and mother according to an occasional practice of theirs, had clubbed dinners, with the joint amount to be partaken at the Gibbon's house. So we all toddled over. . . . In the late afternoon he & Carrie & I walked down to Collis's camp of Louisiana D'Afriques to see their last dress parade. They were to go the next day. I was glad I went. It was a beautiful scene. The day was perfect, the scenery lovely, the music inspiriting, & the Turkish costumes very picturesque. It would have been altogether delightful,

had we not heard that the good news of the preceding day was a lie from beginning to end, & we walked home quite disheartened & silent. Billy whistled a little to cheer us up, & and sang for us in the evening. [Lucy drew a small smiling face to end the sentence.] And my dear, what do you think he said when Ann opened the "Last Greeting" "Shall I sing it in French or German," says he. O! my my. If he'd staid all night I should have more to tell you. But he didn't. Alas. He went in in the 9½ train.[6]

The Louisiana D'Afriques were young musicians from Germantown who had formed a military band that was outfitted in the popular Turkish-styled Zouave costumes. The band continued to wear their scarlet pantaloons, flowing waistbands, and fezzes throughout the war.

◆ ◆ ◆

On the 12th of August Lucy wrote again to Ellen, and the yearning that she had expressed so many times before to be part of the struggle cast its shadow over the spaces between the lines. She wrote to say that both the Chase brothers, Richard and Beverly, had enlisted, and whatever feelings she might have had at Dick Chase's news, her letter to Ellen again expressed her resentment as she hungered to be able to do more than the work women were given. There also had to be a sense of dismay. She hadn't been aware that Dick had been considering enlisting, and she had always assured herself that with his responsibilities at a Philadelphia foundry producing war supplies he would be safe. However much she had allowed herself to think of their situation, it was clear that now she would have little time to be "patient" with him, as Ellen had advised. As she wrote, it was obvious how deeply shaken she was by Dick's decision. Before she reached the last lines of her letter the tone of her words had turned into a fervent declaration of what she could plainly see as her duties in the struggle. At the close she returned to her still heady memories of her experiences in South Carolina to bolster her feelings.

Hill Top. Aug 12th, 1862
Dear Elle,
Dick came out here last night for a letter of introduction from father to Capt. Palmer in Buell's Body Guard, & told us he and Bev. had enlisted! I suppose Bev wrote to you of it on Sunday. We were very much astonished, especially about Dick, as he had always seemed a fixture at the foundry.

I did so ache so for you to sleep with me that night, for who can feel more interested in those two dear fellows than you and I? And now I write to you for no earthly reason except to let steam off!

Noble boys! God bless them for going, a thousand, thousand times! May the Lord shelter them wherever they are. They could not be closer to me in entering this hallowed warfare, if they were my own brothers. You are to be envied to have one of your very own to send . . . when I think of the soldiers "I have enlisted" is always the open sesame to my heart.

Sentimental? You must let us prate, us girls. What else is there for us, but to wish vaguely, & cry blindly, "for those who will never come back to the town." But there is something better, too, what was I saying? Don't look backward, but forward; let us give ourselves to this struggle,—wholly. If we can't do anything now but pick lint & and sew for the hospitals, maybe *sometime* God will turn to us for a noble work. For one I say, *never, never, never* give up! Let every cent, & every friend, & every hope go first! Rather a lifetime of loneliness & sorrow for individuals than miss the redemption of the nation. Kneeling in that poor cabin with those who suffered scourgings at our hands, & listening to that child-like old preacher calling down blessings on their new friends who had come "so far, 'way from de beautiful Norf" to deliver them, instead of cursing every Anglo-Saxon, as he had cause & right to do—I vowed that if I ever forgot them, so might Heaven forget me! & So everyone that joins "the army of the Lord" reminds me that there is to be no interest in this life here, except as a preparation for those duties which must come.

Goodbye, darling. Write oftener to me, we must love each other more, now those others have gone. Bev. I believe is going to Auburn; I am glad you will see him again. Once more, God bless them & you.

Perhaps realizing herself that her emotions had carried her beyond the accustomed limits of their nearly daily exchanges of letters, she signed her full name, "Lucy McKim."[7]

Ellen felt many of the things that Lucy had expressed, but her emotions were complicated by the realities of her own family's situation. Her brother Frank had enlisted and she was conscious that her own impetuous attitude had abruptly changed when she realized that he now could be in danger. On August 21, 1862, she wrote to Annie McKim from Auburn.

My dear Anne,

Perhaps you think this isn't a melting afternoon for the poor soldiers to march around town in, but it is—and the air is full of martial music, which

would just suit young ladies, who are emphatically patriotic—not to say that
we are not also burning with a like ardor—but then there is such a sad side to
everything.

Ah me—I'm afraid this war must break our hearts, before it liberates the
slaves, whose hearts have for so long been of no account.

I pity these young, inexperienced, hopeful things going to such severe
duty. It seems easy enough to sit at home, amidst luxuries, and say 'Go, or be
a coward'—I'm sure it is miserable hard to leave love & comfort, to take one's
life in one's hand and go forth, enthusiasm or not. And women must stay
at home, & sew their bravery into small bags, & roll their energy into hard
bandages, & never do anything chivalrous—except wear bright faces, in hard
times like these. How much life a staunch, thoroughgoing President might
put into the people—But this imbecile whom we have the misfortune to call
our ruler is it not strange, that he will let his chance for Heaven slip thro' such
lax fingers? Fancy Fremont & Jesse[8] in the chair, then not only would there be
willing fighting, but something would come of it. If we deserve all this horrid
retribution, because we have been wicked, I don't see as that is any comfort. It
may be just, however.—

If you are so strict about young men's enlisting, I fear you would lead a
sorry life here—I know several who have no notion of going. Poor Joe Lever-
ing! I can imagine his look of dismay to see you coming toward him with
a regimental roll in yr. pocket. I suppose he *prefers* to be "refined without
blood"—Don't be making a bugbear of yourself Anne—To be sure your life
is in the army, & so you can't see why other people are not able to live under
similar circumstances—but did you feel altogether, bona fide glad, when Dick
and Bev enlisted. Ask Lux if she did. I hated for Willy to go back—for in the
first place, he didn't seem strong enough, & in the next, who cares for the
Union "as it was", and that's all they seem to be fighting for now! And then
think of Dick & B. under that [illegible] Buell!— oh lor! What's the use of
talking?

If Beverly Chase had been older there might have been less of a problem for Ellen, but he was four years younger, and his open attentions
caused her some embarrassment, though she acknowledged that she was
pleased to be his friend. Under the accepted code of behavior, a carefully
supervised "friendship" was all she could consider acceptable. Both she
and Lucy never considered breaking away from the strict sexual mores
of the period, though Ellen had in her letters at least already considered
herself engaged to two young men and thought herself briefly in love with
several others. Lucy was only nineteen when Dick Chase told her he was

leaving, and she had steadily insisted to everyone that she wanted to do "something" before she committed herself to marriage. In her letters to Ellen, what she spoke of passionately was her desire to live her own life— at least for a little longer.

On a visit to Philadelphia, Bev had hovered so closely over Ellen that "his intentions" were obvious to everyone, at least from Ellen's point of view. Her mother, who had heard of the situation in letters from her sister, Lucretia Mott, wrote Ellen that she had to be careful not to encourage him. To lessen her mother's worries Ellen decided that she would break off any contact with him until he was twenty-one, which would mean that they would have no contact for three years. Somehow it seemed to her like a realistic request to make, and having no choice Bev had agreed. The assumption on her part was that for these years they would communicate with each other through Lucy. To offer Bev some consolation in his seemingly hopeless situation she encouraged Lucy to become friendlier with him, scolding her for not responding to his good nature and his obvious sincerity. The afternoon before Bev was to leave for the army he came to the McKim house, and whatever Lucy might have said bravely about her good wishes at his enlistment, their clumsy goodbye left her deeply upset. She wrote Ellen after receiving her first letter from him.

> Since I wrote to you I have seen Bev. once and Dick not at all. Bev. came out the aft. of the day he was to go & staid to tea. We had company—forget who—& of course it was unsatisfactory. I introduced him to the girls & he had quite a long talk with Kitty, who liked him very well, & whom he took quite a fancy to. He went in at 8 o'clock, & I shook hands with him at the front door for the last time—perhaps. I wanted to kiss him, but couldn't, like a great silly, do anything but stand there & feel stunned. That was all. He said a lot very fast, but I didn't hear it. . . .[9]

The summer had been disastrous for the Union, but in Maryland in September McClellan's army stopped an attempt by Lee's army to invade the North at Antietam Creek. It was one of the war's bloodiest battles. Lincoln was aware that Britain, in its concern for the disastrous economic effects among British workers by the blockade of southern cotton, was under increasing pressures to recognize the new Confederacy. The failure of Lee's army made an ultimate southern victory seem less of a certainty. It was at this unexpected moment of success following months of demoralizing failure that Lincoln glimpsed an opportunity to newly define the meaning of the war. On September 22 he issued the first Emancipation

Proclamation. The full effect of the proclamation was delayed until January 1, 1863, and there was much in the declaration that failed to satisfy the most ardent of the abolitionists, but it could result in a final vindication for their decades of struggle. For Lucy the precise wording of the proclamation was less than satisfactory since it did not condemn slavery, but the effect of the document would be the fulfillment of everything she had felt when she first walked among the slave cabins on the Pope Plantation.

On October 1 she wrote to Ellen:

> There ought to be a good chance that we have Emancipation. O! that proc-
> lamation! Is it not worth living for, selfish and imperfect as it may seem to
> Abolitionists? Let us be thankful that we are simply alive, with eyes and ears!
> Let us be double thankful that we are Americans, & Americans of today
> instead of Yesterday or Tomorrow! Indeed, I believe that the only thing I have
> just a little to be sorry for is that I am white, & not black!—except my wom-
> anhood, that 'I bewail in sack cloth & ashes.'[10]

In the fall Lucy began giving more of her hours to instructing young piano "scholars." Eagleswood School had closed briefly the year before so there was no longer an opportunity for her to teach there. The school had finally begun to experience some financial stability, encouraging enough for Angelina Weld to write to Lucy's father to say that they could now think of purchasing much-needed equipment and finance their son's entrance into a university. Their son, however, had fallen ill, and Angelina and her sister were conscious that the demands on her husband's energies had undermined his health as well, so the decision was made to close the school. Later Marcus Spring struggled to keep it open as a military academy for a few years, but any youth who could be considered a likely student was now receiving military instruction in the war itself.

Lucy's foster sister, Annie, had also taught music at Eagleswood, and the sisters set out to turn their piano lessons into a more serious endeavor. On September 23 Lucy and Annie printed up a handbill which they circulated in Philadelphia, announcing that they were still giving piano lessons. Their modestly printed notice read:

> Miss Annie C. McKim and Miss Lucy McKim continue to give lessons on
> the PIANO at their residence, corner of Day's and Cottage Lanes, and at the
> houses of pupils in Philadelphia and in and about Germantown.
>   They have the advantage, as teachers, of four years experience, having
> given instruction, part of that time at Eagleswood Boarding School. They

make *thoroughness of groundwork with new beginners* a point of the first importance. Terms $15.00 a quarter.
REFERENCES:—Prof. B. Carr Cross, Prof. Frederick Molinhauer, George H. Earle, Esq. Hon. Charles Gibbons, William Howell, Esq., and Hon. William Morris Davis.
GERMANTOWN, September 23d, 1862[11]

In the letters that flowed between Lucy and Ellen, often daily, sometimes twice a day, the two young women usually confined their pages to discussions of their personal feelings, and there are only glimpses of Lucy's engagement in music and her attendance at abolitionist gatherings. Her time was so taken up with everything else that demanded her attention that she had only spare moments for the slave songs she had begun transcribing, and she and Ellen had much else to write each other about. In a long, busy letter to Ellen on September 9, 1862, she seemed to have forgotten the emotional outburst of her letter of less than a month before. She could even complain that she was getting old, "I am twenty! Commiserate [with] me!" But a few lines later, though her mood was still playful, the war once again intruded.

> I have had two letters from Bev. since I wrote to you, one coming right on the heels of the other, both in pencil & nearly illegible. Cause of the pencil: he had lost his writing materials. Cause of the illegibility: he wrote on the tiptop peak of a high hill, where the gentle zephers did so gambol about his paper that he was obliged to sit on one end of it & and confine the other with a large rock to keep it down. Them mayn't be his words, but they will convey the idea. He asked for a pair of wristlets, and I straightway knitted him a pair of crimson & chinchilla; lined 'em with red silk, & fastened in the lining of each a little bag of violet-sachet. Just as they were done, what must [his company] A. C. do, but go to LOUISVILLE without leaving a sign of an address, so I can neither answer Bev's letters now nor send him his sleeves.[12]

Only a few weeks after his enlistment, and without any formal military training, Beverly Chase had been attached to the Life Guard of General Don Carlos Buell, whom Ellen had written about with such distaste in her letter to Annie. Buell had bumbled through the war, distinguished mostly for excessive caution, though he managed to bring some semblance of organization to the troops he was given. The letter that Bev struggled to write on a hilltop in the wind was probably written on one of the hills around Chattanooga, Tennessee, where Buell had grouped his army,

hoping to capture the city. When his supply line, a railroad line from Louisville, Kentucky, was cut by southern raiders, he hurriedly drew the army
back to Louisville. It was somewhere on the abrupt flight that Lucy and
Bev lost contact.

There is certainly a poignancy of which she must have been aware herself in her knitting elaborately silk-lined wristlets with a bag of perfumed
sachet for Bev to wear under his thick uniform jacket through the sticking
mud and the grime and rancid sweat of a military campaign, but it was the
only way she could say to him that she did believe in the cause for which
he'd volunteered. She ended the letter with a hasty, half-sheet addenda to
Ellen, "I meant to have written about music, principally, when I began! O!
I've so much more to say, but can't take another half sheet, as it's night."

◆ ◆ ◆

What Lucy probably intended to write Ellen, when she wailed at her letter's close, "I meant to have written about music principally, when I began!
O! I've so much more to say . . . " was the exciting news that two of her
arrangements of the St. Helena songs she had collected would soon be
published. With a steady demand from amateur musicians everywhere in
the country, music publishing flourished both for a handful of large music
firms located in the larger cities, and for small independent publishers
in virtually every city and town in America. In October two of her settings were printed with dignified but ornately designed covers. There was
no publisher credited, only the name George Swain, a Philadelphia music
engraver, in small letters, and on the title page spaces had been left for five
additional titles.

The title page read boldly:

Songs of the
FREEDMEN
OF
Port Royal
Collected and Arranged by
MISS LUCY McKIM

It was almost certainly her father who arranged for the publication of
the arrangements through his work in the antislavery office and the Port
Royal Relief Committee. The publication could perhaps have been moti-
vated by the thought that the songs might be successful enough to earn

always-needed money for the antislavery office. His office had already offered the arrangement of "Go Down Moses" by Rev. Lockwood for sale in April, and its publication could have been the inspiration for her father to arrange for the appearance of Lucy's arrangements. Probably more important was the thought that their publication would be an indication to the people who had contributed so generously to the funding of the activities in Port Royal that the project had already achieved tangible results. The cover design for her arrangements gave a prominent place to a display of the words "Songs of the Freedmen of Port Royal" rather than the titles of the songs themselves, which probably reflects this decision. It was also the many donors to the fund who perhaps had been considered as possible buyers for the songs.

On July 9, 1862, only two weeks after their return from St. Helena, her father presented a long, detailed report of his journey to the island with Lucy to the committee. It was in this carefully written presentation that he described his daughter as "a young lady . . . who had been tenderly and conscientiously reared outside of sectarian pales, on the outskirts of liberal Quakerism."[13] The report was considered important enough to be printed as a pamphlet, and it had a wide distribution. Parts of his talk relating to music were also reprinted in *Dwight's Journal* in the issue of August 9, a month after he had presented his report to the committee.

The letters and notes that he wrote during his hurried days on St. Helena describe innumerable meetings and conferences, and it seems clear that he had little time for gathering musical examples or even listening to much singing. His comments on the music in his talk were almost certainly taken from Lucy's notes. Laura Towne had noticed that during their visit Lucy spent much of her time "busy collecting facts, etc."

In his talk her father first described the singing of the boatmen, emphasizing the religious character of the verses, then went on to speak more fully of one song they had heard that had a strong effect on Lucy.

There was one [song] which on shore we heard more than any other, and which was irresistibly touching. It was a sort of ballad, known as "Poor Rosy, Poor Gal." It is almost impossible to give an idea of the effect of this or any of their songs by a mere recital or description. They are all exceedingly simple, both in sentiment and in music. Each stanza contains but a single thought, set in perhaps two or three bars of music; and yet they will sing it, in alternate recitatives and choruses, with varying inflections and dramatic effect, this simple and otherwise monotonous melody will, to a musical ear and a heart susceptible of impression, have all the charm of variety. Take, for instance, a few stanzas from the dirge of "Poor Rosy." Fancy the line sung in a major key, and the following changed by an easy transition, and with varying inflections, into the minor, and you will have some idea of the effect.

Poor Rosy, poor gal!
Poor—Rosy—poor— gal!
P-o-o-r R-o-s-y, p-o-or gal!
   Heaven shall be my home. . . .

"Poor Rosy, Poor Gal" was the first of Lucy's arrangements to be published. Its appearance was not announced in the *National Anti-Slavery Standard* until November 2, 1862, but she had already sent a copy of the music with an introductory article to *Dwight's Journal*. Her article was printed in the issue that appeared on November 8, 1862. The brief piano introduction was written in simple, hymn-like chords which, as her father described, open in the key of G-major for three measures, quoting the song's melody—then the fourth measure—the melody of the chorus— ended the introduction in the key of e-minor. She marked the rhythm as "andante," although as she described in her article the melody was very popular and she heard it sung in a variety of tempos, depending on the work that was being done at that moment. The repeated arpeggios of the setting have the effect of a softly plucked guitar. She also used the word "barcarole" to describe the rhythm of the arrangement, which her father incorporated into his address. She was employing a common European word that described in musical tones the movement of traveling over water. Traditionally it was the rhythm of songs sung by Venetian gondoliers, but quickly came to refer to any song intended to achieve that lulling, repetitive effect.

Just as she changed the harmony from major to minor for the solo melody to the answering chorus melody of "Heab'n shall-a be my home," Lucy also changed the piano accompaniment from the rolling effect of the barcarole, with its gentle murmur of open chords, to repeated block chords to accompany the chorus. Although the setting of the song and the piano accompaniment are technically simple and easily performed by any competent musician, the choices she made reflect sophisticated musical decisions. For a first publication by someone who considered herself as a pianist rather than a composer, it clearly reflects a highly disciplined musical knowledge. It is not intended to imitate the song she heard, and this is the most sensitive of the decisions she made. She made use of the melody and the words she copied on the island as the inspiration for an effecting song in which the African American art of singing was made comprehensible to anyone familiar with European art song. In her setting "Poor Rosy" became as individual and fascinating as the songs she described in her letters.

In the introduction to her arrangement that Lucy sent to *Dwight's Journal* it was also clear that she was as skilled a writer as she was a musician. Though the musical terminology of her father's earlier piece certainly reflected Lucy's assistance, what he wrote in the *Journal* was similar to the reportage of many at this moment who were hearing slave music for the first time, while her lengthier piece focuses on the music itself. Its statement of her own understanding of slave song is not only acute, but expressed in eloquent phrases. "The wild, sad strains tell, as the sufferers themselves never could, of crushed hopes, keen sorrow, and a dull daily misery which covered them as hopelessly as the fog from the rice-swamps."

The *Journal* introduced her letter with a warmly favorable review of her arrangement.[14]

Songs of the Port Royal "Contrabands"

We had received No. 1 of "Songs of the Freedmen of Port Royal, collected and arranged by Miss Lucy McKim," with the following letter, which speaks for itself. We trust we violate no confidence in printing it. The melody has a simple and touching pathos, a flavor of individuality which makes one desire to know more of these things: and we trust that "Poor Rosy" will be followed by other specimens as genuine.

Mr. Dwight,

   Sir:—In a recent number of your journal there appeared an article relating to the music of the slaves of Port Royal, taken from an address delivered by my father before the members and friends of the Port Royal Freed-men's Association of this city. The extract included the words of one of their songs, beginning "Poor Rosy, poor gal!"

   My chief object in writing to you is to say, that having accompanied my father on his tour to Port Royal, and being much struck with the songs of its people, I reduced a number of them to paper, among them the ballad referred to. I send you herewith a copy of it, hoping it may interest you. Whether to have others printed is, as yet, a question with me.

   It is difficult to express the entire character of these negro ballads by mere musical notes and signs. The odd twists made in the throat; and the curious rhythmic effect produced by single voices chiming in at different irregular intervals, seem almost impossible to place on score, as the singing of birds, or the tones of an Æolian Harp. The airs, however, can be reached. They are too decided not to be easily understood, and their striking originality would catch the ear of any musician. Besides this, they are valuable as an expression of the character and life of the race which is playing such a conspicuous part in our history. The wild, sad strains tell, as the sufferers themselves never could, of crushed hopes, keen sorrow, and a dull, daily misery which covered them as hopelessly as the fog from the rice-swamps. On the other hand, the words breathe a trusting faith in rest in the future—in "Caanan's fair and happy land," to which their eyes seem constantly turned.

A complaint might be made against these songs on the score of monotony. It is true there is a great deal of repetition of the music, but that is to accommodate the *leader*, who, if he is a good one, is always an improviser. For instance, on one occasion, the names of each of our party who was present, was dexterously introduced.

As the songs are sung at every sort of work, of course the *tempo* is not always alike. On the water the oars dip "Poor Rosy" to an even andante; a stout boy and girl at the hominy-mill fly, to keep up with the whirling stone; and in the evening, after the day's work is done, "Heab'n shall-a be my home" peals up slowly and mournfully from the distant quarters. One woman—a respectable house servant, who had lost all but one of her twenty-two children said to me:

"Pshaw! don't har to dese yer chil'en, misse. Dey just rattle it off,—dey don't know how for sing it. I likes 'Poor Rosy' better dan all de songs, but it can't be sung widout a *full heart* and a *troubled sperrit*!"

All the songs make good barcaroles. Whittier "builded better than he knew" when he wrote his "Song of the Negro Boatman." It seemed wonderfully applicable as we were being rowed across Hilton Head Harbor among United States gunboats,—the *Wabash* and the *Vermont* towering on either side. I thought the crew *must* strike up

"And massa tink it day ob doom,
And we of jubilee."

Perhaps the *grandest* singing we heard was at the Baptist Church on St. Helena Island, when a congregation of three hundred men and women joined in a hymn—

"Roll, Jordan, roll, Jordan!
Roll Jordon roll!"

It swelled forth like a triumphal anthem. That same hymn was sung by thousands of negroes on the 4th of July last, when they marched in procession under the Stars and Stripes, cheering them for the first time as the "flags of *our* country." A friend writing from there, says that the chorus was indescribably grand—"that the whole woods and world seemed joining in that rolling sound."

There is much more in this new and curious music, of which it is a temptation to write, but I must remember that it can speak for itself better than any one for it.

Very Respectfully   Lucy McKim

Lucy's "letter" was the first article to be published anywhere that approached slave songs as a distinctive musical idiom.

Unlike the professional arranger's setting of "Go Down Moses" that her father's office had announced for sale the previous March, Lucy's setting of "Poor Rosy" has a fresh immediacy. It still has the feeling of a song, and she has kept the island dialect of the verses, unlike the standardized English of Rev. Lockwood's text. If the melody is sung without her simple accompaniment, with her comments about the way it was sung in the singer's mind, it doesn't suggest the delicacy and the modesty of what Lucy must have heard as she went about the island. The setting, like her letter, was the first serious effort to capture the essence and the unique devotional message of the slaves' music.

◆ ◆ ◆

Lucy could not have been aware that her consciousness of the need to begin preserving the songs she was hearing would mark only the beginning of efforts by others who turned to collecting music on St. Helena. There had already been considerable change in the conditions at Port Royal in the few months that had passed since Lucy and her father visited, and patiently sorting through the continuing confusion Laura Towne had brought some order to the school. The number of students continued to grow, and she and Ellen Murray could not keep up with the needs of so many new arrivals. To aid them McKim sent another teacher to join them. She was Charlotte Forten, who was the first and also one of only a handful of northern free blacks who went to the South to assist in the work with ex-slaves. She was born in Philadelphia in 1837, which meant she was five years older than Lucy. When she came to the island she was twenty-five.

Forten had grown up in the Philadelphia abolitionist community, and she already knew many of the people involved in the Port Royal work. Her father, Robert Forten, was the brother-in-law of Robert Purvis, and with him was active in the Underground Railroad. Forten's family had faced the same difficulty finding a school for her as the other abolitionist families, but the Eagleswood School hadn't yet opened so she was sent to school in Salem, Massachusetts. In Salem, as a member of the town's Female Anti-Slavery Society she was active as a speaker and a fund raiser to support the society's cause. She was an attractive woman, with a slim, delicately modeled face and a watchful, probing glance.

In 1856, when Forten was nineteen, her family suffered financial reverses and she was forced to take a position as a teacher in Salem. When the growing number of pupils at the Port Royal school made it necessary to engage an additional teacher, the Port Royal Committee decided she was the obvious choice to be sent to the island. On October 28 the steamer *United States* landed her at Hilton Head, and the next day she was rowed across to the island. She was to live in the deserted house of a smaller plantation that was considerably less spacious than the large mansion where Lucy and Ellen Murray had stayed, and for her first night she slept in the house occupied by the general superintendent of the work. After their greetings in a large room with a cheerful fire, she and a traveling companion retired to their room for the night, and for her the adventure began the next morning.

The next morning L. and I were awakened by the cheerful voices of men and women, children and chickens, in the yard below. We ran to the window and looked out. Women in bright-colored handkerchiefs, some carrying pails on their heads, were crossing the yard, busy with their morning work; children were playing and tumbling around them. On every face there was a look of serenity and cheerfulness. My heart gave a great throb of happiness as I looked out at them, and thought, "They are free! so long down-trodden, so long crushed to the earth, but now, in their old homes, forever free!" And I thanked God that I had lived to see this day.[15]

Like so many visitors to the island, Forten was immediately drawn to the singing she heard, and she began her own collection of songs in her diary. She was teaching young children, and often she heard songs that the children had heard and adopted from the singing of the adults, or had created themselves for their play. Lucy had also written of the children's singing in her letters, but the transcriptions she had made were of the religious songs she heard among the older slaves. Forten's copies of verses only documented the words, since she was unable to annotate the music, but they present a unique glimpse into the musical world of St. Helena's children.

> They sang in rich, sweet tones, and with a peculiar swaying motion of the body, which made their singing the more effective. They sang "Marching Along," with great spirit, and then one of their own hymns, the air of which is beautiful and touching—"My syster, you want to git religion."

> *Go down in de Lonesome Valley, My brudder, you want to git religion.*
> *Go down in de Lonesome Valley.*
>   *Chorus*
> *Go down in de Lonesome Valley,*
> *Go down in de Lonesome Valley, my Lord,*
> *Go down in de Lonesome Valley,*
> *To meet my Jesus dere! . . .*

> They repeat their hymns several times, and while singing keep perfect time with their hands and feet. . . .[16]

At a gathering of children for Christmas she heard them sing another song which she described as "one of the strangest, most mournful things I ever heard. It is impossible to give any idea of the deep pathos of the refrain,—'Sing, O graveyard!'"[17]

> *I wonder where my mudder gone;*
> *Sing, O graveyard!*
> *Graveyard ought to know me;*
> *Ring Jerusalem!*

> *Grass grow in de graveyard;*
> *Sing, O graveyard!*
> *Graveyard ought to know me;*
> *Ring, Jerusalem!*

She also commented on another of the children's hymns that she found particularly moving.

In this, and many other hymns, the words seem to have but little meaning, but the tones,—a whole lifetime of despairing sadness is concentrated in them. They sing, also, "Jehovya, Hallelujah," which we like particularly—

De foxes hab holes,
An de birdies had nes',
But de Son ob Man he hab not where
To lay de weary head
    Chorus
Jehovyah, Hallelujah! De Lord He will purvide!
Jehovyah, Hallelujah! De Lord He will purvide!

They repeat the words many times. "De foxes hab holes," and the succeeding lines are sung in the most touching, mournful tones, and then the chorus— "Jehovya, Hallelujah!"—swells forth triumphantly, in glad contrast.

Christmas night, the children came in and had several great shouts. They were too happy to keep still.

"Oh Miss, all I want to do is to sing and shout!" said our little pet, Amaetta. And sing and shout she did, to her heart's content.

The quest to preserve and document the musical culture of slavery had begun, and the search would continue so long as slavery was still a living memory for those who had endured it.

9

It is so hard

I stand amid the roar
Of a surf-tormented shore,
And I hold within my hand
Grains of the golden sand—
How few! yet how they creep
Through my fingers to the deep,
While I weep—while I weep!
O God! can I not grasp
Them with a tighter clasp
O God! can I not save
One from the piteous wave?
Is all that we see or seem
But a dream within a dream?

—Edgar Allan Poe
from "A Dream Within a Dream"

The year 1863 would be a time of despair, of death, of victories, hopes, uncertainties, and loss as the war ground on. The struggle seemed now to have become something that would never be finished. For many who were caught up in it, it had become almost as difficult to remember how it had begun as it was to imagine how it might end. For Lucy it would bring a moment of tragic despair. For the newly freed slaves it brought a swelling outburst of joy.

The Emancipation Proclamation took effect on January 1, 1863. For those who were now free it was a moment of jubilee. For others, conscious of the terrible cost of the years of war, it would be a jubilee tinged with darkness. How much more blood would be shed before emancipation could be celebrated by all who still were held in bondage?

For Charlotte Forten on a cold, bright winter day on St. Helena, it was a moment of jubilant celebration with the soldiers of the newly formed first black regiment in the US Army.

> New-Year's-day—Emancipation Day—was a glorious one to us. The morning was quite cold, the coldest we had experienced, but we were determined to go to the celebration at Camp Saxton - the camp of the First Regiment South-Carolina Volunteers whither the General and Colonel Higginson had bidden us, on this, "the greatest day in the nation's history." We enjoyed perfectly the exciting scene on board the *Flora*. There was an eager, wondering crowd of the freed people in their holiday-attire, with the gayest of head-handkerchiefs, the whitest of aprons, and the happiest of faces. The band was playing, the flags streaming, everybody talking merrily and in universal gaiety; and danced and sparkled more joyously than ever before. Long before we reached Camp Saxton we could see the beautiful grove, and the ruins of the old Huguenot fort near it. Some companies of the First Regiment were drawn up in line under the trees, near the landing to receive us. A fine, soldierly-looking set of men, their brilliant dress against the trees (they were then wearing red pantaloons) invested them with a semi-barbaric splendor . . .[1]

Colonel Higginson was Thomas Wentworth Higginson, who had been in close touch with Lucy's father in the weeks that John Brown's wife awaited her husband's execution and lived with the McKim family in Philadelphia. Higginson had studied for the ministry at Harvard, and had no military training, but in his zeal to contribute to the Union cause he taught himself the rudiments of military drill and organized his own company of infantry in Massachusetts. He discovered he had been endowed with a sense of military discipline and within a few months he had become a captain of the 51st Massachusetts Infantry. His energy and instinct for leadership made him so successful that when there was a question about an officer who could assume command of the newly formed black regiment organized at Port Royal he was an immediate choice. On November 5 he was offered a promotion to the rank of colonel if he would take over the command of what would be the first regular black regiment in the Union army. His orders were to recruit and train ex-slaves to become members of a combat regiment. He hesitated, feeling attached to the troop he had formed, but he realized that this was the more important task and agreed to take over the command in South Carolina. He arrived on the islands not long after Forten herself, who continued her account of the day's celebration.

The celebration took place in the beautiful grove of live-oaks adjoining the camp. It was the largest grove we had seen. I wish it were possible to describe fitly the scene which met our eyes as we sat upon the stand and looked down at the crowd before us. There were the black soldiers in their blue coats and scarlet pantaloons, the officers of this and other regiments in their handsome uniforms, and crowds of lookers-on—men, women, and children, of every complexion, grouped in various attitudes under the moss-hung trees. The faces of all wore a happy, interested look. The exercises commenced with a prayer by the chaplain of the regiment. An ode, written for the occasion by Professor Zachos, was read by him, and then sung. Colonel Higginson introduced Dr. Brisbane, who read the President's Proclamation, which was enthusiastically cheered. Rev. Mr. French presented to the Colonel two very elegant flags, a gift to the regiment from the Church of the Puritans, accompanying them by an appropriate and enthusiastic speech. At its conclusion, before Colonel Higginson could reply, and while he was still holding the flags in his hand, some of the colored people, of their own accord, commenced singing "My Country, 'Tis of Thee." It was a touching and beautiful incident, and sent a thrill through all our hearts. The Colonel was deeply moved by it. He said that reply was far more effective than any speech he could make. But he did make one of those stirring speeches . . . All hearts swelled with emotion as we listened to his glorious words,—"stirring the soul like the sound of a trumpet."[2]

For Lucy, the war's bitter realities cast a muffling shroud of darkness over her jubilation at the moment of emancipation. At this moment in January she learned that Dick Chase, only short months after they had met for the last time, had been killed during the battle at Murfreesboro in central Tennessee. Bev also at first had been listed among the missing. Numb with the shock, Lucy sent a despairing letter to Ellen on January 21, 1863.

Hilltop. Jan'y 21st 1863.
Dear Elle. It has been selfish enough in me not to write you before this, all that I could talk about Murfreesboro & things connected with it, for I knew that I asked every day for some news & guessed that you did. I can but ask you to forgive me, for I have no excuse except that to write or speak or hear spoken one dear name gave me a terrible shiver . . . a letter came for me from Bev. evening before last; the first part of which was such a touching attempt to be cheerful that I have not dared to look at it since, as red eyes are not in the programme at Hilltop.[3]

In Lucy's letter she copied the details of Dick's death, which had been sent on by another officer in Dick's regiment, Oliver Hough. It was only one of thousands of sorrowing accounts like it as the war swelled in intensity, but for Lucy that would be no consolation.

> "Of old mess Gus & I are the only ones left together; Ned Taylor being in sergeant's tent, Dick Pancoast and Bev paroled prisoners, Dick Chase—dear boy—dead. On the 29th Co. E & part of C, B, and D being in the front skirmishers, made a charge against a line of infantry who were concealed in a cornfield. After two charges we returned & drew up in line of battle below, expecting perhaps that they would come out, but they did not. At, and before the second charge, the balance of our party had joined us, making us some 200 strong, hardly enough for a brigade. Dick was struck in the left cheek. He just bent slowly forward to his horse's neck & then rolled to the ground. He must have died very soon, for as our party fell back he was unconscious. I was not with him, having been sent back to bring up the reserves. The next day a party of 5 of which I was one, started to recover the bodies. Bev. had gone back to the wagon train. We found them & took them to Nashville, where in Nashville cemetery he is buried. . . Everybody speaks his own details of praise, all how justly due! But in my mind there re one or two lines that utter themselves over & over again & get no further. 'There is none like him, none, nor will be when our summers have deceased' 'None like him, none.'"

With her father's stern admonition that there would be no weeping in the house Lucy could only give way to her grief in her letter. She followed the account of Dick's death with an anguished cry of bitterness at the impersonality of fate.

> O! Elle! The gapes that such stabs make let in a light to see the love that is hidden within us. Didn't you think when all the boys started for the War, that you were all prepared to hear of their being killed at any time? I did. I fancied myself so well drilled—was so certain of being at least calm & philosophical!—But since that first dizzy moment when I saw "Killed,—& R. W. Chase." I have been realizing the fact that I am not so ready to graduate in *nosce te ipsum*[4] as I thought. Death is the last Professor for us poor students. He teaches that one can live and work, aye & laugh and never confess the serge under the silks. "Goodbye, & down with the rebels" they said, brave fellows, "Au revoir" one answered gaily, "we could spare you,—never give up." And took the cup in our hand bright with red, white & blue ornamenting, looking in boldly at the dark draught, and boasting, "bitter you may be, but if it is our

fate we swear to toss you off with a Gloria Patri!" How these long months has the thing stood by us, & day by day we looked at it & imagined we knew the taste.—It is a howling cold day without, with rain & gusts of wind. Poor Bev.! I'm glad he's housed with good Mrs. Powell. He signed himself "Your brother-less friend." I am sick to be with him ever since that fatal [?] day I have been longing to put my arms around him, & tell him as you would a child, "O! Bev! darling don't grieve!" It seems as if he *must* feel some comfort,— if there be any in friends' sympathy—even as far away as Nashville. He is a double charge to me, dear, precious for your sake & for Richard's. Heaven forgive me if I do not prove a faithful friend to him.—I wish you were here, even though your presence would suggest the blank in our future more to me than anyone or anything else now. I know Laura is a sweet good child, but—well it is just "but"—I can't fill it up.

With so much spilling out that she was compelled to say, Lucy took a new half sheet of paper and tried to begin it with an account of social gatherings at the home of friends or at Hilltop. Then she couldn't keep up the light patter and turned again to what was consuming her.

Do not think from what I have said that I grudge my share in the nation's redemption. God forbid! Long ago, I prayed that Liberty might conquer, if for my share I had to give not just my friend or my home but everything that would go to make my whole life's happiness. I trust that it was not mere sound. I trust that no grief will ever shake me from that wish. This one has not, at least. "They also serve who only stand and wait" is true enough. But it is so hard! If one could *only* have something to do. Sometimes it seems as if God could not really know how willing we should be for any work, or he would give us some. Perhaps he will, if we be patient.

She ended with a last sentence squeezed in at the bottom of the page:

I've been such a while over this letter, & as usual have not said what I meant to—would you write to me—

Lucy had been very young when she and Dick Chase had first known each other, but during the previous three years their relationship had rip-ened into something far deeper than friendship, though that was the face they put on their laughter and jokes when they were together with other people. She had chosen not to tell even Ellen, expecting that he would continue to be there in her life. Lucy could tell herself then that whatever would happen next between them, it would happen in its own time and for the moment her life could go on. What she understood now was that she had loved him. The last time she had seen him on a short leave he asked her if she would wear his friendship ring—which in the complicated rituals of courtship at the time meant a pledge. It was short of an engagement, but it meant they were what would be termed sweethearts—that they had made a promise to each other. It was a commitment that Lucy would not have taken lightly. Without hesitation she had accepted his ring.

If Dick Chase had returned, more would have been spoken between them. They would have had time to chart the beginnings in their new relationship. As she wrote in the letter to Ellen, a death like his "let[s] us see the love that is hidden within us." Since, however, there had been no open commitment, by the rituals of sorrow that decided what grief was appropriate to express, she could not make any public show of her mourning. In her family she was expected to leave grief beyond the doorstep—"red eyes are not in the programme at Hilltop"—and it was only with Ellen that she could reveal how deeply she had been shaken. There is no way to know what the future might have been for Lucy and Richard Chase, but for months she shut herself away emotionally, and her anguish at being excluded from any real place in the struggle that had taken his life was only intensified.

Conscious of how much she had revealed to Ellen of her feelings she added a note to the letter: "You must allow this letter to be one of the 'sepulchrally private' ones—"

Her letter crossed with one of Ellen's and she was upset by the tone of Ellen's letter. In her futile anger she flashed at her friend, only to apologize when she wrote ten days later.

> Hilltop
> Feb'y 1st 1863
> Dear Elle, I shall have to get used to beginning my letters "General Apologies No. ____" for in each one I say something which requires one to ask your pardon in the next. One ought not to open her mouth or touch a pen when she is out-of-sorts,—irritable,—all of a jangle. Your letter displeased me, not from any fault in itself, but because nothing, I think, from which I expected a great deal *could* have pleased me that miserable night. Had it arrived at almost any other time than just after I had written, its reticence on a certain subject would have been most grateful; but just then—well it was a sort of mental cold plunge bath; result, the "frigid" scrap. Yet I think you would have allowed me those few lines of ill-temper if you had known what a relief they

were. Friends must suppernate (a figure for the times). Sometimes I think
of the old Scriptural expression about one's heart being a cage of unclean
birds, & how true it may be. Not that I have just made the discovery! Mercy,
no! Nor that I believe such birds to occupy it always—still less. But lately my
discordant-aviary has screamed so I can't hear myself think. Very uncomfort-
able; and main't it mean to want you to feel wretched when you showed so
much more sense & calmness than I? But I really did, & now I'm sorry. Do
write me some sneers and anger as a punishment. The next time I boil as hot,
I shall be careful not to scald you. . . .

Father is in such good spirits about the times, that we are all affected by
them. Cheerfulness & gloom are so contagious . . . We all sing "Hooker is our
leader" in Marching Along, but don't much care for it. If little men can pull
us through, I shall be thankful to be saved from the worship of a great General. We are a Democracy, & if the masses take the anxieties & suffering, the
masses should receive the glory—And why not be hopeful? I am conscious of
a growing sense of confidence in our Cause. Mediation? Let 'em try it. Democrats? Bah! National bankruptcy? Gammon. Compromise?—How are you, J.
B. Crittenden? Giving up the struggle in short? Never, never, never! Not when
Robert Purvis leads a black regiment into the heart of South Carolina. If
there is anything in having moral force & justice on our side and moral obli-
guity & Tyranny on the other, we must succeed. The Proclamation has been
issued, we *shall* succeed. O! This war is a great grand thing! A sharp resistless
cure for a huge disease.

It is only hard not to envy those "terque quaterquw beati"[5] who are a part
of it. Can anyone help being "restless for action?" Is it not almost anguish to
be a comfortable nobody in a heroic age? I have as much influence in the
fate of Greece whose history I read, as I have in the fate of America, that
I love with a love borne of sorrow, whose good happiness is nearer to my
heart than is father or mother or brother or every being under the sun. The
whole cry of my soul is that all the battles may not be fought without my
having fired one shot, that all the pain may not have passed without my having saved one sufferer. It does not require a metaphysician to perceive a most
vigorous selfishness at the bottom of such a longing. Truly I deserve a place
to work for my own satisfaction, but then if I am to be of no use, I will try
to be content that my bungling fingers are brushed to one side. As to those
details you mention I don't care for any of them, because neither the Hospital nor negro school houses would be the best place for me, I think; & as
for being a man—womanhood is as good as manhood anyday—But I don't
mean to talk so much about myself. Let us consider something a little more
domestic . . .

Went again to the opera by invitation—to chaperone Emily Davis;
Charlie & Ike as escort; Ann took herself & C. It was "Das Nachslager [?]
in Grenada" . . . The music is light & pretty, but the play insufferable. We
had good seats in the balcony right in front. There was such a glare &
a heat & the people were so ugly & so dressed, & they all chattered like
apes—it was horrid. Then it was just to close my eyes & shut out all the
noise & glitter & and be at once in a solitary place so so far away, where a
cool dark night brooded over one grave.

 It is late. Goodnight, petite Lucy
Morning: I am reading over what I wrote last night. It appears the last page
has relapsed into the old jargon, but really that evening at the opera was one
of the most painful I ever passed.[6]

Ten days later Lucy wrote again, and again she was struggling against
the tide of her grief. Her pain had been sharpened anew by meeting Bev
at an unexpected homecoming.

 Hilltop
 Feb. 10th, 1863
Dear Elle—This is just a P. S. to my last, to tell you what may not perhaps be
news to you if Laura has got the start of me, but what if she hasn't—you will
like to hear—*Beverly is here*: Last Sat. evening I stopped at Annie Needle's to
see Laura before she left for Baltimore; found her & her mother, Mrs. Baldwin
& the N's waiting for Bev to call. Every particle of strength seemed to ooze
from my joints at the announcement. He had arrived most unexpectedly the
eve. before, & caused a great commotion . . . The new excitement made Edith
faint, & Mrs. Chase's throat paralysis, or whatever it called—return; Bev had
to go out for brandy. You can imagine the scene. Having no clothes but his
uniform, his mother had to go to Burlington for supplies (the next afternoon); in the meantime some were lent to him. Getting these detained him
so long that Laura went off without seeing him. We all left N's, leaving word
where I should be the rest of the day. Went to Spieler's to get Charlie's photo
taken, & while waiting in the crowded little reception room, Bev entered.
I had saved a chair in a corner, in case of need; & we sat there and talked
statistically—e. g. "When did you come? Did Mrs. Needles tell you where
I was? Has thee just left Aunt C's?" etc—blessing the noise around which
made a sort of solitude, & and feeling what we couldn't *think*—let alone say.
Bye & bye he went out for an errand, I agreeing to wait for his return. . . . He
returned & we all walked down to 3rd street where I stayed to lunch with C.,
promising to meet him at Germania.

It was a beautiful program, & Bev listened in a half-famished kind of way. Everything at home was so delicious to him, he said, after that hell in Nashville. The poor boy is really so thankful to be home, that he scarcely seems to think of what has happened. He looks perfectly well—never better & has grown larger & handsomer. His teeth & complexion are as pure as a girl's; his dress, of course, immaculate. In manners he seems exactly the same, except a nervous habit of smiling which seizes him every now & then; and sudden fits of abstraction into which he falls even when one is speaking to him. He winces under allusions to his brother from almost anybody, & I have not heard him speak his name. A little he & I have talked of "him," but not much. I wish I could forget the differences. . . .

On leaving me at 9th & Green, I invited him out for Monday evening (couldn't leave Sunday). He came bringing tickets for Murdoch's last reading. So I put on my things straight away. . . . While Bev went for his night-things (he was to return with me) Mrs. Chase, E. & I had a strange kind of interview. I kept wondering if they too, under their cheerful faces & black dresses, were not perpetually thinking how unreal was presence & how real absence. Then Bev came in, & we rose; and while I stood talking to Edith with my back half to them, I saw him take his mother's face in his hands & smile cheerily at her. We did not go till he had put his arms around her & kissed her over & over & over again. She looked very white, & did not utter a word—he walked several squares silently, then he said, "Mother is wonderful!"

(Now this is *entre nous*: he "will leave no stone unturned," to use his words, "to get a discharge from the army. His health is not sufficient for a private's life. But as getting a discharge is scarcely within the limit of *possibilities*, he hopes to be able to be transferred . . . *would like* to be in a black regiment.)[7]

In one of the newly formed black regiments Bev would have served as an officer, and he believed he would have a better chance of survival. Under the complicated rules relating to the exchange of prisoners in those first years of the war, however, Bev was still technically a prisoner. He had been only conditionally released until someone could be found among southern prisoners held in the North to make an acceptable exchange.

Ellen answered Lucy's letter immediately, now with some of the agitated torment that had almost overwhelmed Lucy. In the summer Ellen had repeated her conditions in a letter to Bev, repeating that she didn't reject his interest in her, but he would have to wait until he turned twenty-one before they could meet again. Now with Bev so starkly affected by his brother's death and the constant threat of his own imprisonment she was torn between holding fast to her conditions and her almost overpowering urge to rush to him.

> Auburn Feb 12, 1863
> Thursday *night*
> My dear dear Luce—
>   Your letter just read, fills me with a strange trembling sort of joy—I am so very glad that that boy is at home. It seems as tho' it might be heaven, I have an insane *yearning* to see him—for a minute—but crush it under. *Do* stay at home until his furlo' expires. I should probably get to Phila. just after he leaves. The 9th of March is now fixed as our starting time. I shall rejoice to see *you*. That at least I am permitted to enjoy!—Lucie do make Bev talk—say just what he thinks & feels, & then remember it, to tell me. I am so thankful, not to be in Phila. now. After my summer letter to Bev I should not want to meet him. I hope I may not, until the three years are up & then—but I deputy you to be counselor, friend, everything to him until then. Let him be a *double* charge to you, as you have said, dear Lux! Does it seem possible that he can be permitted to go back! I can't bear to think of it. As you say, the dead make the living so precious to us ... if you were here, my bonnie Lucy—I need not speak a word. I could just sit by you & we could have a splendid *cry*. My eyes are a trifle dim now, for the 2d time, only the 2d, since Murfreesboro. It is so sweet, so bitterly sweet to know of this dear boy safe.[8]

In a letter to Laura Stratton on January 17 Ellen had written of her own deep feelings for Dick Chase.

> Dick! When I think of a dear, young, beautiful face, which as angelic cannot be much changed—which I can never see again—and lovely violet eyes, which will never laugh into mine again & and pure, brave lips which will never call me "Little Sister" again, and all this grieves me. . . . I loved him dearly & miss him sadly.

    In the midst of the emotional crisis of Richard Chase's death, the second of Lucy's arrangements, "Roll, Jordan Roll," was announced in the *National Anti-Slavery Standard* on January 17, 1863. However meaningless it seemed to Lucy at that moment—there was no mention of it in her letters to Ellen—it was once again some small vindication for the struggle that was being waged to give the slaves their freedom. Again, she had responded to the song as she had heard it, not as it would have been sung by a trained academic chorus, and she again chose to keep the dialect that was part of the song's effect, as she had done in her setting of "Poor Rosy."

March, angels march! March, angels march!
My soul am rise to heav'n Lord,
where de heav'n'e Jording roll.

    Little chillen sittin' on de Tree ob Life,
    Where de heav'n'e Jording roll.
    Oh! roll, Jording, roll Jording, roll, Jording roll! . . .

The arrangement for this song was different in character from her setting of "Poor Rosy." She had heard it sung as a ringing anthem by three hundred worshippers in the Old Brick Church at the Pope Plantation, and she set this melody to a march tempo, with a vigorous, assertive accompaniment. She scored a vocal part for the melody's second section to be divided between women's voices for the opening line, then men's voices joining them nearly an octave lower to finish the musical phrase. To the women's vocal line she added a bright flourish to accent the words "Tree ob Life," and as the men's voices joined them, the piano responded with strong rhythmic emphasis—"the rolling sound" a friend had described. Although she wrote the opening line as "March, angels march!" she titled her setting "Roll, Jordan Roll." The song is usually known by this title, but both Lucy and Charlotte Forten had heard the congregation shout out the song lustily at the Brick Church on St. Helena with "March, angels march!" as its opening line. Lucy chose to use this local version of the song for her setting. With its ringing chords and march rhythm her arrangement matches the fervor of the singing she heard in the church, and as performed by a large chorus her arrangement of this great song would fill a meeting hall with a surge of excitement, though there is no way to know if Lucy herself ever heard it sung.

The front cover of each of the two songs that had appeared included spaces for more titles to be added to her series of "Freedmen's Songs," but only these two were published. In her article in *Dwight's Journal* she had stated that it would be for her to decide whether or not to continue publishing the songs, and the decision not to continue could have reflected poor sales. It seems as much a possibility that the tragedy of the last weeks had too strongly affected her for any thoughts of the songs. She was too upset emotionally to continue—and once again she was left with the sense of her uselessness to aid in the struggle.

◆ ◆ ◆

The weeks passed. Since nothing had been decided between Lucy and
Richard Chase she had to go on with her everyday life. She had only
his ring. She would keep within the limits of propriety and not dress in
mourning nor would she allow herself to cry unless she was alone in the
house. She mourned him as much as she was permitted. She refused all
social engagements, would not meet any of the young men who called
on her, and tried to avoid whatever might give her pleasure. She walked
every morning to the hospital to sew garments for the soldiers, and in the
afternoons she had her "scholars," and she could distract herself with cor-
recting their clumsy fingers.

With the publication of her two song settings and her long article in
Dwight's Journal only months before, Lucy had taken the first steps toward
the collection of the Port Royal songs she had announced to her friends.
With the weight of her war work and her hidden grieving over Dick
Chase's death, there was little she could do, but in the spring and summer
there was unexpected support for her enthusiasm. Philadelphia had been
the home of the southern aristocrat Pierce Butler, and the celebrated English actress Fanny Kemble had met him on her triumphant American tour
in the early 1830s. They married, and she then came to understand that he
was a slaveholder, and with her young children she spent two winters on
the Butler rice plantation on the Sea Islands off the coast of Georgia, only
a short journey to the south of St. Helena. In a series of letters to a friend
in New England, Kemble, an outspoken abolitionist, presented the clear-
est picture of the atrocities of slavery that any witness who had not been
themselves slaves had yet written. Her husband sued her for divorce, and
part of the settlement was an agreement that she would not publish the
letters, though some of them made their way to the press through friends.

Kemble had lived in Philadelphia after her marriage and she was still
popular in the city for her writings and for her enthusiastically received
readings from Shakespeare's plays. Finally, with the divorce settled at last,
she published the letters in England in May 1863, hoping their picture of
slavery would encourage England to continue its refusal to recognize the
Confederacy. The book appeared in the United States in July, only a few
days after the battle of Gettysburg. Her letters caused a sensation. With
Harriet Beecher Stowe's *Uncle Tom's Cabin*, which had been a major influence in shaping both American and English attitudes toward slavery, Kemble's *Journal of a Residence on a Georgian Plantation in 1838–1839*,[9] again
made it clear in the words of someone who had been a witness that there

could be no compromise with slavery, and Kemble's book was passionately received. For Lucy what was significant was that in the book Kemble also wrote of the slave songs she heard on the island where she lived. It was only a day's journey south of St. Helena, and she employed similar words of praise and response for the music that Lucy had expressed in her article. For Lucy, that a figure so widely known as Kemble also heard what she had heard was a certain validation for her vision of a collection of the songs. When Lucy's collection appeared four years later, Lucy quoted from Kemble's book in the review she wrote of the volume, in acknowledgment of the book's importance to her.

Although in the stream of letters between Lucy and Ellen there is no indication of Lucy's continued involvement in the discussions and the controversies over slave songs, it is clear from the committed positions of her later writing that she had been part of the debates and discussions that had followed the appearance of song texts in many travelers' articles. Much of this interest must have been sustained in conversations with her father, whom she had assisted with the descriptions of the slave singing they heard on St. Helena in his report to the contributors to the Port Royal Relief Committee shortly after their return the previous summer. Her dedicated commitment would leave its imprint on what she would write later.

The Emancipation Proclamation also brought decisive changes to Lucy's father's life. The Pennsylvania Anti-Slavery Committee had done its work. When the war finally ended, it was assured now that the slaves would be free. For most of those who had been for so long engaged in the abolitionist cause there was still the certainty the Union would triumph, despite the seemingly endless setbacks. Some who had struggled for this moment decided the job was done and they dropped away—though many of them quickly engaged themselves in other issues. For the women who had been active in the antislavery committees, the next struggle was for their right to vote, and they turned to the burgeoning suffragette movement. William Lloyd Garrison soon was engaged in the causes of both temperance and women's rights. James McKim, however, understood that whatever the emotional effect of emancipation, it was only the first step in an arduous journey to true equality for African Americans. More immediately, the war had to be won, and many in the North now realized that enlisting the freed slaves in the army would both give them a role to play in the struggle and set them on the first steps toward integration in American society through education and meaningful employment. It was also obvious that in the increasingly critical situation the North faced, the freedmen could supply a new and untapped source of troops.

On his trip to South Carolina the year before, McKim had seen uniformed black troops from an earlier attempt to form a volunteer regiment among the freed slaves in Port Royal, and he had been impressed by their discipline and their eagerness to join the newly formed units. When Thomas Wentworth Higginson was given the command of a new black regiment in Port Royal a few months later, Higginson could see that when his troops marched through the streets they were loudly cheered by the black community, whatever emotions they aroused among the whites and the northern soldiers who milled along the sidewalks of Beaufort. McKim threw himself into the work of recruiting volunteers for the rapidly forming black regiments. By the end of the summer his official stationary was headed "Office of the Supervisory Committee for Recruiting Black Regiments." His new address was 1210 Chestnut Street in downtown Philadelphia.

◆ ◆ ◆

Almost three months after Dick Chase's death, and only weeks after Bev Chase's disturbed visit to Hilltop, Lucy and Ellen journeyed to Massachusetts to visit two school friends, Anna Davis and Richard Hollowell. They lived in the town of Medford, close to Boston. Neither Lucy nor Ellen could have had any expectations of what the visit might bring them, or that these weeks of early New England spring would have an effect on their lives. The first excitement was their discovery that there were a great many friends from Eagleswood living in the Boston area. These old friendships had meant so much to Lucy, and in their enthusiasm the four of them decided to hold a party and bring everyone together. There were almost thirty alumni from the school to invite. The party was quickly arranged; a hall was engaged in Boston for the evening of March 16, three musicians were hired, and arrangements made for ice cream and cake. The dancing began promptly at 7:30 pm. It was not only ex-students who thronged the hall; among the guests of honor were their much-loved school director Theodore Weld and William Lloyd Garrison himself. With him he had brought two of his four sons, William and his younger brother Wendell, who had been in Philadelphia the year before, when Lucy had been their guide on their endless tramping through Philadelphia's streets.[10]

As the evening went on with laughter and music, it was immediately obvious that Ellen and William Garrison were attracted to each other. For Lucy, despite the obvious interest of Wendell Garrison, it was too soon for her to leave her period of private mourning. Wendell later confessed to his brother that he had been entranced by her in their earlier Philadelphia visit. They had visited the city when he delivered his nonresistor lectures, and since their families were very close, she would be expected to show them some hospitality, despite their differences of opinion.

A week after the party's excitements Lucy and Ellen journeyed by coach in a heavy spring snowstorm to make a formal visit to the Garrison family's house on Dix Place. William Lloyd Garrison lived with his wife, Helen, and with several of his children, including all four sons and a younger daughter, Fanny. The oldest son, George, twenty-seven, still was undecided about what to do with his life and he was working in the print shop of his father's newspaper, *The Liberator*. Restless years of travels had taken him away from the family for long periods, first to the Minnesota territory, then to Kansas, where he had been witness to some of the cruel fighting between hastily organized bands of abolitionists and the pro-slavery advocates streaming into the territory. The youngest son, Frank, who was fifteen, was at Eagleswood with the McKims' son, Charlie.

Dix Place was a dark, tall, much-used brick building crowded into a row of houses like it on a noisy street steadily being overrun by the flood of immigrants arriving in the city. It was a cramped, busy household. The family had been long used to being short of money, but after thirty years of operating his newspaper almost single-handedly, their father, now in his late fifties, was beginning to show the effects of his age. There would have to be more help from his children. Lucy and Ellen were enthusiasti-cally made welcome. For the abolitionists' children there were nearly as many obstacles to finding a marriage partner as there had been for their parents in finding a school where their children would be secure. William Lloyd Garrison was such a controversial figure that it was even unsafe for their daughter Fanny, now nineteen, to go onto the street without one of the family's male members to accompany her. Now into the parlor walked two blooming, intriguing young women who were themselves daughters of abolitionists, and though it wasn't mentioned openly, it was clear they were unattached. In the Garrison household were his two sons, William and Wendell, who had both come to the point in their lives where mar-riage would be their next step.

Each of the Garrison sons was good-looking, but Wendell was usu-ally considered to be the handsomer of the two. They were both tall and lanky, William a little taller, and each of them wore the customary heavy beards. Wendell was also considered to be livelier than his brother, though Ellen found him "prudish." They both had the same bluff, open faces, generally assuming serious expressions when they posed for the camera. As a possible husband neither of them showed much promise, since they hadn't settled into any kind of career. Their mother would not consider living without her children close around her, so they had gone to Boston schools most of their lives. William left school at eighteen to begin an apprenticeship in a relative's business, determined to have a career in business and achieve more economic security than his father had managed. Wendell, the most intellectual of the sons, completed his studies at Boston Latin and continued to Harvard. Following his graduation in 1861 he had tried tutoring and editing, but he had made no fast plans for his future.

William was even more impatient to be married than his younger brother. He had been very publicly engaged for a number of years to a woman named Lizzie Powell, a daughter of still another abolitionist family, who was making a name for herself as a speaker and activist in the growing women's movement. Hearing Lizzie speak had made Ellen so self-conscious about her own lack of talents as a speaker that she had despaired for weeks. By mutual agreement William and Lizzie had decided that though they could remain friends they would not make a successful marriage, so while they occasionally still met, it was only in public.

Only months before, Ellen had been strident in her dismissal of any of the young men she knew who refused to join the struggle against slavery, but William and Wendell's father, as a committed pacifist, had allied his family with him in a determined refusal to bear arms in any conflict whatsoever. Only the family's rebellious oldest son, George, served in the Union army, enlisting that same year. William and Wendell both were insistent on their refusal to fight. They publicly proclaimed themselves to be "non-resistors," as Wendell had made clear in his talks to abolitionist groups in Philadelphia. In November, 1861 Ellen had written Lucy, "I wouldn't *look* at a nonresistant. What do they suppose is going to become of our firesides?" In May 1862, however, in a letter to her mother, Ellen, now a half-year older, rhapsodized, "What can be compared to the joy of being 21-2 waiting only to say 'yes.'"[11] Whatever decision William Garrison might make in refusing to serve in the war, it was no longer important to her, and she responded to his attentions with obvious pleasure.

For Wendell the question of "nonresistance" had become a cause, and both he and his father had written and spoken out in their advocacy of a "dis-union" of the nation. The southern states would be allowed to secede and be left to maintain the institution of slavery, if they chose. The North would form its own confederation in which slavery was outlawed. The two brothers became eloquent on the subject, assuring each other that their stand required more courage than to simply join the hundreds of thousands of men their age who had chosen to fight to defend the Union.

Lucy and Ellen were invited to stay in the Garrison home for several days, and both brothers singled out the one they had chosen for continued attention. Lucy continued to hold herself aloof from Wendell, but she found that the family was fascinated by her stories and her songs from Port Royal and she found herself entertaining them with considerable pleasure. She and Ellen left without having made any kind of arrangement from Lucy's side to maintain any kind of tie, while Ellen and William immediately began exchanging letters. For Wendell's father the idea of his son marrying a daughter of his friend Miller McKim was so appealing that he began to speak of it as though it were already a reality. Wendell sent a cordial note to Lucy in Philadelphia and she responded a few days later with a formal letter of considerable length describing in great detail many of the paintings she had just seen at a museum exhibition she had visited.

◆ ◆ ◆

The spring and summer of 1863 continued to offer little solace to anyone who supported the northern cause. The Union army in Virginia under yet another inept commander was trapped by the spring's mud and rains. Discipline had broken down and the men lived in filth. Disease was spreading in the camps. The soldiers had not been paid for six months and many had deserted. Although few of the men in the camps could have been aware of it, the conditions for the Confederate armies were as frightful, with shortages of food and what pay they received coming in the form of increasingly worthless Confederate currency. The military situation continued to be stalemated in the East, while in the West the Confederacy was being systematically eviscerated by the grimly determined Ulysses S. Grant and his generals. The last fort on the Mississippi River would soon fall, cutting the Confederacy off from Texas and Arkansas, while Union armies now controlled Kentucky, most of Louisiana, Mississippi, Tennessee, and Alabama.

Once again an uneasy decision was made by the South to break out of the tightening ring by attempting an invasion of the North. The first move had been turned back in Maryland at Antietam the September before, but this time Lee shifted his army further west before moving north, and succeeded in reaching south-central Pennsylvania. The two armies met at Gettysburg and in the major battle of the war from July 1 to July 3 the Confederates were again defeated. In a desperate final effort on the last day of fighting Lee adopted the mass tactics of the northern generals and marched his divisions up a long hillside, open to Union artillery and deadly infantry fire. Just as in the countless attempts by the federal armies to succeed with the same tactics, the day's long waves of repeated, futile charges only left the slope strewn with Confederate dead.

One of the wounded of the battle was Ellen's brother Willie. He had been shot, the bullet entering his chest. The surgeons who operated on him felt they had successfully treated the wound, but to the members of the family who rushed to his bedside they admitted that they could do little about the pneumonia that was sweeping through the tents where men lay recuperating from their wounds, killing many of their patients. Ellen stayed in Auburn, anxious, and as always at moments of stress suffering from crippling headaches. After several weeks Willie's condition improved and though he was gaunt and without strength he was released from the field hospital and allowed to continue recuperating at home.

Only two weeks after the triumph at Gettysburg the North reeled again from another tragedy. For a third time in only a few months Lucy found herself counting the costs of the war she had championed so bravely. The first had been Richard Chase's death and his brother Bev's traumatic state, then the severe wound suffered by Ellen's brother. On July 18 Colonel Robert Shaw led his black regiment, the 54th Massachusetts Infantry, in a futile attack on Fort Wagner, south of Charleston and close to St. Helena Island. Laura Towne and Charlotte Forten had been among the many visitors to the regiment's encampment as they awaited action. In the attack Shaw was severely wounded, and in retaliation for the action by black troops the southerners slaughtered the survivors and threw their bodies into an open pit. After Shaw's uniform and his gold watch and ring were stripped off by thieves his body was thrown in with his men.

One of the wounded who managed to escape was Lucy's friend Ned Hollowell, Shaw's second-in-command, who suffered three bullet wounds but was carried by his men from the battlefield. Both the Hollowells, Ned and his brother Richard, had attended Eagleswood with Lucy and Ellen, and it was Ned who helped them to organize the party for old school members in Boston in the spring. Richard immediately rushed to South Carolina and brought his brother back to Philadelphia.

◆ ◆ ◆

Gettysburg had been such an apocalyptic event that crowds of curious sightseers journeyed to see the battleground. A few weeks after the battle,

Lucy's brother, Charlie, set out on a walking tour to the battlefield with his closest friend, Frank Garrison, Wendell's younger brother. Charlie had been working in his father's office for the summer, and their journey would give him a break before the classes at Eagleswood resumed in the fall. Another school friend named Will Davis would join them. Charlie was fifteen—he would be sixteen in the fall, and the other boys were the same age. It would seem from letters Wendell later wrote to his brother William that he encouraged the trip as a way to meet Lucy again, though ostensibly he joined the others to help with some of the practical problems.

The Garrison family was used to what they termed "pedestrian adventures," since there was never enough money for them to take vacations riding trains or carriages. The brothers, in twos or threes, had walked over most of New England on trips that had taken them hundreds of miles through Massachusetts, Vermont, New Hampshire, northern New York State, and Connecticut. For Wendell it was no problem to walk with the three others, helping them find places to sleep and assisting with campfires and fishing for some of their food. At Gettysburg there were relatives who could help show them the site.

It is difficult to understand how Wendell could lead a trip to one of the great battlegrounds of the war, since he professed not to believe in the war. He felt himself, however, as convinced of the rightness of his pacifist views as the most determined southern patriot believed in the rightness of slavery. Two weeks before they were to leave on their trip he was notified that he had been chosen in the draft for service in the army. The draft was a desperate effort of the North to repair the staggering losses of the unending conflict. The draft aroused widespread anger. Throughout the summer the country experienced protests and demonstrations. New York was the scene of bloody riots in which poor Irish immigrants, drafted into a war they felt had nothing to do with them, erupted in violent outbursts, murdering African Americans they caught on the streets and destroying buildings where the African Americans lived or had received medical care.

To muster at least minimal support for the draft, the government provided loopholes for anyone who could buy their way out of the service, since the government was as much in need of money as it was in need of men. Either a sum would be paid for a substitute who would agree to take the place of the man who had received his draft papers, or a simple tax of three hundred dollars could be paid as a commutation. Wendell reasoned to himself that if he paid for a substitute, which cost five hundred dollars, he would only be sending someone else to fight in the war which Wendell didn't believe in. The cheaper tax meant that he could be subject to further draft calls, but he chose it as an immediate expedient.

In the first days after the tragedy at Fort Wagner the Garrisons had been frantic for news of their son George, since following his enlistment he had been assigned to the second of the Massachusetts black regiments, the 55th Massachusetts Infantry. His regiment had also been sent to the St. Helena area and was held waiting in reserve during the Fort Wagner attack. When word finally reached the family that George had not seen any of the fighting, his father again wrote him, this time trying to shame him into giving up his army career by insisting that his first duty was to consider his mother's feelings, who still refused to accept the idea of her children not being around her. His absence was causing her endless worry. Garrison certainly was fervent in his desire to bring slavery to an end, but it would have to be someone else's son who would bring it about. When George had enlisted, his father wrote on June 11, 1863, "It makes me tremble, in regard to the effect that may be produced upon the health and happiness of your mother should any serious, especially a fatal, accident befall you. Her affection for you is intense, her anxiety beyond expression."[12]

◆ ◆ ◆

Lucy's brother, Charlie, had been raised with as much freedom as his sister, and although their mother was sincere in her Quaker faith, Charlie was like most other American teenagers of his time. In a letter to her Irish friends the year before, Lucy wrote that he was learning to "play on the banjo, a real American instrument. Did you ever hear it?" She also praised his skills with the "bones," comparing him favorably to the performers in the minstrel troupes, though it is difficult to know how often she had been to see a minstrel show. "He also plays the *bones* quite wonderfully, almost as well as they do at our negro minstrels."[13] On his visits to Frank in Boston he asked to be allowed to attend the minstrel shows himself.

They left for their walking trip on July 28, sleeping in barns or farmhouses where they were invited in. On the winding dirt roads, Gettysburg was less than 130 miles away and they walked slowly and comfortably through the golden summer, stopping to fish and to swim, cooking any fish they caught to supplement the food they had brought with them. Charlie had a small notebook, and he kept brief notes on their progress. After walking through the Pennsylvania Dutch countryside, and visiting a coal mine in Pittsfield, Pennsylvania, they reached Gettysburg on August 5 about 8:35 a.m. Only a month had passed since the battle, and though the bodies had been buried, the hills and fields were still littered with the battle's debris. They found Ellen's brother, Willie, who was still in the general hospital close to the battlefield. Willie was overjoyed to see friends and told them he was eager to be released in time to be in Philadelphia for the wedding of Lucy's sister, Annie, on October 1. Charlie's diary continued[14]:

> After staying there an hour or so we walked toward the battle field with Frank [a relative of the Garrisons], who was so kind as to show us some of the principle features. We visited the cemetery and Round Top. Dead horses, shallow graves, shells, cartridge boxes etc. were the principle features. We ate our dinner on Round Top and after picking up some relics and looking at the extensive fortifications, we came back to town where our knapsacks were. We walked about eight miles on or around the battlefield.

At night at the farmhouse where they stayed they met two army topographers making maps to show Meade was right to let Lee go. There had been a storm in the North over the failure of the Union General George Meade to press after Lee's beaten troops, and the debate raged for several months. Meade's defense was that his own troops had suffered so heavily that he wasn't certain he could succeed if he engaged Lee again. In Harrisburg the boys were accosted by a drunken officer, but Wendell managed to calm the situation before there was a serious altercation. They walked through the mountains to Lewiston in eastern Pennsylvania; then with enough walking already behind them they took "the cars" for some of the homeward journey.

Charlie's last entry gives the flavor of their nearly month-long journey.

> August 21, 1863
> After walking three miles we stopped and went swimming. After coming out we prepared to a wood nearby and ate our "frugal meal." After dinner Wendell took sketches of we three boys separately but just as he was finishing, a violent thunderstorm came up and we were obliged to retreat to a leaky shanty and during the pelting rain we sang vociferously. However it soon slacked and we started for the station house which we reached without a "dripping." We are now waiting for a train for Phila. in which we hope to return home.

Home was the McKim house at Hilltop, where Charlie's mother and his sisters were expecting his return.

10

A Simple Leaf

Give all to love;
Obey thy heart;
Friends, kindred, days,
Estate, good-fame,
Plans, credit, and the Muse,—
Nothing refuse.

Tis a brave master;
Let it have scope:
Follow it utterly,
Hope beyond hope:
High and more high
It dives into noon,
With wing unspent,
Untold intent;
But it is a god,
Knows its own path,
And the reaches of the sky.

—Ralph Waldo Emerson

When Wendell, his younger brother, Frank, and Lucy's brother, Charlie, reached Philadelphia, Wendell followed the boys to the McKims' house in Germantown where Lucy and Annie were alone to greet them, since their mother was away on a short visit. Lucy hadn't seen Wendell since March, when she had kept him at a distance, but months had passed. She was not aware that Wendell had helped arrange the pedestrian excursion as a way for him to meet her again, but she responded more pleasantly this time. During the weekend they were joined by Fred Dennis, who would marry

Annie a month later, and the two women were spending most of their time up in the attic of the house, patiently sewing Annie's trousseau in the devastating heat. Lucy attempted to describe the chaotic visit in a letter to Ellen on August 31, 1863.[1]

Saturday morning it was fearfully hot. The pedestrians were expected the next Monday, but accidentally dropped in upon us at nine o'clock this day, sunburned & warm. They had passed the previous night at Roadside [the home of the Motts]. Mother was not yet at home, & when Ann and I had got 'em off to their rooms & baths, we looked at each other and wept. . . . When the youths appeared, there was no way but to take the whole cargo of 'em to the 3rd story west, & let them watch the interesting process of trousseau making. After lunch we adjourned to the parlor, & while Wendell was playing the Raw Recruit madly on the piano & everybody else whistling and crashing bones, mother *did* appear. Never did I hail a sweeter vision! Frank kissed her & Wendell looked as if he wanted to.

I can't describe to you the way time passed until Monday when Wendell, Frank & Charlie went to town sightseeing, and Fred left—except that we melted. If you ever arouse my worst hatred I can not wish you a greater punishment than entertaining a parcel of men through a series of hot August days. I wished myself in the cold, cold ground unceasingly.

The evenings were passable to be sure. I wore that green grenadine with the great dewy earrings, & Wendell said I put him in mind of Undine (particularly from the aerial style of my gait & willowy figger.)

Fred & "Wendy" got on finely together, & Fred thinks if he (Wendy) wasn't a non he'd be prime. This wretch & Ann expended their best energies in trying to make me laugh, but I defied 'em & didn't once gratify them with the ghost of a snicker.

Sunday evg. pa & ma went to bed leaving four of us nicely paired off; W. & I on the slips, & A. & F. in a distant corner whence I could occasionally hear audible smiles. Time wore on—really I can't tell you everything, for I should never finish. Tuesday morning we were to husk corn under the trees at the upper end of the garden, but once family rested, everybody fizzled out but the bloody man & me, so we were tete a tete again.

Cher amie—Nothing Happened!

With Wendell and the two boys away on Wednesday, two Eagleswood friends, Ned and Amanda Hollowell, stopped at the house. Ned was on crutches from his wound at Fort Wagner and Lucy and Ned were soon in a "wild talk" that Annie felt was definitely a flirtation, but that Lucy insisted was "only a high time." Ned had news that Bev had been offered a 2nd lieutenancy in the 34th regiment.

In her letter Lucy went on to describe a concert in the evening, and the games and talk and walks that filled the rest of the days were what a young couple would usually consider as "courting." Lucy, certainly stirred by her talk only a few hours before with Ned Hollowell—still suffering from his wounds and deeply shaken by what he had experienced at Fort Wagner—seemed almost half-mocking in her account of the stir she was causing, but as she assured Ellen at the close of the letter, no commitment had been made. She was still "L. McKim, toujours."

> . . . W. & I had our seats together, this time they were in a romantic corner of the piazza. Music—bass sextet—quite fair, two or three admirables, especially a March Funebre from Don Sebastian. Got home late, but didn't go to bed for some time, for W. seemed quite impossible. Gay time.
>
> Friday was spent quietly, only varied by a couple of walks, one in the mng., one in the aft., both in a gentle drizzle.
>
> Played Muffin in the Ring with great success. I called W. "honey," & Ike Davis went home & told everybody he was sure etc. etc. The boys left next morning, protesting they had never had such a good time. We certainly got very well acquainted.
>
> Wendell is *admirable*—unimpeachable—as perfect as this flesh allows.
>
> Ma Cherie, je suis L. McKim, toujours.

As Fred Dennis had made clear, he couldn't see Wendell as a possible suitor for Lucy; Wendell was a "non," as Lucy knew. For her it was a difficult impasse. In her heart she was committed in every way to the struggle for emancipation and she still was trying to conceal her suffering over the death of Richard Chase, who had been dead for less than a year. The contradictions would have to be resolved over the next months.

◆ ◆ ◆

Encouraged by the new warmth he sensed in Lucy on the visit to Hilltop, Wendell wrote to her immediately after his return to Boston. He was burdened with the weight of his own feelings and was uncomfortably conscious of the busy talk connecting him with Lucy among his family and people they knew. Simply that Lucy and Ellen had paid a visit to Dix Place and that William and Wendell had been present was enough to fill a moment's gossip for friends. In impulsive haste, in his letter he declared his love for Lucy, and asked her to marry him. Upset that he had so misread her attitude—as she interpreted his letter—she returned it to him immediately, with her own letter explaining the impossibility of there being anything between them. She could never be anything but honest, and her letter was probably as difficult for her to write as his letter had been for him.[2]

Hilltop, Sept. 4th, 1863

Dear Wendell:

Your letter received last evening lies before me.

I wish indeed that you had revealed to me your thoughts when you were here; for the part I must bear in this discussion of them is so equivocal, it might have been easier spoken than written.

Would that I could wholly and without reserve return at once the love you offer me, which I deeply feel to be a crowning honor. But it is impossible. Instead I can only beg you to accept a harsh but faithful explanation of my feelings. I like you very much; better than any man I know. You excite in me the warmest admiration and respect. But I *love* no one. I feel strong and independent alone. Life is brimming with excitement and occupation. The world seems wide before me. I am so young: freedom is so sweet: I cannot part with it.

There may be a partial cause for this unimpressibility, which it is only candid to state.

For three years I had a dear and intimate friend. Last December he was killed in a cavalry charge 'in' Tennessee; and although we were not engaged, and indeed most likely never would have been, his death was a great shock to me. Since then my susceptibilities seem to have been paralyzed.

Wendell, it must pain any woman to put aside the greatest gift a man can tender her. But it seems as if it never could have pained anyone as it does me now, knowing so well the value of what it laid before me. My judgment as well as omens . . . seem to urge me to alter the ungracious reply I have given you. Even a vague fear besets me that I am willfully thrusting away what may be the greatest happiness of my future. But I dare not—I ought not—for your sake as well as mine, pronounce otherwise than I have done, without the coincidence of unmistakable affection.

Reading over at this point, it seems as if a hope of something different for the future was covertly held out. Such an intention was not in my thoughts. I would not allow myself to do anything of the sort. A veil hides all our morrows; can we then promise what they shall bring forth? Even *guesses* at changes are weakening and delusive.

Forgive this hard, unsatisfactory letter. It contains the nearest approxima-
tion I can make of my sentiments. A word less would have been unjust to us
both. In any case believe me most truly your friend.

Lucy McKim

What had passed between them was never spoken to anyone else, and
on the surface everything continued as it had been before. On September
8 Charlie wrote to Frank about his interest in the minstrel shows appearing in Philadelphia.[3]

September 8, 1863
If father is willing I shall certainly go to [Carncross?] to hear Dixey's Minstrels, and hear the celebrated song of Dan Emmett's entitled "High Daddy"
or "I won't go home anymore"—I have never heard the Buckley Brothers,
although I should like to very much.

Lucy bids me say that the next time she goes to town the music she promised you shall be mailed.

Please remember me to Wendell

A few days later Lucy was surprised by a visitor, and described the
moment in a letter to Ellen on September 15.[4]

I was peacefully making chemises in the library; everybody else was upstairs,
when the bell rang. Becky informed me "A gentleman to see Miss Lucy, &
prefers not to send his name;" I went to the parlor profoundly wondering; a
tall figure in blues held out two hands; it was Bev! He has been working all
summer for this 20 days furlough, with which he meant to surprise everybody. I had just got a good letter from him in which he never mentioned a
word of it. He had come from Columbus on tenterhooks for fear his little
secret had somehow reached the light; stopped at the Continental for repairs
& started for Hilltop. His boyish delight at my complete astonishment was
very funny. I took him right back to the library & went on with my work,
while we had a long pleasant talk.

Despite his high spirits at being with Lucy again Bev's news was disquieting. By the terms of the prisoner exchange agreement he was still
a southern prisoner, waiting hopefully to be exchanged. He had been
forced to decline Ned Hollowell's offer to join his regiment. He told Lucy
that there were men still waiting to be exchanged since the first battle of
Bull Run two years before, and Bev was only a private, without important

friends in Washington. He was hopeful he might soon be exchanged and that the regiment being assembled by the son of the Welds from Eagleswood, Lewis Weld, would "hold out the first hand to him."

For the rest of his brief leave Bev was her companion for concerts and social calls. At the same time Lucy had to answer the letter she had received from Wendell in answer to her letter of September 4. She finally felt herself ready to answer on her first "writing day" after Bev's arrival.[5]

> Sept. 20th, 1863 Hilltop
> Dear Wendell:
> I have been waiting quite a while before answering your letter, in order to have a good 'think' over it, and over matters connected with it. And now this Sunday afternoon finds me pen in hand, trying to put in words—as I can't in drawing— the conclusion to which I have come. You will pardon me, I hope, for reverting once more to a subject which can hardly be a pleasant one for discussion for either of us. And I take courage to say what I must, because your last letter was so kind and disembarrassing.
> It does not seem to me right, after the expressions of feeling that have been made that we should correspond. The two strong opinions that support this opinion are these:
> 1st. If after a lapse of time during which letters had been regularly exchanged—let it be six months or three years—I should find myself quite unchanged while you remained the same, that discovery would no longer be an honorable justification for the continuance of a refusal on my part.
> 2nd. If, on the contrary, a series of congenial letters should have induced a complete alteration of sentiment in me, could I be certain that I loved the man identically with the correspondent?
> I fancy I see your generosity knocking away prop no. 1. But that ought not to be. It seems trite and feeble to say 'love another', yet let me say it! Indeed I am not worth running a risk for. There must be many better women! I should always regret having told you the *whole* truth, did it prove to be a hindrance to your seeking and *finding* happiness elsewhere.
> As to the second consideration, it sounds mortifyingly selfish, I have dressed the thought twenty ways, in vain! Some forms will be unlovely in any garb. Unfortunate as it is, however, it is conclusive.

She continued her letter with comments on news he'd included and thanked him for music that he'd sent. She also had her own news—her music classes were full, and she "scarcely expects to have time to think, after the 1st of October." She ended with a final insistence that this would be the end of their correspondence, but asking him to send a final letter to confirm the agreement.

> Even after all I have said I shall hope for one more letter from you saying that you understand my motives for discontinuing a correspondence that in every other way would have been a pleasure.
>   Yours truly
>   Lucy McKim

On October 1, the hours Lucy and Annie had spent on the bridal trousseau finally could be counted as part of the general display, and Annie married her tall, handsome Lieutenant Fred Dennis. It was the first marriage in the family and Lucy was more shaken by it than she at first understood. She wrote a disconcerted letter to Ellen on October 10.[6]

> If I come on for a couple of weeks Christmas may I sleep with you one night? ... What's your general idea of a Polonaise? Did Chopin's illness & Mme. Sand's nursing him ever put you in mind of G and—sh, sh—Pro, I mean— Progressive friends you know! How are you—* * o my eye.
>   Don't say I'm incoherent. Believe I'd be very jolly if somebody was around to help, but I think I kind of miss Annie. Do smile—deal gently with the erring.
>   Lucy

Two weeks later, on October 25, she wrote a long letter, still without mentioning the exchange of letters with Wendell, but half-jokingly reporting that she had been surprised by a conversational exchange with a guest at the house, who reminded her that time was passing. She would celebrate her twenty-first birthday the next week. She continued her letter with a description of her chaotic daily schedule, which could justify some of her emotional turmoil, and also noted that she had had to go to the doctor for a throat ailment.[7]

> .... I had not thought myself *venerable* exactly until the other night, when a guest said he thought a girl was hardly fit for marriage at seventeen, but if she waited until past twenty, why—"it was leaving it almost too late." I need an inspiration, in faith. Pens are awkward instruments to one given over to piano playing & teaching. Three hours every morning do I thread the mazes of Gutmann, Chopin, Schumann. Three hours every afternoon—with from 1 hr. & ½ to 2 hrs. walking distributed between them—do I help limpsy infantile paws to extract five-finger exercises from the suffering ivory. Between

whiles (seems to me that don't look correct when it's written) so far have
been fully occupied with resting . . . Next week gymnasium class begins.
Chas & I enter for six months. The class is Miss Hopkins's at Germantown.
Have also begun a course of medicine under Dr. Hering for throat. This you
needent speak of. How's your health, fellow sufferer?.

She also wrote to other friends and family members, and on November 8 she was obliged to confess to Wendell's sister Fanny, to whom she
was writing in Boston, that she was having trouble with her eyes again,
but she also notes that she still is hearing as much music as possible. The
pianist "Wolfsohn" she mentions was the well-known concert artist Carl
Wolfsohn who appeared with the country's leading orchestra societies in
concerto performances.[8]

My old ailment of weak eyes has returned with the autumn winds and autumn
work. I find on Sunday—writing day—that when I have scribbled awhile to
satisfy Annie's insatiable cravings my unfortunate orbs are quite used up.

She continued to say she was taking one lesson a week from Wolfsohn
and that she

. . . enjoyed them & him so much. A brilliant Polonaise of Gutmann, of
Chopin's waltzes & opus 53 (Best) have been under consideration so far. The
musical opportunities here this winter promise to be quite good. At present
we have the German opera & Gottschalk; expect more German & the Italian
opera, the Germania has begun, & the first classical soiree is announced for
this month.

Through all of this activity she continued to abide by the agreement
she had made with Wendell, and if they had contact with each other it
was through members of the family. She continued to write to Fanny, and
Wendell wrote to her younger brother, Charlie. Although Lucy had not
referred to any differences between herself and Wendell about his "nonresistor" views, even before the visit to Hilltop Wendell had already been
concerned that Lucy's father had expressed his disapproval of Wendell's
public appearances supporting his position. In a letter to his brother William on August 23 Wendell argued his side of the issue.[9]

Mr. McKim regrets that I have thus recorded myself on the side of the peace
doctrine, thinking that . . . I may be hampered of my free will hereafter by the

recollection that I am committed. Of course, I cannot show him how thoroughly I have investigated the question, and am far from deeming that I have probed it to the bottom; but with my present understanding of its scope I feel acquitted of all injury to my fellow-man when I embrace the doctrine of love to all the race, and complete obedience to the laws of God.

Whatever Lucy and Ellen had written to each other in their years of friendship about their attachments or flirtations, they had never seriously declared a determination to not marry someone sometime. For women like them it was considered to be the natural progression to womanhood. In her own letters Lucy had only asked of the world that she have a little more time to live her own life. It was Ellen, two years older, who first made a decision. In February 1864 she wrote to her mother and father.[10]

> Boston Feb 17th—'64
> My beloved Father and Mother—
> I wish I knew how to tell you what for two days past, I have been longing to tell you—that William Garrison has asked me to marry him, & that I have promised to—I wish I knew of your full consent and satisfaction, it is all I need. Sister is not yet ecstatic. She holds her opinion about the Altar fires, but it is because she does not know this brave strong man, so eager to do what is right, at whatever cost.
> I know *you* will be as happy as I desire; if there were any reason to think otherwise, my peace would be greatly disturbed, for I long to make my offering of a son-in-law to you, as acceptable and excellent as my sisters have done before me. Do not fancy that I have acted impulsively, or blindly in this, not that I do not strive to appreciate how serious and irrevocable the step is. For a long time I have been thinking of it, and I have tried to use my judgment instead of my feelings . . . There is no conflict in my mind, & as far as I hear you are gratified, you to whom I owe everything & whom I love and revere with my whole heart, I shall forever be at rest—
> I don't want it to be generally known quite yet—Of course Dix Place will have to be informed and our Eliza and the boys—I shall write a little note to Mrs. Hall & Lucy & that is all . . . Please do not send it to Phila. for I want to get a little accustomed to it first. William made Fanny his immediate confidante, & she came up yesterday, bringing me the sweetest welcome—They are all so cordial & noble, I am certain to be well cared for & I shall do my best to deserve their esteem. I pray that Dr. Taylor will make me well and strong, so that I can hurry home & *learn to keep house*—
> Goodbye my dear Parents—
> Your loving daughter Ellen W.

Ellen's letter to Lucy telling of the engagement arrived a few days later. That it was William Garrison, Wendell's older brother, seemed only what had long been anticipated, since they had been open about their attraction for each other since the visit Ellen and Lucy had paid to the Garrison household the spring before. Eliza was Ellen's sister, living close to their mother in Auburn. A few days before, Ellen's mother had received a letter from William asking for their permission to marry Ellen, and she had not suspected that there was any serious connection between them. She had known William for most of his life, and her first surprise was that his letter was not signed with his accustomed "fraternally yours." There was no question that she and her husband would approve of Ellen's decision.[11]

My darling child—
　　We were taken entirely by surprise, by W. L. G.'s letter which reached us at Eliza's on Friday—It was unexpected to me, because I supposed he was "as ever, fraternally yours"—and I felt somewhat at a loss how to answer it—
　　We can sincerely welcome a son whose record stands as fair as his, but it is no small thing to relinquish to another, our last little daughter—We could not read your sweet and tender letter unmoved nor without much solicitude, but you have not decided hastily and it wd. be far from our wish to interpose any objections in a matter in which we have always been disposed to leave your judgment entirely unfettered—knowing that whatever promoted your happiness, would ensure ours.

Wendell had accepted Lucy's conditions, and they didn't meet, but he remained in contact with the family through letters to Charlie. In a letter to Wendell's younger brother Frank, Charlie reported on a letter and a gift Wendell had sent him. Charlie's banjo playing had progressed to the point where he was reading music scores for his pieces.[12]

March 15, 1864
... Wendell wrote me a splendid letter the other day, in which he sent Willie Davis some stamps, and me the pieces "Young Recruit" and "Perfect Cure." He said you had finished the 7th Book of Vergil and were about to commence Xenophon; you will go into college like a breeze, I've no doubt.
　　Last Sunday I went over to Camp William Penn. The troops have exchanged their shelter tents for barracks, and are now in comfortable quarters near Mr. Mott's. They are upwards of two regiments; Gustavus Adolphus Scraggs & I think that comparing the white and the black drummers, the latter are by far the best, don't you? Their drum major (got up "regardless")

reminded me of a conceited turkey cock more than anything else, strutting along as though he were "some".

With the announcement of Ellen's engagement to William there was now more intense pressure on Lucy over what was for most of their friends her inexplicable refusal to accept Wendell's suit. William felt he understand something of the situation, and he wrote to Ellen that Lucy and Wendell shouldn't see each other again if it was only to accept a relationship that would bring little to either of them. Ellen, half-agreeing, answered, "If Fate doesn't mean that he shall have her, it was cruel to let him love her."[13] William also wasn't certain that Lucy loved his brother, and he was concerned that the families now were putting too much pressure on her. In her story of the Garrison children, biographer Harriet Alonso wrote[14]:

> That the McKims exerted pressure on Lucy was made evident to Ellie during a visit where Miller and Sarah McKim spoke endlessly about Wendell and hinted about the possible union between him and Lucy. At one point the two embarrassed their daughter before her friend, who reported "she colored up to her eyes, when her father mentioned him; she declared the reason was physical, & not in the region of the heart." . . . Ellie conceded that "If Lucy in not in love, her father & mother are. Her father thinks *she is*, and *doesn't know* it. She talks of it, reasons with herself, & wonders if the strong yet not impulsive feeling of admiration that she is conscious of, may be the divine love—I am afraid it is not, if she can take it to pieces so calmly."

A darker sense of tragedy also weighed on Lucy in these months. No suitable southern prisoner could be found as an exchange for Bev, and he was returned to the South. He was sent to Andersonville Prison, where thirteen thousand desperate Union prisoners were huddled on twenty-six acres of filthy mud. They lived in rudimentary shelters and the only source of water and sanitation was a polluted open stream that ran through the encampment. Sometime in March Bev died of starvation. Lucy once again was forced to face the dilemma of her own convictions that the war must be fought, and Wendell's equally strong insistence on nonviolence as the way out of the blindness of the struggle.

What seemed certain was that Lucy herself did not know if she was in love with Wendell, and she was also finding her life of music and teaching fulfilling. Unlike Ellen, who had faced only her own confusions without her engagement, Lucy could imagine herself earning a kind of independence with work of her own. Finally in June, Wendell, in spite of a promise that he would give her a year to reach some decision, made a trip to Hill-top to confront her. He was conscious when he began to speak that Lucy still was not determined to accept him, but on July 2 he wrote to William that "when the word was uttered by me, there came a revulsion, a collapse of predeterminations, and like kindred drops we mingled into one."[15]

On June 26, 1864, Lucy wrote to Ellen to reveal her attachment to Wendell, at the same time pledging her to secrecy, since in the complicated rules of courtship and engagement she and Wendell could not declare themselves until his older brother William had married Ellen. Her letter began with their usual banter, talking about William, but then she abruptly changed the subject.[16]

> Speaking of Wm. reminded me of Wendell, who is here, & a piece of intelligence I have for you . . . As usual, I stop your mouth before hand with a promise of secrecy—seriously, Nell. And now from this prelude I fancy you have half-guessed that I have been a "good girl," & "sensible," & not "romantic" nor "unreasonable." Anyhow it is quite true that I've promised & agreed to love Wendell and be very happy & very thankful. Do you know I think almost as much of him as you did when you were here in the spring! Indeed I even fancy that I prefer him to William—but I don't want you to think me extreme.
>
> We have come to the decision to have nothing but an "understanding" until after your wedding at least for several reasons. So limit yourself, please, to discussing it with William alone "until further notice." . . . Well, goodbye petite, & wish me joy in one of your own good letters. I told Wendell that he ought to be very grateful to you. Father & mother seem quite satisfied! Charlie won't know. Aren't you glad we shall be sisters? I don't know why God has been so good to me—perverse that I was! Ever yours, L. McK

Ellen, stunned and overjoyed, immediately replied, squeezing her response on the narrow strip of paper that was the only thing she could lay her hands on, and refusing to give in to another of her crippling headaches.[17]

> *June 29, 1864*
> *Lucy—you dear dear one—*
> *First to do it, & then*
> *to tell me of it! Altho' I am*
> *half blind with a headache,*
> *I must write these lines*
> *if they are my last—It*

is evening, & I've left mother
reading Augusta's letter of
particulars to run up to my
own room, & embrace you
& kiss your little ring for you
& say how you make me
more than happy—I'm so
glad!—I was bitterly afraid
you would try to be surer
of yourself & so postpone your
joy, & perhaps let it slip
altogether—
Now see if you'll ever
regret it! Don't I know
Wendell—don't I know that
he is next to the very best man
for a husband that could
be born—of course he is
& if you'll only make him a
decent wife—that's the question.
. . . . you are very good to say
I may talk it over with Wm.
I wouldn't say one word to
him about it if you desired.
I could keep shady [?] but
won't he stand on his head five
minutes!

Ellen was overjoyed that since they were marrying brothers, "you are making yourself my sister," and half-seriously proposed that they have a double wedding.

. . . I didn't know I
had set my heart so on having
you & Wendell come together
but your good news has discovered
it to me—O—won't you
have to go through a course of house
work now!

Wendell wrote his brother William on July 2, when their arrangement was decided, that his mind had been made up since the winter of '62–'63, and that he had thought of the trip to Hilltop at the end of the previous summer as a "courtship." He had, however, been as reticent about their agreement as Lucy had been, and in a letter congratulating him on his choice, his father expressed his surprise, since he hadn't noted any alteration in the conduct of either Lucy or his son.[18]

> Boston, June 30, 1864
> My dear Wendell:
> Your letter, addressed to your mother and myself, announcing your matrimonial engagement, was a surprise to me, if not to her. Most sincerely do I congratulate you upon the choice you have made, believing it in all respects to be a wise and good one. Lucy has always held a high position in my respect and esteem; and now I shall be permitted to love her as a cherished daughter. She is comely in person, and possesses, I think, all those qualities of mind and heart desirable in a wife suited to your tastes and wants. She has large self-respect and self-reliance, an amiable disposition, great purity of character, a high ideal standard of goodness, and an affectionate nature. As the daughter of two of my earliest and most beloved friends, to whom I have been attached by the tenderest ties, she will ever have special claims on my regards. You both kept your secret so well that your announcement is not only exceedingly pleasant, but a charming surprise. . . .
> Having said this much in her praise, I will now say that I think she has done wisely and well in accepting your overtures. I may be blinded by a father's partiality, but I hold you in such high esteem that I should not care to tell you all I feel . . . Nothing, therefore, remains for me to do but give you and Lucy my blessing, and to invoke upon you both the benediction of Heaven. May your union be consummated in due season, and the results of it prove that you were drawn together by magnetism of love which binds kindred souls beyond all possibility of separation.
> How delighted Ellie, the bosom friend of Lucy, will be to hear of the match! To her, I am sure, nothing would be more desirable. And how pleasant it will be to all the families concerned in it.

Two weeks later Garrison also wrote to Lucy, apologizing that while visiting friends at their home in Melrose a "slow fever" had kept him from writing.[19]

Boston, July 11, 1864

My dear Lucy,

I have hitherto esteemed you as the worthy daughter of parents who, for more than a score of years, have stood among the highest on the list of my most cherished acquaintances. Now and henceforth, if Heaven permit, I am to love you as a daughter, through your plighted troth to Wendell, yet to be consummated in wedlock. Though taken by surprise at the intelligence—for how well you and he kept the secret from me of your ripening union! I am as much delighted as any prospective father-in-law ought to be in such a case. I hope Wendell has said as much to you in my behalf; for I meant to have sent you my approval and blessing at a much earlier date. But since I have been laboring under a slow fever which at one time I was apprehensive might assume a typhoidal form....

Of course, our thoughts are largely absorbed in the approaching nuptials between William and Ellie. I believe theirs is a genuine love-match, and therefore feel assured it will work well for the families. William is as "happy as a king"—or, still better, as happy as Wendell manifestly is when extolling you to us in his letters, and telling us how he is overflowing with bliss! At one time I was afraid all my grown-up boys would live and die bachelors; but two of them have resolved not to do so, and, should George be spared to return, I trust he will soon follow their good example. As for Franky, see if he do not find a lassie to his taste, in good season! ....

The word spread quickly, though Wendell and Lucy continued to say little about it themselves when they were with friends. A few days later a friend of the family named Agnes Harrison, now Lady MacDowell, met Lucy during a visit to Philadelphia and she wrote to her sister in England about Lucy's high spirits.[20]

July 17, 1864

... On Friday Lucy McKim came to spend the day ... we had a jolly talk. Lucy is just as bright and vigorous as usual. In the evening we sat on the piazza – Ellis going over some of his European travels with Lucy ... Then Lucy played over bits of Mendelssohn, Mozart, & Beethoven till bed time—when we retired to our rooms—to talk ethics till two hours later—in fact it was nearly two o'clock when I stole along the passage to my room.

A month later she met Lucy again, this time with Wendell.

Aug. 22, 1864

On Saturday afternoon I had to go over to the church to practice, but by walking quickly I hoped to get back in time to receive Lucy McKim who was coming over to bring her fiancé to be introduced here. They had however arrived & been shown "the estate," and admired new walks & roads with Ellis. We had quite a pleasant evening. Lucy (whom any one would mistake for Minerva, if they were not aware that the latter had been long since deceased) was just as handsome & logical & strongly practical as ever, in spite of the "sweet madness" which is supposed to attack people in her position. We had a small talk in my room while I was doing my hair. It is unnecessary to say that she spoke of "Wendell." She stood balancing a book on her hand in the most Hypatian attitude, delivering herself of some very elevated philosophical statements. I listened till she informed me very seriously that his letters were quite the finest pieces of letter–writing she had ever read—that she had read them critically, & *using judgment*, had come to that conclusion. When I burst into a fit of irreverent laughter, she after a moment's perplexed hesitation was obliged to join, & then we went downstairs to meet the critically and "judgmatically viewed" letter writer himself. He is a good fellow, excellently suited to Lucy, more imaginative than she, & just formed "to dove-tail" with her into a very fine noble married life I think . . .

Since Wendell and Lucy had agreed there was no "engagement," there couldn't be a ring, but on July 25, in a small, crumpled envelope Lucy sent him a leaf she had worn in her hair. It was a kind of token that soldiers and their sweethearts exchanged, something that the other had worn as a sign of their attachment, and for Lucy it said what was in her heart.

◆ ◆ ◆

As the weeks passed Lucy lived at home, doing her share of housework, which she disliked intensely, continuing her morning hours of practicing, and spending her afternoons with her piano scholars. In the first weeks of the summer she had found once more as had happened in the summer before, that she was drawn back to her dreams of collecting songs. The previous year it had been Fanny Kemble's book of her life among the slaves on her husband's Sea Island plantation that had made its way into every parlor discussion. Now it was an account of life on St. Helena Island, the island Lucy had visited, that appeared as a two-part article titled "Life on the Sea Islands" in the May and June 1864 issues of the *Atlantic Monthly*.

The author was Charlotte Forten, the teacher who had come to the island to join Laura Towne and Ellen Murray only a few weeks after Lucy's visit. It was a signal accomplishment for an African American woman to appear in the pages of the country's most distinguished journal, and her pieces attracted considerable interest. Lucy's response later was to ask Forten to review *Slave Songs* when it at last appeared, and Forten's warm and spontaneous review included phrases from Lucy's first writing about the songs two years before.

Forten had turned to her diaries as the material for her pieces, and the writing had a fresh directness that caught the breathless mood of her experience. For Lucy, the account of Forten's sojourn on the island was certainly familiar, since she had made the same journey herself only short months before Forten's arrival. She could read of the plantation houses, the Brick Baptist Church, the dirt roads, and the moss-covered oaks she had seen herself. Forten recounted a visit with a small group to the Episcopal Chapel, where Lucy and the others with her had fled their open carriage to take refuge from a rainstorm. Forten commented that the chapel's organ was "not as out of tune as all the pianos on the island," and a woman in her party played the organ while the gentlemen sang.[21] She decided that while it was pleasant to hear the old New England hymn-tunes, the music "did not thrill us as the singing of the people had done."

What would have been of even more interest for Lucy was that the articles included the texts to seven slave songs, among them songs she had heard herself, including a version of "Roll Jordan Roll." Forten's notation of the text differed from the setting Lucy had published of the song two years earlier, but it concluded with the chorus similar to what Lucy had transcribed[22]:

> *Oh, march, de angels, march! oh, march, de angels, march!*
> *My soul arise in heab'n, Lord*
> *For to her the ven [sic] Jordan roll.*

For Lucy in these months, with Ellen's wedding approaching and her own engagement known to the world, the slave song collection was certainly not where her thoughts lingered. But if Forten's writing caused her to think of it now, again the question hovered—how could she bring it about with her life turning in these new and entirely unknown directions?

◆ ◆ ◆

Lucy's father still was working to alleviate the situation of the teachers on St. Helena and he was as immersed in his efforts to recruit volunteers for the black regiments being trained for the army. The situation with the freedmen was rapidly evolving, and McKim was now employed by the Pennsylvania Freedmen's Relief Association, continuing his close contacts with Laura Towne as he endeavored to give her whatever assistance he could from Philadelphia. One of her most serious problems was the unsuitability of the Brick Church as a school. It had been constructed as a church, with most of its space the single large chamber for worship, and all the classes on every level were crowded together in a noisy scene. Forten soon found that the large room had no chimney and the winter days often were dauntingly chilly. A primitive stove they employed in an attempt to warm the room only filled the room with smoke. The church was in use on Sundays for services, which meant the school materials had to be removed at the end of each week's instruction.

It was clear to McKim that something had to be done to help Towne, but he was also aware of the lack of building materials on the islands. His decision was to make use of the building materials and the facilities in Philadelphia to construct a large wooden-framed school and then dismantle it and send it by coastal steamer to St. Helena. The previous summer, under the terms of an expropriation act authorizing the seizure of the island's abandoned plantations, the plantation properties had been offered for sale. With Laura Towne's aid and encouragement, and her steady opposition to any attempts by the federal authorities to discourage purchases by the slaves who had worked the land, three-quarters of the island was acquired by the freedman. With Towne there to oversee the project and to provide her own money, fifty acres across the dirt road from the Brick Church were purchased from its new owner to be used as a site for the new building.

It had been a difficult year on the island. On January 7 Towne wrote in her diary[23]:

We have no milk, and at times no wood. There is nobody, not a single hand— not one man up and well enough to get these things. All the boys are getting sick also. It is a tight time. I am nearly ill too. Every evening I fold powders and every afternoon I take my way down street and stop at every house, giving medicine at the door.

On February 7 she wrote to her family explaining why she had asked them to send her things from the family home.[24]

Our room is nearly as ill-built and open as a rough country stable.... and our only bit of carpet being in our parlor floor, we have bare boards in our rooms with the air rushing through every crack, and sunlight along every board visible where the sun shines under the house. This is comfortless and cold as you cannot imagine, who have not had uncarpeted floors since you can remember. When we first came here, and for a time, these things were endurable, but year after year it is hard to live so.... You know what South Carolina fare is. We are just in the oyster hole again, and having nothing else we are sick of the sight of them. I was going to send home for butter, for we have had neither butter nor milk for some time—so much less than last year.... We had a cow sent to us and were happy, but she was a jumper—and our fence such as you might expect—and she jumped and ran, after our feeding her for three days and getting just one quart of milk. Her feed, too, was a heart break—we are not sure of it from day to day—none to be begged, borrowed, or bought, so her escape was a relief.

On May 21 she wrote of damage from a Confederate raid on a nearby island.[25]

Charlie and Harriet Ware rowed us over to Hunting Island, Ellen taking an oar. We saw the splendid new lighthouse, blown up by the rebels, the magnificent beach with trees washed [up] and standing on their roots high above water, or lying, roots in the air. I tried to row coming home, and persisted a long time so as to do my share of the work, but it was rough and I grew frightened so I gave the oar to Ellen.... While we were away here, Morgan Island was visited by the rebels and all the people carried off! The Winsors rowed over to the blockading boat to give the alarm. The captain replied that he was put there to blockade and not to defend the coast, and he would do nothing. They say that he has not half force enough to work his boat....

Despite the difficulties and the threats, Towne would not leave the island or Ellen Murray, though she understood the pleadings of her family, who had never considered that she would spend her life away from them. She returned to her home for a few weeks in the fall, visiting everyone and reassuring them that her work was satisfying every need she might have, and that her health was good, despite the climate and the insects. The work on the island would go on, and Lucy's father would continue his efforts to keep the school open as a way to realize his own dreams of a better life for the freed slaves. The pieces of his prefabricated schoolhouse arrived at the island at the end of the summer, but it would be Christmas before Laura Towne could find the labor to have it erected and then made ready for her students.

◆ ◆ ◆

With their futures at last decided, Lucy and Ellen continued to write comfortably to each other, their new situation not affecting their long relationship, but giving them fresh excitements to write about. On July 21 Ellen wrote to Lucy, expressing her happiness at the turn in their lives.[26]

> I couldn't help laughing the other day, over the particulars William sent me! He had been to New York, & had a lovely talk with his brother, & was amazed to find he had been rejected once "but not hopelessly." (Ah indiscreet Lucille!) & that so long ago. but he (Wm) had not said a word to me—while the grass was not growing green under his feet . . . Fanny writes that "he is jolly & gay as possible." & it is you, young lady, who have done part of it. That other sister thinks she is fortunate—so do I. I think we all are—I cannot sleep at night for thinking so & planning & laughing to myself.
>
> I watch the moonlight on the floor, & go dreaming with eyes wide open while everybody else in the house is snoring. There is such a healthy reality about the visions. They are no air castles, no wild flights of fancy, but it is really, soberly true, that you are going to be my sister . . .

A letter from Lucy three weeks later continued their mood of relaxed teasing, asking for some needed information about her dress for Ellen's wedding, now less than a month away.[27]

> Hilltop Aug. 11/64
>
> I wish you would send me a note the minute you get this & satisfy my doubts about wearing a lilac or a green sash with a wedding dress, and also enclose— if you *can* spare it (I'm serious) that little turquoise ring. Wendell's in a stew about mine—that is he would be if he knew what a stew was, & wants me to be sensible & go to the jewelers with him & be fitted—like for a pair of shoes! But my *romance* forbids this . . .
>
> Nellchen, you don't know how much I like Wendell! It really surprises me. So you want to know how I write "when the tenderness bubbles up." Little skeptic! I verily believe you think I don't know how to say anything tender. But remember, ice will burn. Ask Wendell if I'm not mellifluous & saccharine! And his epistles? They're just as opposite to what you'd think—well, wait till I come—can you?

11

I am no good at last words . . .

No more I seek, the prize is found,
I furl my sails, my voyage is o'er,
The treacherous waves no longer sound
But sing thy praise along the shore.

I steal from all I hoped of old,
To throw more beauty round thy way;
The dross I part, and melt the gold,
And stamp it with thy every-day,

I did not dream to welcome thee;
Like all I have thou camest unknown,
An island in a misty sea,
With stars, and flowers, and harvests strown. . . .

—William Ellery Channing
"The Harbor"

With their engagement now openly acknowledged, Wendell and Lucy could let themselves put aside the conventions and polite restraints that had inhibited their correspondence in the first months of their courtship. They could indulge themselves in the playfulness of lovers. Wendell was working in New York as a staff writer and fledgling editor for the *Independent*, a journal published by a family friend, and he was living in a room in downtown Manhattan. He was also intensely lonely, and as he wrote her on July 17, certainly with considerable hyperbole, his week centered on their exchanges of letters.[1]

... before describing what has happened to me since Wednesday, let me show you what advantages you have in this correspondence. You can put the finishing strokes on your letter, or even write it entirely, on the morning of its going to mail. I must write on the appointed day, before 8 P.M. You receive my missive on Monday & Thursday; I yours on Tuesday and Friday. Imagine my feelings last Friday when, on entering my office in the morning, I missed the familiar hand. I was outraged. I could not suspect you of being unpunctual, when you begin letters before the time; I refused to think of you sick, or in peril, or suffering on some tower staircase . . . and I should have been quite miserable except for the prospect of the afternoon mail, which did indeed content me. Look at my calendar:

Sunday, the joy of writing to you.
Monday, reading your last letter
Tuesday, reading your letter of Sunday
Wednesday, writing to you again.
Thursday, reading your last, and, as on Monday, fancying you engaged in devouring my letter of the day before. (Me flatte-je?)
Friday, reading your Wednesday letter.
Saturday, reperusal, and wishing it was Sunday!
There now, be merciful, and don't keep me waiting.

In her notes to him she signed herself, "Wholly thine."

◆ ◆ ◆

To give her life to Wendell, however, did not mean that Lucy's lifelong friendship with Ellen would end. For women like them, their lives were as defined by their relationships with each other as they were by the new relationship with a husband. Since they both would now be married it would mean that they would continue to share the experiences that awaited them. In a letter answering Lucy's heartfelt response to Ellen's letter telling her of her engagement to William, Ellen wrote to Lucy from New York to make it clear that nothing between them would change.[2]

New York Feb. 25
Thursday
At the risk of any number of ferocious headaches, savage and vengeful at the liberty I take of writing by evening light, I must say to you how welcome

& grateful your precious letter received tonight is to me. I read it at dinner, & could have kissed it & prayed over it, so sweet & warm it is. There is
a little time now before we go to the Artists' Reception which I devote to
you, although I leave my newly arrived mother downstairs. I wish I could
have sent you a little note by the brothers, but it was impossible, & not as
if I could stop writing to you, my always dearest Lucy. And as if I had told
William *anything* except that I will promise faithfully to have his slippers
warm for him provided the wool business keeps us supplied with fuel. You
creature—my mind still serves me. Ah me—I dread that you may no longer
repay confidence in this art [*sic*] if you are not to me the very very same as
ever, my happiness will be blighted—William said I wish you would feel as
happy & as easy with me as you are with Lucy—whereupon I said—I will—
but dear Thicky—I know it makes little difference in our minds when people
are engaged. . . . I couldn't possibly love another sufficiently to drive the love
I have for you away from my heart where it has been for so long. Don't say I
must be divorced from you, in order to marry William. . . .

It had always been understood that Ellen would be the first to be married. William was the older brother and their wedding would have to take
precedence to Wendell and Lucy's, whenever that might be. What was of
almost as much importance for Ellen and William was that he was busily
engaged in a newly founded wool business, so they could plan to be married, even though financial anxieties would occupy their thoughts as the
months passed. The wedding was held in her parents' parlor in Auburn at
the end of the summer, with Lucy and their families present. At his sister
Fanny's request a day after the wedding ceremony, while Lucy took an
afternoon nap, Wendell sent their older brother George an account of the
days at Auburn.

When William had arrived three days before the ceremony, he found
Ellen lying in her bedroom. She was helpless with a serious chest cold,
and another of the migraine headaches that so often inflicted her at any
moment of excitement or stress. By the time Wendell arrived it was the
headache that was more worrying.[3]

. . . I reached Auburn on Tuesday, and found that Ellie's nervousness has so
gained upon her that there was a general fear of her inability to endure the
service on the morrow. She, however, had no idea of baulking, though it was
deemed prudent to recall the invitations to the reception after the ceremony.
The three days previous had been wet and dismal, save occasional intervals of
rain and cloud. Ellen was kept very quiet and betrayed no worse symptoms. . . .

Lucy was to participate in the ceremony, but upstairs as the guests gathered, Ellen was so weak that Fanny and Lucy had to lift her from her bed and hold her up as they dressed her. It was with their help that finally she was able to walk down the stairs. Wendell described the scene in the parlor.

> In the small parlor were decorations of autumn leaves and branches, interspersed with many bouquets contributed by generous friends. The piano at one side was covered with bridal presents, numerous, elegant, and costly— many, of course, not appearing, as they had been sent to Boston.

Among the guests was the bridegroom's father, William Lloyd Garrison, but his wife was not well enough to see her son married. Lucy and Wendell led the procession, Fanny and Ellen's brother Willie followed, with a cousin, Emily Mott, and Frank Wright coming after them. Ellen and William came last and the ceremony was conducted as they stood in a corner of the room by a minister who had long been a friend of the families. For the Garrisons it was a moving occasion seeing one of the children at last married.

> The ceremony was purposely shortened for Ellie's sake . . . and the responses of the bride and groom were distinct and unfaltering. Ellie stood up throughout, and sat for the rest of the evening, or stood, as she felt weak or strong. . . . Father's eyes were somewhat moistened, and if he did not rub them to see if he were dreaming, he was at least puzzled to realize just what was taking place. Though I, too, saw the tie knotted, I can hardly swear I have a married brother—the same I left so beaming & happy on Thursday morning. Ellie was bright and without a headache the next day. . . .

In the weeks of preparation before Ellen's wedding there had been another series of defeats by the Union armies, and the discouraging news hovered as a grim background to the family's happiness. In an undated letter to her friend in these months Lucy wrote that she had seen the name of yet another friend wounded in battle, but she attempted to find some kind of cheer in their situation.

> You mustn't believe anything but the best reports! We're not going to fail, after all! I have been awfully blue since Sunday, but today [Saturday morning] I mean to do better. Surely Providence didn't mean to let so much noble blood be shed in vain just because our leaders are fools. Then you know, Elle,

our courage—hat of us women, I mean—is chiefly shown thro' our cheerfulness, so cheerful for the army's sake let us be.

The country was further traumatized by the election approaching in the fall. Lincoln seemed certain to be defeated, and the opposing party offered peace to the South. Then in the last weeks of the summer, newspapers across the North blazed with news. On August 4 a Union naval force captured the city of Mobile, the last important port still held by the South, and on September 2, General William Tecumseh Sherman led his troops into Atlanta, and widespread fires destroyed the city.

The war would now take on a different character. Within days after his victory, only allowing his troops a short break to catch their breath, Sherman persuaded Grant to let him take sixty thousand of his men on a raid across the north of Georgia to capture the city of Savannah on the Georgia coast only forty miles south of Port Royal. He would advance without concern for his supplies. His men would seize whatever they needed from the homes and plantations they passed, and they would destroy everything else. By the time they reached Savannah two months later, Georgia was in ruins, and the South realized that it was facing defeat. Sherman's men then turned north, their columns trailed by a ragged army of newly freed slaves who outnumbered his troops as they rushed from the plantation cabins to freedom.

Writing in her diary on St. Helena, Laura Towne described the condition of the newly freed slaves who made their way out of Georgia behind Sherman's troops.[4]

Another great crowd of negroes has come from Sherman's army. They are utterly wretched in circumstances—clothes all torn to rags, in some cases children naked, A steamboat load came to the village to-night, and they are crowded in the church and into all the people's houses. It is astonishing with what open-hearted charity the people here—themselves refugees from Edisto two years ago—have received these newcomers right into their houses, and to that most jealously guarded place—their "chimbly." A "chimbly" here is a man's castle, and the privileges of this coveted convenience are held sacred. To lend a "chimbly" to a neighbor is to grant him a great favor, yet these people are welcomed to the "chimblys." I asked our Brister if he found any friends among the refugees from Georgia. "All friends tonight," he said, "but I hain't found no family . . ."

The presidential election was held during Sherman's advance north, and instead of his feared defeat, Lincoln was elected with a solid majority. Eighty percent of the soldiers who voted supported him; in Sherman's army 90 percent of the votes went to Lincoln. He became the first president to be reelected since Andrew Jackson in 1832. Towne rejoiced in her diary, "We are overjoyed at Lincoln's victory in this fashion. He has all the states but three—*Kentucky!*, New Jersey, and Tennessee. Is it so?"[5] When Sherman's army announced the fall of Savannah on December 22, he declared that the city was a Christmas gift for the president.

The encouraging progress of the war finally offered some hope to the small group of teachers and supervisors on the islands, where they still were blockaded by a ring of southern troops. Laura Towne in a letter to her family on December 18 could relate the exciting news that the prefabricated schoolhouse Lucy's father had sent to the island was almost ready for her students.[6]

> Our new school-house is now being hurried forward pretty fast, and we hope to get in by the first of the year. How happy we shall be, nobody can tell who has not taught in a school where he or she had to make herself heard over three other classes reciting in concert, and to discover talkers and idlers among fifty scholars while one hundred and fify more are shouting lessons, and three other teachers bawling admonitions, instructions, and reproofs. Generally two or more of the babies are squalling from disinclination to remain five hours foodless on very small and tippy laps—their nurses being on benches too high for them and rather careless of infant comfort in their zeal for knowledge. . . .

The dismantled building was erected beside the dirt road. In the photos taken as it was completed it had the appearance of a large, imposing structure, with its distinctive New England church-like wood façade. In reality it was more modest, but its raw lumber soon weathered and the school became a much-visited sight along the road, closed in by the oaks and their streamers of moss hanging from their wide stretched branches.

◆ ◆ ◆

The mood also lifted for Lucy. In December she traveled to Boston for a long overdue visit to Ellen, and before her departure she wrote a hasty note which in its near-incoherence suggests her own state of mind at the seriousness of Ellen's married state.[7]

12/12/64
My dear not-quite-forgotten Nell,
    Don't upbraid me till I have you safe in my grasp, and then you may—if you have the heart to. And first, let's speak of that same reunion, as of all

things in the near future it is the sweetest to think upon. Fanny—or William it was—wanted to know just when I should arrive at Boston. Well, I mean to leave here, if all goes as it should, on Friday the 23rd, of December, in the 11 o'clock train. Wendell is to ascertain which is the pleasantest night route to Boston from N. Y. & whichever he decides upon I shall take, letting you know at what time I shall reach Boston on Sat. mg.

A few weeks later, on January 26, 1865, Wendell wrote again to his brother. He and Lucy had now been engaged for seven months, and there was still little sign of when his financial situation would improve enough for them to marry. His letter expressed his discouragement at their situation, though Lucy, who was conscious of the general custom of waiting out a year of engagement before a marriage, did not share his impatience.[8]

. . . we ought now to be man and wife . . . . but we fix no time with confidence. My position [on the staff of the New York *Independent*] is in itself little permanent, and I must wait for the new sphere to open.

At the moment the war was over, as Richmond still smoldered and the men of both armies could at last breathe with relief at the thought of returning to their homes in time for the spring planting, the mood of jubilation was shattered when Lincoln was assassinated on April 14. In a letter to her sister three days later, Lucretia Mott expressed the stunned mood of the country.[9]

Was there ever such universal sorrow? The "mirth" of the days before so suddenly "turned into heaviness." Men crying in the streets! As we opened our paper, the overwhelming news stunned us, and we could hardly attend our household duties . . . Such a display of mourning as now in the city, was never before . . .

In the flood of outrage, fear, dismay, and turmoil that followed Lincoln's assassination by a southern sympathizer, the authority and the tempered spirit he might have lent to the monumental task of creating the union anew out of the emotional and physical aftermath of the war was lost. For most of the exhausted soldiers, returning at last to their homes and families, their feeling was simply that they had survived the most devastating war that had been fought in human history, and most people in the North shared the mood of the returning veterans. They were joyous that the war was over at last, they were sorely pained by the losses they had suffered, and their mood of satisfaction that the union had been saved was a salve for the sores of the assassination and their apprehensions of the future.

◆ ◆ ◆

There is no way of knowing how Lincoln would have dealt with the problems of Reconstruction, but for the abolitionists like McKim what was clear was that the immediate problem was food and clothing. Then they would begin the efforts to find some kind of work and make the beginnings of a system of education for the freed slaves, who numbered in the millions. It was thanks in part to the experience gained in Port Royal and on St. Helena Island that the new Freedmen's Bureau, which would have to deal with these same problems but now on a much larger scale, could be finally considered as one of the successful efforts of the Reconstruction era. The bureau itself operated for only a short period, from 1865 to 1872, but it was supported by a number of smaller agencies working with the same purpose. The effects of their work, even if the efforts of the bureau itself were short- lived, were crucial support for the millions of men, women, and children who had made their way to freedom, often simply by trailing after the columns of the northern armies, babies in their arms and their few ragged possessions carried in bundles.

Lucy's father had faced these challenges in South Carolina in 1861–1862, and he had learned his way through the complicated procedures involved in commandeering food supplies, of bringing medical aid, of maintaining schools—staffing them and supplying them. In his work recruiting volunteers for the black regiments he had dealt with the issues of payment and providing stable employment. It was these experienced workers like McKim who made the efforts to aid the freedmen function with an unexpected level of success for the brief years when there was political support for what they had undertaken. He moved from Philadelphia to New York to become the corresponding secretary of the American Freedmen's Relief Association, and though he was in new offices, he realized that he was only facing problems he had encountered often before.

His new work, however, only satisfied a part of McKim's concerns for the challenges facing the country at the war's end. The agitators' aims that had drawn him to the antislavery cause were still strong, and he was determined to find a public platform where men like himself could make themselves heard. He decided to seek funds not only from the many supporters who had helped his work on the islands, but from newer contributors who might have similar interests. His aim was to establish a national magazine which would express the views of those who shared his convictions and would aid the cause of the freedmen. As with any of the work relating to abolition or emancipation that went on in Philadelphia, his proposal quickly reached the ear of Lucretia Mott. When they talked about his project she quickly noticed that when her old friend spoke of his proposal he was presenting a speaking platform for men.

In a letter to her sister about his plans for the magazine she made it clear that she wasn't entirely sympathetic in her support. Although the proposed title could be interpreted as a response to the new mood of the country, as Mott makes clear what McKim envisioned was a "Reconstructive Union" of a wide gathering of reformist groups, and she also makes it clear that she finds things in his proposal unsatisfactory.[10]

> Miller is much interested in the new Union Association, and the paper to be called the "Nation." They are now collecting money on a large scale from some never before called on, and who have contributed freely. Miller would like for all the Anti-Slavery and freedmen's societies to be merged in this—a Reconstructive Union. He sent an appeal to our "Friend's Association," I told him it was objected, that woman was ignored in their new organization, and if it really was a reconstruction for the nation, she ought not so to be, and that it would be rather humiliating for our anti-slavery women and Quaker women to consent to be thus overlooked, after suffering the Anti-Slavery Society to be divided in 1840 rather than yield, and after so claiming our right so earnestly in London to a seat in the "World's Convention." He was rather taken aback, and said "if there seemed a necessity for women," he thought, "they would be admitted," to which the impetuous reply was, "*seemed a necessity*!! for *one half* the nation to act with you!"

The issue of rights for women would emerge again and again over the next decades as large numbers of the old abolitionist coalitions determined to fight only for freedmen's rights and to ask the women once again to wait until that issue had been settled. For the women who had for so many years led the struggle against slavery, the attitudes of the men they had worked beside amounted to treachery.

Although McKim succeeded in raising a substantial sum for his proposed magazine, he wasn't able to raise enough. He learned of another group that was also trying to raise funds for a new magazine that would approach many of the issues that concerned him, but intended to open the pages to a broader range of cultural issues. The group was headed by a New York journalist named Edwin L. Godkin, and he had determined that the sum of money needed would be one hundred thousand dollars, which was a very large sum for those days. His magazine would be published weekly and it would be concerned with the day's politics, literature, science, and the arts. He intended to position the new journal somewhere between the seriously considered and widely respected pages of Boston's *Atlantic Monthly* and the generally less serious but highly successful illustrated issues of New York's *Harper's Weekly*.

Godkin was nine years older than Wendell, a large, burly, bearded man who had emigrated from Ireland in 1831. He studied law, then traveled widely in Europe before returning to New York and becoming a journalist for the *Post* and the *New York Times* in 1862. He had a wide acquaintance among the intellectual world of the period and his contributors included Frederick Law Olmsted, the architect of New York City's famed parks, and Charles Eliot Norton, distinguished professor of art at Harvard, writer, critic, and an ardent supporter of progressive social reform. At the time Norton was approached by Godkin he was also acting as editor of the prestigious *North American Review*. Godkin had succeeded in raising a good part of the money he needed, but he found himself in the same dilemma as McKim. Neither of them had raised enough. The obvious answer was to combine their ideas and to pool the funds they had. Wendell still was struggling as a poorly paid staff writer for the *Independent*, and although the journal had a very unprepossessing reputation his months working there had given Wendell useful experience. As part of the arrangement to join their two efforts, the magazine was to be launched with Godkin as general editor and Wendell as literary editor, which was interpreted to mean that he would be responsible for much of the magazine's content.

The first issue of *The Nation* appeared on July 6, 1865. The opening sentence of their column offering news of "The Week" was an indication of their intention to offer a different kind of journalism to their readers. They wrote:

This week has been singularly barren of exciting news.

News writing like this could certainly set a new standard for honesty in a journal hoping to reach large numbers of readers. The cost for a year's subscription was three dollars.

The first months of the magazine were as filled with uncertainty as the beginning of any new journal is liable to be, but both Godkin and Wendell seemed to have been born with an instinct for the kind of journalism they had proposed, and the magazine quickly began attracting readers.

Politically it was much more radical than its appearance would have promised, but the series of crises in the effort at Reconstruction called up a wide spectrum of opinion. By the fall it seemed clear that *The Nation* would survive, and it would finally be possible for Lucy and Wendell to be married.

Four days before their wedding in December Lucy wrote Wendell a "last letter." Her implication was that there would be no more letters, since they would never again be parted. The letter began with the details of presents they'd received and of excited visits paid to friends. The final page of the letter closed[11]:

> This aft. I go to call in to the Petersons & the Dorseys & Brookers. Those are the last. Anne & Carrie & Fred follow in the evg. . . . Father has gone to see about the lunch, etc. The express will bring out all my dresses for repairs. Wilkinson's before bedtime. My bonnet is finished, tried on, & pronounced a success. In short things are winding up. Mother & I have had a last talk. She is so happy because I am to marry a good man,—so am I, for that matter! Dear, dear Wendell—how can I love you enough?
>
> This is the last letter I shall write; but I am no good at last words.
>
> O! if your wife only makes you always glad that you wooed and won
> Lucy McKim

Their marriage took place in Philadelphia on December 6, 1865. Since she and her family were so much a part of the Philadelphia community and the Garrison family was known throughout the country, they were married in a large public ceremony at the Unitarian Church at the corner of 10th and Locust streets in downtown Philadelphia. Ellen quickly noticed that Lucy was wearing a gleaming ring, and when they had a moment together they agreed that they could congratulate themselves on their marriages. They would also congratulate the two brothers who had been fortunate to win them.

There was a reception at the Dennises' given by Annie and her husband, Fred, and then Lucy and Wendell took the train to New York to begin their life together in his rooms at 115 East Tenth Street.

◆ ◆ ◆

In the first months of their marriage Lucy lived with Wendell in Manhattan. She took over work for *The Nation*, both to lighten the demands on Wendell in these early months and also to have something to do herself that would keep them close. In a letter to her father from Lucretia Mott's daughter Maria Davis in December 1866, she spoke of Lucy's reviews in the magazine, which probably were for children's books. McKim scholar Dena Epstein[12] suggests that the pieces she was referring to were two that had just appeared. The first, in the issue of December 13, was a review of "Fiction for the Children" and the second was "More Juvenile Fiction," which appeared in the next week's issue, December 20. As was a common practice at the time, none of the articles in the magazine were signed; longer pieces like travel letters generally were published under an author's signature, though it was generally understood that in most instances these were pseudonyms.

The tone of the two reviews certainly was similar to some of the decided opinions Lucy expressed in her letters to Ellen. As Epstein noted, "The reviewer had no patience with moral tracts masquerading as stories, saying of *Frank Stirling's Choice* and its author, a Miss Bulfinch: 'Anyone who knows will assure Miss Bulfinch that boys like Frank Stirling are impossible . . . [they are] girls in boys' clothes, or rather the female Sunday-school teacher's ideals in boy's clothes.'" Another review which may have been by Lucy was of *The Song Book*, a collection of British and American songs in the issue for April 12.[13] After praising the choice of British songs and sighing somewhat ruefully over the American selections, the reviewer commented: "We have the amplest material and the broadest variety . . . [not forgetting] the beautiful and entirely unique Negro melodies that are now reaching us from every part of the South."

All of the articles, however, have clearly been edited, almost certainly by Wendell, who was doing his job as literary editor, and at the same time also writing many of the other articles and reviews himself.

◆ ◆ ◆

With both Lucy's father and her husband now working in the city it was impractical for them to remain in Philadelphia. The family had been planning to move for some months, and they finally had found a house closer to New York. Wendell was earning little at the magazine, and as a newcomer to the city and its musical world Lucy was unable to contribute with her music lessons, but if the two families were to have a home together their economic situation would be more manageable. Ellen and William had spent their first months with the Garrisons in Boston, so it was only to be expected that Lucy and Wendell would come to a similar decision with her parents. It was also agreed that Manhattan was too expensive for

them to consider. When they did find a new house in New Jersey, it was
no surprise that it was in a planned community, again with the same ideals
of communal cooperation that had been central to so many of the ideals
the family stood for. The new home was a large, imaginatively designed
house in the new community of Llewellyn Park, in West Orange, a reasonable journey directly west of New York with a depot for the local trains to
Manhattan a comfortable walk from the house. Sarah McKim wrote to
Charlie on June 7, to describe the work that was going ahead to make the
house ready, work that had been delayed by considerable rain.[14]

> June 7 '66
> My dear Charlie
>   I promised thee that thee should hear from some of us this week, and now
> before breakfast I seat myself for that purpose.
>   . . . We are all in a tolerable state of health considering the state of the
> weather and the much we have to do before we can be comfortably settled.
>   The constant rain has been very much against our making headway. The
> painters, carpenters, and all are so kept back in consequence.
>   After all is fixed our home will look lovely I think—the house is rather
> fanciful for my taste—it was built by an artist—it has funny kitchen roofs—
> and clustered chimneys & Bulls eyes windows, and niches for statuettes and
> all sorts of artistic arrangements that don't quite suit my plain taste— still I
> don't doubt I shall be able to accustom myself to them and be quite comfort-
> able. The park is beautiful, and the views from our house are lovely, a boating
> lake not further much from our house, than Mr. Wedner's was from Hilltop.
> I can see from my chamber window—and where I have fancied I shall see
> thee and Tom skate. Rabbits and small squirrels I judge abound in the park,
> but whether allowed to shoot them or not I cannot say. Our horse is lovely
> and decidedly handsome and about as fast and gay as [Stick?] used to be,
> only more gentle. It's a famous place here for beautiful homes and handsome
> carriages. The leaves are so fine that it makes driving pleasant. But I must be
> brief as it is nearly time for Father to be off. And also time for me to leave for
> the Park. Lucy and I go over to the Park every morning [and trust] the work-
> men and do all we can to look forward on the good times when we can all be
> gathered once more around our fireside.[15]

Llewellyn Park still exists today as a secluded community of classic
older mansions and elegant newer homes in a wooded hillside area at
the edge of the community of West Orange in central New Jersey. At the
entrance to the park is an elaborately styled 1850s stone cottage, with the

exotic air of a gatehouse to a Scottish hunting estate. The roads and the houses in the central area of the grounds have been built along a twisting, wooded ravine called The Ramble, which has paths, wooden benches, and gazebos, again in the mid-nineteenth century romantic style. The Garrisons' new home is still there on its wide grounds, with its stables behind the large main building. The "funny kitchen roofs" Sarah McKim described are high, steeply pitched gables set closely together which give the roof line a look of startled surprise. The house is built of wood, painted now a bright yellow, with floor-to-ceiling windows typical of the times. There is a classic porch leading to the front door with a graceful carriageway, which would then have been graveled, curving against it.

The "lake" Lucy's mother describes is across the road that passes the property. It is a broad, beautifully shaped pond with grassy banks, a path with rustic benches and a gazebo which have retained the style of the original structures, and would certainly look familiar to her if she were to look out of her upstairs window today. The window would be a perfect vantage point to watch the ice skating on winter days. The new house, despite her misgivings, was to become the family's home for nearly a century. Lucy's music books were found in the house ninety-five years later, long forgotten on a shelf in a closet.

◆ ◆ ◆

In the fall Charlie entered Harvard, returning home for a visit and to arrange for some things to be sent ahead. He also spent part of his time with friends on the house's broad lawn playing what he called either "cricket" or "baseball"—there was considerable confusion about the name—a new sport that he had taken up with considerable enthusiasm. His father wrote him at the college.[16]

> September 11, 1866 Harvard
> ... Your mother, Aunt & Lucy are working on your things, getting them ready to send by the trunk ... the cricket marks are disappearing from the lawn, and all traces of your short stay with us will soon be gone. In fact we all miss you very much and often express to each other our wish that you were here.

In families like the McKims at this time, the parents wrote often how much they missed their children, but in reality their children generally spent long periods away at school or for extended visits with other family members. In his father's short letters to Charlie over the fall months there

were glimpses of Lucy's activities. In November she was also away, spending time with Wendell and his family in Roxbury. In his note to Charlie
on November 3, 1866, her father expressed his hopes of having her in New
Jersey again in mid-November, but understood that Wendell desired to stay
a week longer. "Well—let her do it while she is young."[17] A few days later, on
November 7, his mother wrote, hinting that there was more news still to be
told, and also agreeing to let Lucy stay as long as she wished. "We miss Lucy
greatly, but am glad for her to have a good vacation. It will be the last probably she will be able to have for some time—as the enclosed note will show."

The discreet note from Charlie's father was to inform him that his sister
was pregnant. His mother's note on November 12 was more open about
the news. Lucy had been in Boston for some weeks, however, and it would
have been easy for Charlie to come from Harvard, just across the river
from downtown Boston, to visit. She could already have told him the news
herself.[18]

> Nov. 12, 1866
> I am very glad thee has had dear sister so long near thee, tho, I suppose
> thee couldn't be very much with her. By the time she reaches home it will
> have been 5 weeks since she left us. I want her to take a trip to Phila. some-
> time this winter, as thee has learned from Father she has a prospect ahead for
> next spring that will keep her closely bound to home for many a long day.

In October, only weeks before the announcement of Lucy's pregnancy,
there had already been concern over Charlie's schooling. After only a few
weeks at Harvard he wrote to his father to express his disappointment
with his studies. At this time, despite its reputation, Harvard was a small,
inbred institution which devoted much of its classroom hours to studies
of classical languages and histories of religion. It was noted for producing ministers, teachers, and lawyers. Although Charlie was enjoying other
things, among them friends and playing on the baseball team, his interests
now were focused on architecture. He was aware that he would receive a
much better preparation for a career as an architect if he left Harvard and
studied in Europe. In a carefully written letter to his father on October
19, 1866, which included much news about his activities with the baseball
team at college, he presented his arguments for being allowed to study in
Europe with considerable eloquence. Charlie was now nineteen.[19]

> Seeing that the course here is now three years and that in no event could I
> think of graduating, it struck me that it would be a saving of time and money

to spend only one year here and then go abroad to Freiburg or whatever place thee should decide upon, and graduate there, since an additional year here would not enable me to graduate, whereas the same time abroad at Freiburg or elsewhere might be employed to much better advantage seeing that their schools are finer.

The arguments about Charlie's desire to study in Europe continued through the winter. His father expressed his exasperation at the situation in a note to Wendell on February 9, 1867.[20]

I am much exercised about Charley. I shall be sorry to disappoint him but if I understand his views & wishes I see no help for it.

The fact is that he is strongly bent on going to a Paris school and is perfectly sure that it is the best thing for him.

Despite his father's determined opposition, as happens often in a conflict like this between father and son, its resolution was Charlie's departure for Europe the next September.

◆ ◆ ◆

In the early months of her pregnancy Lucy continued to write pieces for Wendell, and in January 1867 she traveled with her mother from West Orange to Philadelphia to visit the Motts. The family spent so much of their time together that it is difficult to follow the events of their everyday lives, since none of them is known to have kept a diary, and they only wrote letters to each other when someone was away. Her mother's letter to her husband relating the events of their trip to Philadelphia is one of the slim records we have of one of their visits to friends, and it is also a revealing description of the difficulties of winter travel, even on the new railroads between central New Jersey and Philadelphia. Ed Davis, whom they were particularly pleased to meet, was the husband of Maria Mott; Roadside was the Motts' rambling house outside of central Philadelphia. Marianne, the niece who greeted them first, lived in the house next to the Motts, with a connecting passage between the houses.[21]

Roadside, Jan. 12/67
My dear husband,

We have just got up from dinner table and now Mr. & Mrs. Mott & Ed. Davis are taking naps and Maria reads her paper. I will sit down and tell all I can think of since we parted yesterday morning.—

We took the cars at Newark & fell in with a truly kind and polite man who looked after our comfort on the way to Kensington—he supplied us with hot sticks of wood every now and then from the stove, placing them under our feet & thereby keeping us as warm as toast all the way to the city—another lady feeds myself— not Lucy, she didn't want any—

. . . Ed. Davis couldn't meet us at Kensington but sent a young man in his employ up to see after us. He escorted us to the new station on [Birk?] St. and after waiting a half hour or more we came out here. [A friend] met us with his carriage and before we were seated in it Marianne Mott made her appearance running down to welcome us. She came right over with us & a most thoroughly hearty welcome we had first from Maria at her porch step, James Mott at the door and dear Lucretia just inside her parlor. . . . Loss of sleep together with fatigue made me very chilly & a plate of soup saved from their dinner was most grateful to Lucy and myself—then we sat & talked steadily on till tea time—all hands. I was not "wrapped" quite as well as I should be , and took a trifle of cold which was scattered pretty much as soon as I had my tea—I never felt in greater haste for any meal in my life I was so thoroughly cold—I felt as tho I could swallow tea pot and all—certainly I was greatly comforted after drinking two cups of scalding tea & eating some very hot tomatoes. Lucy & I retired a little after 9 oclk & slept so well we felt all right today. . . .

When James and Lucretia Mott went to their Quaker meeting Lucy and her mother began a round of visits to friends, often dining at different houses. Her mother's letter ended on a note of solicitude.

Lucy will write herself. I hope you are comfortable and shall hope to hear from you soon.

Neither Lucy nor Wendell may have realized at that moment that their marriage and Wendell's work at *The Nation* would be the answer to the question that had faced her for so long, how to undertake the collection of slave songs. There were optimistic signs pointing to a solid future for the magazine, and Wendell could use its pages to reach a much wider audience who might be able to contribute to the material Lucy hoped to gather. Also she had seen the magazine articles that had been published and the travelers' accounts of the slave songs that were appearing with some regularity in the daily newspapers. She had as well been aware of the discussions that had been stirred by the questions of authenticity and authorship that the songs had raised. It seemed certain that there would be an audience for the book. It was a moment of opportunity for her to turn again to what she had wanted for so long. With her baby coming she realized there would be little time for her in the years to come, and with all of this in her mind it could have been sometime in the next few weeks that she proposed the idea to Wendell.

12

The Making of *Slave Songs of the United States*

Walk in, kind Saviour,
  No man can hinder me!
Walk in, sweet Jesus,
  No man can hinder me!

See what wonder Jesus done,
  No man can hinder me!
See what wonder Jesus done,
  No man can hinder me!

O no man, no man, no man,
  can hinder me!
O no man, no man, no man
  can hinder me!

Collected by Lucy McKim on St. Helena Island, July 1862
  In *Slave Songs of the United States*, 1867

In a letter to his brother William on April 29, 1866, Wendell discussed at length William's criticisms of what had been accomplished with *The Nation* in its first months of existence. To his spirited defense of the magazine's many achievements Wendell added as a separate note:

> ... She [Lucy] has furnished me an idea which I shall acknowledge in its place.

The idea was almost certainly the book that was published a year and a half later as *Slave Songs of the United States*. It fulfilled the dream that

Lucy had already expressed of publishing a collection of slave songs at the time her arrangements of two of the Port Royal songs appeared in the fall of 1862, five years earlier. In those same months she had written Laura Towne on St. Helena to ask her for more of the songs for the collection. Although Wendell was to join the project wholeheartedly, it was from Lucy that the spark had come. He had never shown any particular interest in slave songs, and aside from the informal singing he did as part of the family's parlor entertainments he doesn't seem to have had a special interest in music. It could also have been that Lucy first spoke of it at this moment, knowing that with the birth of her child she couldn't expect to turn to the book for many years in the future.

It would, however, be months before they could actually begin the work, with so much else occupying them in the first months of their marriage. Wendell was now living as a member of the family at Llewellyn Park, though this necessitated long train rides to and from the magazine's offices in Manhattan. The community was still being built on the newly cleared land, and it was surrounded with forested slopes that rose into somber hills beyond the winding roads of the park. Although the family had some feelings of isolation after the closeness of the community they had known in Philadelphia, the naturalness of their setting at least provided them with some of their recreation. Often on the days he had free from the office Wendell walked on the dirt roads into the hills. A letter from Lucy's father to Charlie, who was still studying in Europe, portrayed the family as comfortably domiciled in their new home to celebrate their traditional Christmas. The friendly tone of the letter, however, didn't prevent his father from allowing himself a final, exasperated gibe at Charlie's lengthening absence.[1]

Dec. 30, 1866
Dear Charley,

I promised to write and tell thee about our Christmas at home, so here is the fulfillment. . . . I think no one was disappointed in the result [of the opening of the presents]. Indeed there was a surplus for each one, & that was because all my presents were given out Christmas Eve—nobody was so bent on an old fashioned Chr. morning discovery as I. But I determined to have some fun even if I am grown up and laid away on the married shelf. . . . A few days before I sent John [the hired man] to hunt up some laurel or holly on the mountain. He said he knew what they were. Imagine my horror when he appeared with his arms full as they could hold of [a neighbor's] precious rhododendrons & other choice shrubs! However as long as they were cut, we put them up over the pictures & in vases & everywhere, & I tell thee, they made a show.

Wendell took a great long walk over the mountains after the presents were distributed. We had a good turbot for dinner & prime mince pie. The only drawback of the whole was that there should have been absent anyone who ought to have been here.

Lucy added a rushed note to her father's letter:

It is very cold, with fine sleighing. Skating is flourishing on at least 3 park ponds I know, & likely on others that I've not seen.

Very affy, Lucy

To judge from the dated letters from their first approaches to possible contributors to their proposed collection of Port Royal songs, it would have to have been in these last weeks of December, perhaps while the family was assembled for Christmas, that Lucy and Wendell began planning the volume. It was only a few weeks later, in early 1867, that the first letters presenting their idea began reaching others who might be able to contribute songs.

It was also evident from the responses of the individuals that they chose to contact that Wendell divided the list into the names of the people whom Lucy knew personally, and a second group who could be expected to respond to an inquiry from the editor of a New York journal, but would possibly have ignored a query from a woman they didn't know. Wendell wrote to the military commanders and professional men on the list. Lucy wrote to the friends who had shown an interest in her earlier song settings. In South Carolina when Laura Towne took friends back to Beaufort after a visit on April 27 she picked up the mail for the island and found Lucy's letter.[2]

I was in Beaufort yesterday, taking back the [Hescocks], who have been here spending two days, and I brought back the St. Helena mail. Think of my having at least a peck of letters and papers to bring over, and only one little note among it all for myself, and that one from Lucy McK. Garrison, who with Charlie Ware and others, is going to publish words and music to all the freedmen's songs they can collect, and wants my collection.

Lucy was now expecting their first baby, and it may have been her pregnancy that caused her and Wendell to look for someone else to work with them on their proposed volume. It could also have been that she considered herself too inexperienced to take on the whole responsibility of the editorship. She was conscious that she had been on St. Helena for less than a month, and she was aware that there were others who had lived and worked on the island for longer periods. Many of them, she knew, were collecting songs themselves, and there was a chance that they had gathered a larger number of examples. When she and Wendell considered who might be qualified to help with editing the material, they didn't have far to look. One of the writers who had been contributing to *The Nation* since its earliest issues in the summer of 1865 was a man named William Francis Allen who had worked with his wife as a teacher on St. Helena the year after Lucy's visit. Allen was to play a large role in their work as the collection began to take on respectable dimensions.

In these months Allen was just at the beginning of his long career as a distinguished classical historian, linguistic scholar, teacher, and writer. In his mid-thirties, he was nearly a dozen years older than Lucy. He was born in Northborough, Massachusetts, in 1830 into a Unitarian family, and when he began his studies at Harvard he was considering a career as a minister, but chose instead to become an instructor of classic languages and a writer. When he graduated from Harvard in 1851 he traveled to Europe and continued his classics studies in Berlin, Göttingen, and Rome. After his return in 1856 he accepted a position as vice-principal at the English and Classical School in West Newton, Massachusetts. Like many Unitarians he was a conscientious objector and did not consider enlisting in the Union army, but after the passage of the draft laws in the summer of 1863, as a form of alternative service he traveled with his wife to St. Helena to supervise one of the new plantation schools. He was tall and trim, handsome and assured, with patrician features and a direct, almost amused glance. At the time he worked on the island he was still clean shaven. After he left St. Helena he worked for the Sanitary Commission in Arkansas and Missouri, then returned to South Carolina after the fall of Charleston in the winter of 1865 to teach again, continuing to collect songs throughout the years he lived in the South.

Allen and his wife, Mary Lambert Allen, lived on a plantation on St. Helena from November 1863 to July 1864, a period of nine months, while they taught school as employees of the Freedmen's Aid Commission. Like most of the later arrivals at St. Helena he already had some knowledge of the singing that others had heard on the island, As the articles on "Contraband Song" by Lucy and her father that had appeared in *Dwight's Journal* had suggested, nearly every person who visited the islands or had been in other areas of the South where there were freed slaves had written about the songs they had heard. There had as well been some response to Lucy's published arrangements.

In the journal Allen kept of his months on St. Helena there is no mention of the writing Lucy or her father did of the songs, but he noted that he had read an article published only three months before his own arrival in the August 1863 number of the *Continental Monthly*. The article, "Under the Palmetto," was written by a Unitarian minister named Henry G. Spaulding, who had been dispatched to St. Helena by the Sanitary Commission to report on the conditions of the freedmen. Most of the article discussed the particular situation on the island, but it also devoted four pages to the singing he heard. There were melodies and abbreviated texts for five of the songs. Allen himself was a musician, a skilled flutist, and he also enjoyed singing. He had already taught himself to sing "The Lonesome Valley," one of the songs from the pages of the *Monthly*, before he embarked for St. Helena. Nothing he had read, however, prepared him for the richness and the power of the musical experience that waited him.

Allen and his wife landed at Hilton Head on November 8, and a week later he visited a "praise house" for the first time. He used the term "deaconed out" to describe the common practice of the preacher reciting lines of a song for the gathered congregation to sing after him.[3]

> ... They were just beginning a hymn, which the preacher (a stranger), deaconed out, two lines at a time. The tune was evidently Old Hundred, which was maintained throughout by one voice or another, but curiously varied at every note, so as to form an intricate intertwining of harmonious sounds. It was something very different from anything I ever heard before, and no description I have read conveys any notion of it. There were no parts properly speaking, only now and then a hint of a bass or tenor—no effort at regularity, only this one or two voices kept up the air—but their ears so good, and the time is so perfectly kept (marked often by stamping and clapping the hands) that there was very seldom a discordant note. It might be compared to the notes of an organ or orchestra, where all harmony is poured out in accompaniment of the air; except that there was no bass. Exhortation, Prayer, another hymn, benediction, and then a "shouting song," I believe they call them, beginning "Good Morning," at which all began to shake his hands and move about the room to measure.

He left out his diary for his wife to read, and he added a footnote to the page in fairness to her less enthusiastic opinion of the singing.

Mary says I draw it too strong. I tried to describe the *character* of the music, and I think I have—I haven't said that it was beautiful, and I must hear it again to form a fair judgment. She noticed more discord than I did.

His judgment of the slaves' songs on further hearings was that the music *was* beautiful, and he found it moving and instructive. Within a few weeks their songs became part of his everyday life, and he soon witnessed his first "shout," which introduced him to a form of the slaves' musical expression that was different from the other singing he heard. The first time he heard the "shouting" was on Christmas night, when he and his wife went to the shout that he was told was a yearly custom. Many visitors had written their impressions of the shout, including James McKim, but Allen noted that the shouts were no longer held often, and his description was particularly detailed. Earlier in the day, before the shout was to be held, he asked a Mr. Eustis about what he might hear and was told that "so far as he knew (and he is a native of South Carolina) it is not only peculiar to these islands, but to some plantations," and in his journal Allen conjectured, much as McKim had done at the shout he witnessed on the island the year before, that perhaps "it is of African origin, with Christianity engrafted upon it just as it was upon the ancient Roman ritual."

. . . We went to see their regular Christmas shout in Peg's house last night. They had a prayer meeting first, and were so late that we went back to the house, and when we went out again at 10 ¼ wandered around for some time in the bright moonlight for them to finish an endless St. Martin's. At last they cleared the room and began, and a strange sight it was. The room is no more than ten feet square, with a fire burning on the hearth, on one side of the hearth sat old Moses smoking his pipe peacefully, on the other stood Peg and Sandy, her husband. On one side of the room is a table, and in front of it stood young Paris (Simmons), Billy and Henry, who served as *band*. Billy sang or rather chanted, and the others "based" as they say, while Jimmy, Lucy, Joan (Moses' wife, and a fine striking looking woman), Dick, Anacusa, and Molsy (daughter of Jimmy and Lucy, and a very nice intelligent woman), moved around the room in a circle in a sort of shuffle. This is the shout. Some moved the feet backward and forward alternately, but the best shouters— and Jimmy, I was told today "is a great shouter,"—keep the feet on the floor and work themselves along over the floor by moving them right and left. It seemed tremendous work for them, but Jimmy remarked to me to-day of the young people shouting "dese yere people worry demselv—we bebber wory weselv", and I saw that the most skillful ones moved very easily and quietly.

The shouters seldom sing or make any noise except with their feet, but work their bodies more or less; while the singers clap their hands and stamp their right foot in time . . .

When Allen could take time from his duties in the classroom and the chores of woodcutting, water drawing, and rough furniture making for the derelict house where he and Mary were quartered, he spent hours listening to the singing around him. He asked people to repeat songs he hadn't heard before, or verses that he couldn't make out, and with his flute as an aid he notated the melodies. In the schools on the islands there were regular singing sessions, and in the first weeks Allen used these times to ask his scholars to sing to him.

> . . . I find that a song . . . is a recreation to them, and lets off superfluous steam. As I do not know their songs yet, I let either Flora or Ellen or Patty from Hope Place start it up, and the others join in singing with great spirit, very loud, and in perfect tune. Everyone sings, and I do not know that I have noticed a discord. It is very odd to see them sing, swaying backward and forward in their seats to mark the time, and sometimes striking one hand into the other, or the foot upon the ground.

In his diary on March 14, 1864, he commented that a copy of the *Continental Monthly* including the article that he had previously read had appeared on the island, and he compared what he had found with Reverend Spaulding's discoveries.

> The *Continental* arrived the other day, and I was interested in looking at the music in "Under the Palmetto." I have heard all the pieces but one, and they are quite correct, except that he called them all "shout tunes," while only one of them is and that he gives only in part, and that differently from what I have heard.

The pages of Allen's diary include his transcriptions of the words and melodies for twenty-one songs. Often when he didn't understand words he asked the singers to clarify what they had sung by repeating the verses, though frequently he found he was presented with a variation on what he notated before. With his enthusiastic interest in the music and the experience of the work he'd already done on St. Helena, Allen was of immeasurable help to Wendell and Lucy. Over the spring and summer, without his tireless efforts to edit the music and prepare the texts it is difficult to see how the book could have been finished.

Allen was also of inestimable assistance to Wendell and Lucy by bringing to the project another of the workers who had been on St. Helena,
Charles Pickford Ware, who had been mentioned in Laura Towne's letter
to Lucy. Allen and Ware had both been on St. Helena at the same time,
and Charles—or Charley, as everyone on the island knew him—was still
employed as a supervisor at an isolated plantation named Coffin Point,
where he worked in close association with Laura Towne and Ellen Murray. Eye trouble had forced him to return to Boston for a few months
before returning for the cotton harvest in the fall. When he landed at St.
Helena he was only twenty-two and as inexperienced in the rudiments of
cotton cultivation as most of the other supervisors who were sent to the
island, but he quickly became part of the plantation's work force. He came
with his sister Harriet, and he stayed on the island until returning per-
manently to Boston in 1872. Before volunteering for the service in South
Carolina he had studied at Harvard, where his father was a distinguished
professor of divinity. Ware slowly overcame his initial lack of knowledge
about growing cotton by his willingness to listen to whatever the field
hands, with their long, resentful years of cotton cultivation, could tell him
about what he should be doing.

Ware was popular with everyone in the island community for his cheerful, responsive manner, even including the new freedmen who quickly
learned to be patient with his hopeless ignorance of cotton cultivation
in his early months as a supervisor. He and Allen were cousins, and they
had grown up knowing each other. They met often in the months that
Allen and his wife were teaching school at a plantation close by. Allen was
aware that his cousin was also collecting songs, and Ware spent much of
his spare time over the next three or four years gathering whatever songs
he could find. Of all those who worked on the island Ware had a longer and fuller experience of the St. Helena songs than anyone else and he
had gathered considerably more examples of the singing than his cousin.
With his manuscripts added to the material they had already collected,
the book that Lucy had long dreamed of would immediately take on a
respectable substance.

◆ ◆ ◆

Ware's answer to his cousin's note on March 21 asking if he would join
them in the proposed book was positive and enthusiastic. He had recently
been approached by others about publishing his songs, but the new project was more interesting for him, since Allen had offered to take on the
onerous work of editing his material. Ware concluded his letter with the

familiar, certainly consciously understated plaint that transcribing the melodies now and then caused him "a little perplexity."[4]

> March 21, 1867
> Dear William,
> Harriet handed me a note from you, to answer for her, as much as a week ago. I began a note to you, was interrupted and—the usual story—it was never sent.
> I have about 50 songs of St. Helena, words and music . . . over 40 of them written out with some care, the only essential defect that I notice being the omission of a few verses which I had forgotten. It has been suggested to me to publish these, and as I have had but little occupation this spring—my eyes are troubling me—I had decided to do so, & only put the matter off because I hoped to be able to make a visit to St. Helena, where I might complete and correct my collection. Of course my collection is entirely at your service; I am very glad to have the editing performed by hands so much more competent to the work than mine . . . I forgot to mention it in my last letter, but if a month is too long to wait, I will write them out again for you.
> I send a sheet which I find lying around—part of the rough draft . . . The music I wrote out on sheets, with numbers referring to the words, no words inserted—only one tract [sic], of course. I pitched the tunes so that none ranged higher than E, with one or two exceptions, in case of great compass in the tune, in favor of F. When I knew that the same tune was sung in two or three different ways—on different plantations—I introduce these variations. Some of the tunes were somewhat difficult to write out, the musical accent & the emphasis causing a little perplexity now and then . . .
> Charles P. Ware

At the same time Allen was continuing his journalistic writing to augment his small income as a teacher. His first article in *The Nation* was a piece titled "State of Things in South Carolina," and he continued to publish regularly, signing his articles as "Marcel." Following the months of teaching in Charleston he had accepted a position as an instructor at Antioch College in Ohio, a struggling religious institution in only its fifth year of operation. He left Antioch at the end of the fall term, and in the spring took a teaching position at Lucy and Ellen's old school, Eagleswood, which had opened again after the war. He was very poorly paid, and the journalism helped him get through the spring months. He noted in his journal that in 1866 for the terms he had taught at Antioch and at Eagleswood he was paid $1480, and his writing for *The Nation* brought him in an additional $91. In 1867 his teaching, first at Eagleswood and then in the fall with his new appointment at the University of Wisconsin in Madison, earned him $1500, while his year of writing articles for Wendell added an additional $186 to his income. The advantage of Eagleswood was that it was close enough for him to go into New York often, and in his diary for the spring he made quick jotted entries noting his trips. Despite the demands of his work in the classroom he traveled to the city on every possible occasion, taking either the ferry or the train from nearby Perth Amboy. Generally he met with Wendell, though it is difficult to know if they talked about the work on *Slave Songs* or about his other work as a contributor to the magazine. The entries, however, make it clear that the work on the songs took much of his time.[5]

Allen's first journal entry mentioning Wendell in the spring is on February 11, but he notes only that they met and doesn't write about the meeting. It was shortly after this, however that he wrote to Charley Ware, so it probable that he and Wendell talked about the possibility of doing the book at this meeting. They met again on March 8; then on March 23, two days after Ware had replied to Allen's proposal, Allen sent letters to both Ware and Wendell. Without Ware's material it was doubtful if they could be certain of having enough songs to continue, and it may have been for this reason that Wendell and Lucy didn't begin to contact possible contributors before Allen assured them of the willingness of Ware to make his songs available.

Wendell received the answers to much of the correspondence at *The Nation*'s office in New York, while Lucy added her part of the work at Llewellyn Park. She was now in the late months of her pregnancy and she was confined to the house. Her mother mentioned in a letter to Charlie, who was away at Harvard, that Lucy had even more work to engage her in the house for the moment. On April 7 she wrote[6]:

> I don't doubt but that thee is thinking very strangely of our silence. Lucy had been meaning to write to thee several days ago—but she has had so much writing to do for Wendell.

Wendell was suffering from a boil on his hand, which was extremely painful, and he had been a prisoner in the house for over a week. The boil had been lanced and the pain relieved, but he still was unable to move his fingers. Lucy was not only taking care of all his office correspondence, but was responding to the answers to her letters concerning contributions to the book, and she also had to "wait on him between times."

◆ ◆ ◆

On April 11 Allen notes that he just had written to the Garrisons, and two days later he added that he visited them in Llewellyn Park, but no record of their meeting seems to have survived. On April 20, at Eagleswood, Allen noted in his diary, "Charley Ware spent night. In eve. looked over over Port Royal songs w. him." From that point the songs came up again and again in his diary entries.

> April 23 In eve. read Mary's Port Royal letters
> April 25 read Port Royal letters—also in eve.—Letter for Garrison
> April 28 Walked in woods. Finished Caesarian for *Nation* (Long's Hist.) & copied negro songs.

The article he mentioned was a review of a new book for the magazine. On April 28 and 30 he noted that he was again copying songs, and at the same time he was teaching *Agamemnon* and revising the text of his Latin grammar, soon to be published.

On May 4 Allen was in New York to meet Wendell, and in the evening on his return he went back to copying the songs. If, as the journal indicates, Wendell was in New York that day for the meeting, he could have missed the birth of their first child, since Lucy went into labor and their son was born the same day. In a letter to his mother on June 23, Wendell could report that their six-and-a-half-week-old Lloyd, named for Wendell's father, was doing well, though his mother was having some trouble with her digestion.[7]

> . . . the baby got his carriage yesterday (bought with Grandpa G's money, and so really his gift) and takes both rides and long naps in it, so that Lucy can sit on the piazza and read beside him. Lloyd certainly resembles his namesake more than any known person—so much so, Lucy mischievously says that she sometimes feels very much embarrassed in handling him. He is mostly very good in his behavior, and allows his mother a considerable latitude in her diet, indeed she only needs to consult her own digestion which is not all that could be desired.

With so much of the work on the book now in Allen's hands there was no interruption in the copying and editing of the songs. On May 10 he noted an exchange of letters with Wendell, and then on May 20 he wrote:

May 20 In aft, Again. Wrote. In eve. wrote preface to Slave Songs—Rain—Letter for C. Ware

Allen had begun his preface before the collection of the songs was complete, obviously intending to return to it again as the months passed. On June 21 he noted that he was once more copying songs, perhaps from new material he'd received from Thomas Wentworth Higginson. The book was complete enough, however, for them to approach a publisher. On May 26 Wendell wrote his mother[8]:

> I saw my friend Prof. Allen yesterday. Our collection of slave-songs is growing rapidly, and we shall produce, I think, a book of great value. Counting those with and those without accompanying music, I reckon we shall have not fewer than 100 songs. Mr Scribner, of New York will probably be our publisher.

The term at Eagleswood ended on June 26, and the next day Allen and Wendell met in New York for another talk with Charles Scribner, whose publishing house was growing rapidly. In a letter to his brother Frank, however, on June 30, Wendell conceded that they would have to seek another publisher.[9]

> On Thursday Prof. Allen & I made our final call on Scribner to get a definitive answer in regard to our Slave Songs. Mr. Scribner lacked nothing in good will, but he said his regular business had assumed such proportions that he could not do justice to a side issue like ours— in which, besides, he did not see his way clear to a return for his outlay, tho' this alone wd. not have deterred him.

Earlier in the month, in the issue of *The Nation* for May 30, 1867, Wendell concluded a discussion of aboriginal music and its comparison to the songs of the southern slaves with an announcement of their project.

> We are able to announce a collection, based on the Port Royal hymnology, and including the songs of as many Southern states as are obtainable, which will be published either in the course of this year or at the beginning of the next. The words and (whenever possible) the music will be carefully reproduced, and it is the aim of the editors to make the volume complete in both respects. Any information relating to the subject would be very acceptable to them, and may be sent to Mr. W. P. Garrison, Box 6732, N. Y. Post-office

The responses to the letters that Lucy and Wendell sent to people they thought might be helpful in their search began arriving within weeks of their query. Thomas Wentworth Higginson, who had been associated with Lucy's father since the John Brown raid, was one of the first people they had contacted. He responded quickly, informing them that he had also been considering publishing something about the songs, but his piece would be only an article, which would appear later in the spring in *Atlantic Monthly*. He encouraged their project, and freely offered them the use of any of his texts. He also promised any help that he could give them as their work progressed. Higginson's name was so well established with the readers they hoped to attract for their collection of slave songs that the association would be of considerable value.

Wendell found occasional disappointments with people who had been to the islands in recent years. They answered with some sadness that they didn't hear the people singing in the way that they had heard about from visitors only a few years earlier. The instinctive sense that Lucy and the others shared, that they were capturing a moment that was fleeting and that this burst of creativity would be influenced by the schooling and the new possibilities of travel that were already reshaping the freedmen's world, was true. Southerners themselves and other collectors continued to journey to the South over the next decades, but they soon accepted the reality that the great spirituals had been found. So much had changed in the new society that was emerging, and in ways no one could have anticipated.

◆ ◆ ◆

Lucy sent personal notes to Laura Towne and to her uncle John, who had written her several years before about the songs he had heard among the African Americans living close to his home in Delaware. She wrote to him in the hope that he might have additional materials. Her uncle's long and serious answer on April 20, 1867, expressed his wholehearted belief in their project, but he also brought up an issue that would be frequently discussed as the years passed and the slave spirituals reached larger audiences. How original were the slave songs? How much did the spirituals borrow from white hymnology and the store of white church melodies that the slave singers certainly had known in their years of servitude? He also quickly emphasized that the songs as sung by the black church congregations were much superior to the singing he heard by the white Methodists, whom he refers to sardonically as the "the Inferior race."[10]

Of some of the Songs sung by colored folks about here, I know only the name; of others a *Chorus* or a *Stanza* at most; and of the music merely a short passage or cadenza here & there—that is *by memory*. Indeed I have not always been sure *when* I heard a *negro* song. And I would advise you to avoid being deceived on this point by the name or reputation a piece may have as of that class. So many of them pass for such which are really of *white* origin & composition, both in the poetry & the music—especially the so-called *religious* songs. For instance, "*Wake up, Jacob*, day is a breaking" is an old Camp meeting hymn of the white Methodists, though deriving most of its spirit & relish (for our ears) to the peculiar vocalisms of the negroes. And many of their favorite melodies, as well as the *words* are only parodies & imitations— though often decided improvements—of those they have learned at the "white" meetings. *Gideon's Band*, as sung by the colored people about here, is a *grand* thing compared with the same piece, as it is in the Books, or even in the most fervent Methodist meetings of the *Inferior* race.

In his letter her uncle goes on to discuss the work songs he has heard, and how much closer they seemed to him to be of a true African nature. He pointed out that in his experience the *purest* music of the black workers he heard were their work songs and chants. His observations are interesting, for much of the African American song that would develop later, including the blues and sanctified gospel song, had their roots in these spontaneous, often as quickly forgotten songs of labor.

Some of the best *pure* negro songs I have heard were those that used to be sung by the black stevedores, or perhaps the crews themselves, of the West Indian vessels, loading and unloading at the wharves in Phil. & Baltimore. I have stood for more than an hour, often, listening to them, as they hoisted and lowered the hogsheads & boxes of their cargoes; one man taking the burden of the song, (and the slack of the rope), and the others striking in with the chorus. They would sing in this way more than a dozen different songs in an hour, most of which might indeed be warranted to contain *nothing religious*—a few often—"on the contrary, quite the reverse"—but generally rather innocent and proper in their language, and strangely attractive in their music; and with a volume of voices that reached a square or two away. That plan of labor has now faded away in Phil.—at least, and the songs, I suppose, with it . . .

After the announcement of the forthcoming volume of slave songs that appeared in *The Nation* for May 30, 1867, Wendell took on the job of receiving the letters from those who responded. Arriving later were the promised songs from Laura Towne. She sent with them a letter to Lucy on June 8, explaining the delay, but also expressing her interest in the project. Ellen Murray had copied the songs so that they could be sent to Lucy as quickly as possible. Laura also described the new songs that she was encountering daily.[11]

> June 8, 1867
> My dear Lucy,
>   ... My book was so heavy in the binding that it was expensive to send by mail, so Ellen Murray volunteered to copy out the songs for you. She has copied out every one, so you lose nothing by not having the book itself. There are many more that the people sing now, for they are constantly either reviving old ones or inventing new ones. I do not know which; but I have neither the words nor tunes....

Thomas Wentworth Higginson's article, titled "Negro Spirituals," appeared in the June issue of the *Atlantic Monthly*. It was a lengthy, informative piece, and it was given prominent place in the issue. By this time everyone in the newly united states had been inundated by books, articles, poems, and songs about the war, but Higginson's interest and his obvious excitement in his experience of hearing the songs in the tents around the camp brought a refreshing vigor to his texts. Most important, his celebrity insured the article of a broad readership.

In the islands Higginson's headquarters was a large tent with a desk and a patched-together chair in one end of it and some scavenged blankets spread on wooden crates as a bed in the other. He served continuously until he was wounded in an engagement on the Edisto River, probing the defenses of Charleston, in July 1863, then returned again to the islands after his convalescence. Of all the people who spent part of these years in the South Carolina islands, Higginson perhaps lived most closely with the newly freed slaves, but he nevertheless felt that he had been unable to penetrate the complex responses he was presented by the black recruits. For him, the watchful mask of pleasant gaiety that he often encountered could perhaps be simply the expression of "happy children," as other northern visitors had described the freed men and women they met, but he also noted the new troops' quickness and their hunger to learn anything about the new society they were certain they soon would be entering.

Higginson described writing down the words of songs that he heard around him in the shadows as he made his night rounds through the tents of the camp, while the singing seemed never to stop.[12]

. . . Writing down in the darkness, as I best could, perhaps with my hand in the safe covert of my pocket,—the words of the ballad song. I have afterwards carried it to my tent, like some captured bird or insect, and then after examination, put it by. Or, summoning one of the men at some period of leisure,—Corporal Robert Sutton, for instance, whose iron memory held all the details of a song as if it were a ford or a forest,—I have completed the new specimen by supplying the absent parts. The music I could only retain by ear, and though the more common strains were repeated often enough for us to fix their impression, there were others that occurred only once or twice.

The article included the texts to thirty-six spirituals and a fragment entitled "Hangman Johnny." Higginson accompanied the texts with an engaging commentary, including references to Scottish balladry and the possible origins of some of the songs' expressions in African words. He was careful to emphasize that the preponderance of songs he heard in the camp were religious in nature, and he also noted that the songs were continually being replaced by new versions or by new songs themselves. The most significant of Higginson's comments on one of the songs was his description of how he succeeded—at last—in finding among his men one who had composed a new song and how it had been adopted by the other men. For many weeks he had been asking in the camp about who had composed their songs, but without success.

. . . On this point I could get no information though I asked many questions, until at last, one day when I was being rowed across from Beaufort to Ladies' Island, I found myself, with delight, on the actual trail of a song. One of the oarsmen, a brisk young fellow, not a soldier, on being asked for his theory of the matter dropped out a coy confession. "Some good spirituals" he said, "are start jess out o' curiosity. I been a-raise a sing, myself, once."

My dream was fulfilled, and I had traced out, not the poem alone, but the poet. I implored him to proceed.

"Once we boys," he said, "went for tote some rice and de nigger driver kept a-callin' on us; and I say, 'O, de ole nigger-driver!' Den annuder said, 'Fust ting my mammy tole me was, notin' so bad as a nigger-driver.' Den I made a sing, just puttin' a word and den anudder word."

Then he began singing, and the men, after listening a moment, joined in the chorus, as if it were an old acquaintance, though they evidently had never heard it before. I saw how easily a new "sing" took root among them.[13]

William Allen included Higginson's description of the creation of a new song in his introduction to their book. The lack of musical annotations for

Higginson's otherwise exciting song texts would be a distinct disappointment for many readers. With the song transcriptions in their *Slave Songs*
collection, its editors could rectify this omission.

◆ ◆ ◆

After the term at Eagleswood ended, Allen spent some time traveling in
upper New York State to visit his family, then settled in West Newton for
the summer. In his journal he noted on July 22 that he and Charles Ware
had looked over the songs together, and during the next months his journal again included mentions of the work on the still-incomplete book.
On August 14 he wrote, "Spent day & eve. revising songs. Rain in eve." On
September 5 he noted that he was thirty-seven years old, and added that
he'd exchanged letters with Wendell and Charley.

There was a notice of the coming book in the summer. In the July 20
issue of *Dwight's Journal* the editors reminded the readers that the journal
had introduced the slave songs to them some time before.[14]

THE SONGS OF THE FREEMEN.
Our readers may remember that about five years ago we published a letter from Miss McKim of Philadelphia (now the wife of Mr. W. P. Garrison)
describing the songs which she had heard (and partly taken down) among
the recently freed people of the Sea Islands. Much larger collections were
afterwards made by Prof. Wm. F. Allen, of West Newton, and his cousin Mr.
Chas. P. Ware of Milton. These three are united by common agreement, and
have very largely increased by accessions from all parts of the South. The
basis still remains the "spirituals," such as were furnished the *Atlantic* by Mr.
Higginson, who has kindly turned them over to the persons named above,
that they may publish them, words and music, in one volume. The collection will be edited by Prof. Allen, who has written a preface of some length
to illustrate the songs. Messrs. A. Simpson & Co. of the Agathynian Press, 60
Duane Street, New York, intend to give the work their imprint (a guarantee of
the highest style of typography), provided they meet with sufficient encouragement. The cost per volume will probably not exceed $1.75, and will be
much less to those taking several copies. Orders may be sent to the firm with
the above address. No one will question the urgency of preserving these transient productions of a highly music race, and they will commend themselves
for actual enjoyment to all lovers of music, as well as to lovers of the curious.

When the summer ended, William Allen took up his new appointment as professor of ancient languages and history at the University of Wisconsin, and he and his family moved to Madison. It was a prestigious appointment and he had little time now for the work with Lucy and Wendell. The proofs for much of their book, presumably of the music sections, were ready in September, and Wendell was also pressed for time with his own responsibilities at *The Nation*. Lucy was eager to take her son Lloyd, now four months old, to show to Ellen, and with Ellen close at home with her baby daughter, Agnes, in Roxbury, not far from the center of Boston, it would be helpful if Lucy could bring the proofs with her. Charles Ware was planning to return to St. Helena, but he was still in West Newton, and with so many of the songs coming from his collection it would be natural that he would want to look at the proofs with Lucy.

On September 17 Ellen wrote a long letter to her mother recalling Lucy's visit to Roxbury, and it is an illuminating document of what was expected of a woman's life—which certainly was not an involvement in something like reading proofs for a book, a task that was considered outside the bounds of a woman's given task of mothering. Ellen could only find a moment to begin the letter because her own daughter, Agnes, was asleep, and the letter began with her confession that she and her husband had made careful preparations for Lucy's arrival. William had been twice to the railroad station waiting anxiously with a carriage for their arrival, when on a more careful reading of Lucy's note Ellen discovered that they would be coming the next day.[15]

> . . . . it was all our stupid blunder. On Thursday they were on time & had stopped at Aunt Charlotte's in Providence for breakfast. Lloyd is the dearest little 4½ months—with elegant *violet* eyes, long long black lashes, a large broad nose precisely like Wendell', & marked eyebrows like his—a sweet delicate mouth—rather large—& a cunning dimple in his chin—his head is long and narrow—his hair is dark & not much of it—& his skin is clear but not so fair as Agnes.

Lucy had arranged the visit at just that time intending to do serious work on an important collection of slave songs, but for Ellen, and seemingly for everyone else in the family, the only thing of interest for them was Lucy's baby. Ellen's letter seldom strayed from one or another of the babies in the house.

He [Lloyd] is just the kind of baby to hug—& he smiles & is good. I begin to think sons will do very well—Lucy is real handy with him, and having no nurse he keeps very tidy & straight.

She has plenty of food for him. Agnes was like a little bird cooing at him when he first came—she stood by him & laughed & said "dear baby," & kissed him & he laughed & crowed at her—

Now they are all gone & it is a whole week since I began this letter—it has been absolutely impossible to get it finished—but you will know what's the matter—Lucy & her mother & the baby all had such colds with the N. E. E. winds that they rather pined for their native atmosphere—

Mrs. McK. coughed in a really severe manner & looked very pale & was miserable, Lucy thought they'd better make a short visit this time & come again when it was milder—We couldn't bear to have them go so soon, but little Lloyd had quite a cough & they were not easy any longer—we had a lovely time while it lasted, tho' there wasn't much that was consecutive, as you might say, about it—for Agnes kept me on the steady trot from morning 'till night, & Luce got tired out & had to take naps—Just as we might get comfortably settled to comparing notes & having a good time splash! would sound from a shoe into the water pail which I had forgotten to place *on the bureau*, or our Agnes would squirm thru the crack of a door that had been left unlatched to hear Lloyd, or climbed *up*—The little boy was as good as could be—I fixed up Agnes' basket cradle for him & he lay in that usually at mealtimes, or our goodnatured Mary wd hold him after the toast—He feeds very nicely—

The only occasion when Lucy and Ellen were able to be by themselves was a theater night when they saw a noted star perform in *School for Scandal*—finding on their return home that Agnes had been crying for an hour, "but we had a real good time . . . that was about the extent of our sprees." Ellen went shopping with Lucy's mother who bought Agnes a box of blocks, with the comment that "she never saw a child with so few play things, &.I felt as if I had been very remiss . . ."

Since Lucy had come to work on the proofs of the book there must have been some time when she worked alone, but the only mention of Lucy's work in Ellen's letter was her reference to meeting Charles Ware when he stayed to dinner after he and Lucy had spent the afternoon working on the proofs, though the work seemed to make less of an impression on Ellen than her husband's skill at carving the chicken for their dinner.

Mr. Chas. P. Ware took dinner with us Sunday, & Wm. carved his two R. I. chickens very creditably—CPW is son of Mary Ware & nephew of Dr.

Putnam's wife (now dead). He is a fine young man who has spent three years among the Freemen at the South & is helping Lucy & others arrange The Slave Songs in a book—he & Lucy read proofs most of the afternoon—Mrs. Dell brought a western friend to tea—a Mrs. [Class?]—daughter of some well-known abolitionist who suffered for the truth—she was decidedly western in accent & costume.- being dressed in black silk *very* low neck & short sleeves with a black waist overwaist which was about as good as nothing— She was half a head shorter than your stumpy daughter—& as stumpy again!

It's difficult to choose which of Ellen's casual asides best characterizes her complicated relationship with her mother—who had long been disappointed in her daughter's lack of interest in her own social activism—her belittling dismissal of the guest as the "daughter of some well-known abolitionist who suffered for the truth," or her description of herself as "your stumpy daughter." There seemed to be no curiosity at all as to what Lucy was engaged in with the proofs for the book that she had brought with her from New York.

◆　◆　◆

As he'd anticipated, William Allen's new position at the University of Wisconsin took most of his time, but he noted in his journal on October 4 that he had worked again on the preface. His introduction had now expanded beyond the description of the songs themselves to include an extended discussion of the language spoken on the island, and finally, as a kind of appendix, he added useful "Directions for Singing." His part of the book was now ready, with the final details left in Wendell's hands. On November 14 Wendell wrote Lucy to say that he had completed his own work with the new proofs and described the arrangements for reviews. With proofs ready, the book at last was finished.

During these weeks their publisher, A. Simpson & Co., had kept the public informed of the book's progress through the advertising columns of *The Nation*. On October 10, when it was listed as "In Press," the title had been shortened to *Slave Songs of the South*, probably to fit it into the column width. On October 31 their book entered the company's current list, and on November 14 the book was presented to the reading public with its full title in an advertisement of its own under a heading reading "The Most Remarkable Collection Ever Made." A week later, on November 21, the advertisement announced in bold letters FIRST EDITION NOW READY, with a descriptive paragraph:

"One hundred and Thirty-Six Songs (words and music) from all parts of the South, never before published or brought together; historically of the greatest value."

William Allen received one of the early copies. His diary note on November 26 was a calm, "Finished examinations. Looked at Slave Songs. In eve. to see Thos. Hill."

Lucy McKim's St. Helena Island, June 1862.

"I am keeping a diary as I must tell you everything when I get home instead of writing it now, as there is so little time. I have also copied down a number of the wild sad songs of the negroes—tunes & words both."

Lucy McKim's letter to her mother from St. Helena Island, June 12, 1862.

The beach at Land's End where Lucy McKim and her father landed on St. Helena Island on June 8, 1862.

"The weather could not be finer. So far it has not been as warm as we had it just before leaving home. . . . five contrabands, viz, old Joe, Jerry, Gabriel, Pompey, & John Cole rowed us to Land's End, singing all the way. . . . There we got ashore, the darkeys carrying the gentlemen on their backs & pulling us up in the boat."

Lucy McKim, letter to her mother, June 12, 1862.

The unpaved beginning of the road from Land's End to the Pope Plantation where Lucy would spend her first nights.

"The first part of the way was through young cotton fields, blackberry-wildernesses, but soon we entered the 'Pine Barren,' a smooth broad white road through a real tropical forest. . . . Just wait till I get home to get off over live oaks, magnolias, hanging moss, & superb foliage."

Lucy's letter to her mother, June 12, 1862.

The ruins of the old Episcopal Church
where Lucy took shelter from the rain.

"All of a sudden it began to pour like one stream & me almost wholly wet by the time we arrived at a small Paradise in the shape of a deserted church surrounded by oaks. . . . A most delightful half hour was passed there, talking and playing on the organ, which strange to say had not been destroyed. I never touched an organ before, queer experience to have there for the first time. . . ."

Lucy's letter to her mother, June 12, 1862.

The ruins lie at a curve of the road, now paved, halfway between Land's End and The Oaks, where Lucy would stay.

The Brick Baptist Church.

"Perhaps the grandest singing we heard was at the Baptist Church on St. Helena
Island, where a congregation of three hundred men and women joined in a hymn—
    Roll, Jordan, roll, Jordan!
    Roll, Jordan roll!
It swelled forth like a triumphant anthem. That same hymn was sung by thousands of
negroes on the 4th of July. . . ."
    Lucy McKim, letter to *Dwight's Journal of Music*, November 8, 1862.

The church is one of the few buildings on St. Helena constructed of brick at this time. It was built by the slaves of the Pope Plantation in 1855 and stood close to the plantation house where Lucy stayed for the first nights of her visit. The building was a large church hall, with a balcony in an upper story where slaves were permitted to stand during the services, and where they would not be seen by their masters and their families.

Oak trees near the site of The Oaks, main house of the Daniel Pope Plantation. The house where Lucy stayed no longer exists, and no large plantation house has been built to replace it.

Gravestones of Pope family members beside the Brick Church. The house was also the quarters of Laura Towne and Ellen Murray. On June 13, 1862, Towne wrote to her family mentioning Lucy McKim's visit:

"You do not know how comfortable and even elegant our apartments are, now that we have all the furniture the cotton agent had in his half of the house. There are no other such accommodations in this region, and we shall be foolish to go away for anything but health. . . . Mr. McKim is taking notes, and will tell everything, I fancy. Lucy is a very nice girl and she is busy collecting facts, etc."

The old house behind the site of the Pope Plantation house.

For several days Lucy's father considered spending more time on the island, but others working there finally convinced him it was too dangerous to stay. He wrote his wife on June 13, 1862, before he made his decision:

"Lucy does not know of my purpose to stay, but she will be delighted to hear of it for her heart is wholly in the work, and she is as happy as she can be. I left her in [?] Pope's Island 'at home.'"

The site of the "Yard" on the Pope Plantation. The land, across the road from the Brick Baptist Church, was purchased by Laura Towne and became the grounds of the Penn School.

"And did I have a splendid, glorious, splenderific, magnificent, nice time? My dear, these are feeble adjectives. . . . I enjoyed myself so much that in recollection there is a halo around the sea-sickness & an ecstatic thrill in every flea-bite! . . . one can slowly realize that one lives in a cage, until accident sets you flying outside. . . . I will go on from our first luncheon at 'The Oaks.' The rest of that afternoon was spent in visiting the "Yard," which down there refers particularly to the enclosure containing all the outhouses—i.e. stables, corn houses, cotton house, chicken house, cabins of the house servants, etc. & the Quarters. . . ."

Mansions on the old streets of Beaufort, South Carolina. Although Lucy McKim
mentions visits to Beaufort in her letters, she did not include any comments about
the city. Laura Towne recorded her impressions shortly after her arrival three months
before Lucy.

"The streets are lovely in all that nature does for them. The shade trees are fine,
the wild flowers luxuriant and the mocking birds perfectly enchanting. They are so
numerous and so noisy that it is almost like being in a canary bird fanciers."
    Diary entry, April 12, 1862.

Charlotte Forten, who arrived in Beaufort in the fall, shared Laura Towne's favorable impression of the city.

"Beaufort looks like a pleasant place. The houses are large and quite handsome, built in the usual Southern style with verandahs around them, and beautiful trees. One magnolia in Mr. French's yard is splendid—quite as large as some of our large shade trees, and with the most beautiful foliage, a dark rich, glossy green."
    Diary entry, October 28, 1862.

"It is difficult to express the entire character of these negro ballads by mere musical notes and signs. The odd twists made in the throat, and the curious rhythmic effect produced by single voices chiming in at different irregular intervals, seem almost impossible to place on score, as the singing of birds, or the tones of an Aeolian harp. . . . The wild, sad strains tell as the sufferers themselves never could, of crushed hopes, keen sorrow, and a dull, daily misery which covered them as hopelessly as the fog from the rice swamps. . . ."

Lucy McKim, letter to *Dwight's Journal of Music*, November 8, 1862.

13

Sweet, Wild Melodies

Nobody knows de trouble I've had,*
*   Nobody knows but Jesus,*
Nobody knows the trouble I've had, (sing)
*   Glory hallelu!*

Verse 1. One morning I was a walking down,
*   O yes Lord!*
I saw some berries hanging down,
*   O yes Lord!*

2. I pick de berry and I suck de juice, O yes Lord!
Just as sweet as honey in de comb, O yes Lord!

3. Sometimes I'm up, sometimes I'm down,
Sometimes I'm almost on de groun'.

4. What makes ole Satan hate me so?
Because he got me once and he let me go.

Nobody knows de trouble I've had,
*   Nobody knows but Jesus,*
Nobody know the trouble I've had,
*   Glory hallelu!*

*I see

Collected by William Allen in Charleston, South Carolina, 1865
No. 74 in Slave Songs of the United States

216   Sweet, Wild Melodies

Although the publication of their book went unnoticed by either *Atlantic Monthly* or *Harper's*, the nation's leading journals, it was widely reviewed elsewhere. As was the usual custom the reviews were unsigned, but it was generally understood that authors took advantage of anonymity to promote their own work. Lucy reviewed it herself and with Wendell wrote a longer second review. Another of the St. Helena Island group, Charlotte Forten, who was cited in the book, was also among those who responded warmly to its publication. Lucy's review, "The Hymnody of the Blacks," appeared on November 24, 1867, in *The Independent*, the journal of religious thought and opinion in New York City where Wendell had been employed before joining *The Nation*. Her opening paragraph made it clear that she had been aware of the many accounts of slave songs that had appeared since her first song settings and article letter of five years before.

> Ever since the occupation of a Southern port by our troops, the fame of the music of the negroes has been straggling slowly northward through all sorts of channels—through letters, magazine articles, through private descriptions, and, occasionally, through illustration. Specimens of the words of the songs have frequently been printed, specimens of the music, with but three or four but illy [*sic*] known examples, never till now. If only in the light of a curiosity, therefore, we welcome the volume before us—the first collection of songs, words and music, that has ever been attempted, and before opening its lids, we may thank the editors for their efforts to save from oblivion a portion of the wild and unique minstrelsy that is now rapidly passing away under the influence of the new civilization. The names of the editors of the collection are sufficient vouchers for its genuineness. All have spent more or less time in the South, and two of them, Messrs. Allen and Ware, were superintendents of Port Royal plantations for protracted periods.[1]

As other reviewers also noted, William Allen's introduction to the volume was so extensive and dealt with so many of the musical and social issues the music presented that it was more effective simply to quote him than to attempt a lengthy paraphrase. Lucy immediately turned to his discussion.

> The songs are introduced by an essay from the pen of Professor Allen. This, which is both vivacious and exhaustive, tells all of the history of the songs that is known, describes the manner of their singing, and closes with an account of the dialect of the Sea Island negroes. Most of the songs are religious—"sperichills" (spirituals) as the colored people call them—and of

these Port Royal furnishes the largest part. "I never," says Mr. Allen, "fairly heard a secular song among the Port Royal freedmen, and never saw a musical instrument among them. In other parts of the South, 'fiddle-songs,' 'devil-songs,' 'corn songs,' 'jig-tunes,' and what not, are common; all the world knows the banjo, and the 'Jim Crow' songs of thirty years ago. We have succeeded in obtaining only a very few songs of this character ... It is often indeed, no easy matter to persuade them to sing their old songs, even as a curiosity, such is the sense of dignity that has come with freedom."

Lucy's comment was that "These 'sperichills' have been described by people who have heard them as breathing the very history of slavery," and she continues with a quote from her own article in *Dwight's Journal* in the fall of 1862.

These wild, sad strains tell, as the sufferers themselves never could, of crushed hopes, keen sorrow, and a dull, daily misery, which covered them as hopelessly as the fog from the rice swamps. On the other hand, the words breathe a trusting faith in the future—in "Canaan's fair and happy land," to which their eyes seem constantly turned.

Her description of "people who have heard them" hearing within the spirituals the story of slavery is certainly a personal reference to her own experience on St. Helena. She then caustically turned to an article that had appeared recently in the popular journal *The World* which had somehow reached the conclusion that the songs were an indication of the slaves' contentment with their lives. "It evidently knows equally little of the religion and the music of the miserable."

She concluded her review by assuring the readers that the importance of the collection lies in the musical transcriptions. Through the notes of the songs the readers will be better able to understand the words, though they may have already been familiar with verses like them from earlier publications. She does obliquely suggest that it may be difficult for some readers to fit the transcriptions of the melodies to the texts, "as nearly as is possible from the notes."

In quoting from this introduction we describe the songs, in part. To give an adequate idea of them in words is out of the question. Everyone will be curious to find for himself—as nearly as is possible from the notes—how the often spoken-of "Poor Rosy" and "Roll, Jordan Roll," sound, as well as the unfamiliar "Rain fall and wet Becca Lawton," and "Jericho, do worry me," and

"God got plenty o' room," what the songs of Colonel Higginson's regiment are like—the words of which he has already published in the *Atlantic Monthly*: and what, also, the Louisiana songs, "Auror Bradaire," [and] "Lolotte," with their negro-French patois, our readers have been already made familiar with the general style through their frequent publications in the newspapers.

In her final sentences, to add a further voice of praise for the slave songs themselves, Lucy quoted from Fanny Kemble's description of the music she heard thirty years earlier.

In recommending the book as a curiosity in literature, as a valuable bit of history, and as a collection of remarkable musical ideas,* we feel that we do not go beyond the truth.

*"The high voices, all in unison, and the admirable time and true account with which their responses are made, always makes me wish that some great traditional composer could hear these semi-savage performances. With very little skillful adaptation and instrumentation, I think one or two barbaric chants and choruses might be evoked from them that would make the fortune of an opera" *Mrs. Kemble's "Life on a Georgia Plantation,"* p. 218.

The review that she wrote together with Wendell appeared in the November 21, 1867, issue of *The Nation* under the title *Slave Songs of the United States*. Lucy and Wendell's review was shorter than might have been expected, but in an early sentence they suggested that in the book itself Professor Allen had contributed a lengthy introduction, though they believed that readers perhaps would unhappily say "too soon rather than too tardily at the introduction's conclusion." The tone of the review was respectful of its readers, at the same time answering, at least in Lucy's mind, many questions that had been raised about what lay behind the spirituals and their musical characteristics.[2]

In what are perhaps the most important passages of their review they take up the question that had been raised about the spirituals from their first appearance in print—their authenticity. It is a question that is still sometimes asked in our own time. Their answer clearly reflects Lucy's serious engagement with the songs and their musical character and just as certainly carries on the tone and decision of what must have been lengthy discussion with others in her circle. The term "peculiar" in the 1860s generally had the meaning of "unique," and was not generally considered negative.

The negroes in their turn imitate the whites, but they show their peculiar musical genius as much in their imitations as in their compositions. A "white tune," so to speak, adopted and sung by them—in their own way—becomes a different thing. The words may be simply mangled, but the music is changed under an inspiration, it becomes a vital force. Hence the difficulty in according authorship: that is to say how much is pure African, how much is Methodist or Baptist camp-meeting. Where did the camp-meeting songs come from? Why may not they as likely emanate from black as white worshippers? Doubts such as these, in the absence of certain proof, can alone account for the admission into this collection of songs like "The Old Ship of Zion," "Almost Over," and several others of the same stamp. Suggestive as they are, they are the least interesting of the collection. The host of unmistakably negro compositions, of which "Poor Rosy" and "Becca Lawton" are two pertinent examples, are a reward to the slowest decipherer of notes and the most backward conceiver of tempo. The opening songs are rich in illustrative variety. What better adaptation of music to words than in "Jehovah—Hallelujah"—"De foxes have a hole and der birdies have a nest"? What more rousing than "Blow your Trumpet, Gabriel" and "Praise, Member"? What more truly spiritual than "The Lonesome Valley"?

In the description of one of the songs it is clearly Lucy who is writing, since it presents a vivid glimpse into the circumstances where she heard it. Although she uses the word "we," Wendell had not been to St. Helena with her. The anecdote does not appear in the surviving letters she sent to friends, and might have come from the diary she promised to Ellen, but which has never been found.

Then there is the quaint "O deat' he is a Little Man," which we remember ourselves to have heard sung by a crew rowing across the ferry from St. Helena to Beaufort. The fugle [sic] man of that occasion—a fellow of inky blackness, with the sweat of a summer's day streaming from every pore, and his eyes squinted into the sun's glare—as he poured forth, energetically, "O Lord, remember me; do Lord, remember me."

They ended their review with two wishes.

We shall be disappointed if many of the airs do not become popular and the effort of the editors to make that permanent which is now transient be not crowned with signal and merited success.

The first wish that there would be an audience for the spirituals they had so lovingly preserved would be fulfilled beyond their most optimistic dreams in only a decade. It would, however, be longer before their own work in making this possible would receive the "signal" success it deserved.

Charlotte Forten's personable and positive review of the book was published in the December 1867 issue of *The Freedmen's Record*. It was, like the other reviews, unsigned, although its references to her own experiences on St. Helena made it immediately identifiable. She quoted the sentences beginning "The wild, sad strains tell...," which appeared in Lucy's review, certainly unaware that Lucy was quoting her own article written in 1862. Forten wrote:

> We are very glad that these songs, which are too rapidly losing favor among the freedmen—are thus collected and preserved, for they make a most striking, curious, and valuable addition to the history of slavery in the country. Professor Allen says, "Our title, 'Slave Songs' was selected, because it best described the contents of the book. A few of those here given (Nos. 64, 59), were, to be sure, composed since the proclamation of emancipation, but even these were inspired by slavery. All, indeed, are valuable as an expression of the character and the life of the race that is playing such a conspicuous part in our history."[3]

The heart of Forten's review was a lyrical paragraph drawn from her articles "Life on the Sea Islands," published three years earlier, recalling her own rich memories of St. Helena, and it served as a reminder of the experiences that had brought the book's editors together in the work.

> To those who have been fortunate enough to hear these songs sung by the freedmen themselves, this collection is one of peculiar interest, and recalls vividly the many and varied occasions on which the sweet, wild melodies, have touched and charmed them. The sunset row from island to island, when we first arrived, in the golden glow of October, with our crew of sturdy boatmen, their jet black faces, strongly relieved by scarlet shirts, and in some cases by white kerchiefs tied over the head, the more effectively to protect them from the heat; ... the great gathering under the grand, moss draped old oaks, on the Fourth of July, and on the glorious "Emancipation Day," that celebration which has been so often described, but whose sublime significance, whose deep and soul-stirring interest can never be fitly spoken; the midnight "shout," in the roughly boarded "Praise-house," lighted only by the red glare

of a single pine knot, which, indeed, did *not* light, but only served to render more visible the darkness embodied in the weird forms, flitting through their strange, barbaric dance; these are a few of the never to be forgotten pictures which rise before us, and awaken almost irresistible longings to behold again the realities, as we glance over the familiar words, and listen to the familiar airs of these songs.

Forten ended her review with her pleased understanding that the book was already a success.

This valuable book will, doubtless, be much in demand. We are informed that the first edition is already very nearly, if not entirely, sold. The publishers are about to issue a second edition, which will, we hope, find as speedy a sale.

It is difficult to assess at this point whether or not the book had sold out its first edition. So little attention was paid to the book over such a long period that it was assumed it had done poorly. Her review would have been written some time before the journal's publication at the beginning of December, and her optimism was borne out by the publisher though there is always room for considerable hyperbole in advertising. In the advertisement for the book in the literary column of *The Nation* on December 5, a new edition was announced:

SLAVE SONGS
OF THE UNITED STATES

———————————

A NEW EDITION
Of this popular work will be issued in a few days.

———————————

    The Press says of it:
"We welcome the volume before us—the first collection of negro songs, words and music, that has ever been made."—*The New York Independent*
"They have no sort of resemblance to the so-called negro songs of the cork minstrels, and, as a rule, are much more attractive."—*N. Y. Citizen*
"The verses are expressive, and the melodies touching and effective. There is no doubt the book will receive wide attention."—*Brooklyn Standard*
"Possesses a curious interest for students of African character."—*N. Y. Tribune*
"These endemical lays are, in fact, chief among the signs and evidence of the normal African character."—*N. Y. World*

"This collection contains many excellent ballads that might readily be supposed the work of our best composers."—*Le Messager Franco-Anericaie*

For Lucy and Wendell, William Allen and Charles Ware, there would have been considerable satisfaction at the news of a second printing, which meant that the first printing had sold out in only a few weeks. There was, however, no further announcement of the promised new edition. Simpsons & Co. had been an active publisher of medical texts and quarterlies, and their advertisement in *The Nation* at the beginning of the new year on January 2, 1868, presented as its sole offering "The Quarterly Journal of Psychological Medicine and Medical Jurisprudence." The firm's name was now Moorhead, Simpson & Bond. There was always uncertainty in the publishing world of this period, and *Slave Songs of the United States*, despite its promising initial sales, no longer had a publisher. There would be a second edition, but it would not be until four years had passed, and by then the news it had for its readers had become already familiar.

14

Now *do* not disappoint us!

I asked of Time to tell me where was Love;
He pointed to her footsteps on the snow,
Where first the angel lighted from above,
And bid me note the way and onward go;
Through populous streets of cities spreading wide,
By lonely cottage rising on the moor,
Where bursts from sundered cliff the struggling tide,
To where it hails the sea with answering roar,
She led me on; o'er mountain's frozen head,
Where mile on mile still stretches on the plain,
Then homeward whither first my feet she led,
I traced her path along the snow again;
But there the sun had melted from the earth
The prints where first she trod, a child of mortal birth.

"Love"
—Jones Very

Lucy was now busy with her new life as a young mother with her first child, and she was as distracted from thoughts of the work on the book as the others who had shared the effort. William Allen was in the early months of his new academic career, and Charles Ware was now helping with the cotton crop on St. Helena. Wendell was committed to his fledgling magazine and was also helping his wife with their new baby. In the late spring Lucy wrote to Ellen to congratulate her on the birth of her second child, a son, Charles, who was born on June 19.[1]

June 22, 1868

My dear Ellen,

Unencumbered congratulations to you, dear old thing, for accomplishing your mission in such a highly creditable manner! A boy! Now perhaps the family Garrison are to have a little practice at that gender, they won't be calling Lloyd "sissy" all the time, & "her" & "she." Poor dear uncle George never recovered from the effects of his niece all the time he was here.

What a few facts I have to write about! Do make William or somebody give us the details [about the new baby]. Wm. did not do very well for a first letter, but we pine for a second. "Head like a pyramid." That is nothing. Their heads are always dreadful at first. Lloyd's was jammed down over his eyes, but it soon rose, to comfort his anxious parents ...

I wish I had time to write more, but Lloyd sits in his carriage on the porch, bothering mother and Ellie, who is ironing, so I dare not take the time.

P/S. Lloyd is learning to whistle—truly! and really accomplishes a note once in a dozen blows or so. It is very funny.

During these months Lucy found she was pregnant again, but now there were complications, and there was concern that she wouldn't be able to bring the new baby to term. After a silence of some weeks she had a reply from Ellen. It was an anxious letter, responding to Lucy's difficulties with the new pregnancy, while at the same time half sardonic in its description of the wonder of a new baby—when it is sleeping. Lucy would lose the baby in a miscarriage some weeks later, one of the series of miscarriages that would take a severe toll on her body. Ellen answered her with a wondering account of her own delivery.[2]

August 21, 1868, Auburn

Beloved Thicky,

... I feel so lost when so long a time passes writing to you, as I might feel if I had gone to breakfast without washing my face, or as if some other daily task had been neglected. Is it not many years since we met, and shall we ever meet again? Your last letter came as near perfection as such things are permitted to come, in this life—it was almost like your dear living presence, & if Fate had not suddenly arrested it should have been speedily answered. To be sure, Theo arrived precisely according to calculations! but without the previous warning I had been led to expect, & so my mundane matters were not fully closed up. I wonder when you will wake your mother at 2 oc. in the morning & prepare to hold tight to something, & expect the worst & then almost before you know it you find yourself still alive to the joy of seeing two tiny red fists striking about in the air, & hear a funny little wail which is like sweet music?—

That's the way it happened to me & now the horrors that followed are over, & I can begin to enjoy things as I did before that 14th—I am convinced it was *walking*, no matter how tired up to the very last, that made the terrible pangs *comparatively*, so few, and you must be sure to remember that!—It is the most delightful thing in the world to have your own baby, when he is sound asleep as mine is at present—but when you have to toss her about, with her gaining a pound a minute & and you sick as well, & when you can't hide behind the thickest tree & et a fine ripe plum (of which you are no end fond, & there never was a crop like the one this year!) without her finding it out, & turning most green in consequence, then with the eighth or the tenth the romance must wear off . . .

. . . It is bad news to hear of you so delicate, dear Thicky. I'm afraid you'll have to give it up this time, if nothing but lying still will save it.

Rest assured however, that you can't know what happiness is, until you have *two*!—& so much easier to take care of two, than one . . .

By November Lucy had recovered sufficiently to feel herself more able to deal with the events of the house, and she responded to a letter from Charlie with sisterly questions and advice. His letter on November 2, 1868, was a long and detailed description of his travels in France, which he titled "Visit to a Chateau on the Loire." The letter seemed to his sister to be a start of a promising travel essay, and she responded to it as she might have done to a manuscript submitted to *The Nation*. Beneath her testy questions, however, there is a glimpse of the constraints she was feeling with the isolation of her new life in a place where she knew almost no one. She was hungry to know about *people*. As the days passed she had no one in Llewellyn Park except the baby, her mother, and their cook.[3]

The tour was the very thing for a rest, and "Among the Chateaus" with those beautiful names sounds awful enticing. O, we want to hear a *great deal* more about thy visit to Chateau Neuf! How you live there, more about the people, who is 'Joubert'? are there any demoiselles? how thee was received? is the old fat Mine, the only one in the family? what kind of a bedroom thee has; what sort of servants there are; what thee and Jourdain do all day, what the 'hifalutin" civilities were, etc., etc., ad infin.

By the way, "Among the Chateaux" would furnish thee enough material for a short series of letters to the A. M.'g News [?]. There isn't the least need of crowding all thy facts into one letter. Dilute a little, take a few items and enlarge on 'em.

In the winter Lucy found she was pregnant again, and if all went well, her second child would be due in September. In her father's letters to Charlie it was clear that she was staying even closer to the house. Her piano had been moved into the sitting room and she usually played for the family in the evenings, though the mornings of earlier years when she had spent hours in absorbed practicing had ended with her son's birth. In a letter to Charlie on February 7, 1869, her father described the response to her playing from little Lloyd, who was now nearly two years old.[4]

> We are all well and little "Dot" [Lloyd] as he finds himself is lively. He talks a great deal about his Uncle Charley! . . . He is very fond of music and makes his mother play him his favorites over one after another without intermission. "Mama, play 'Will you, Will you little Boy,'" "Mama, play 'Cluney Clark,'" "Mama, play 'Bully's (?),'" "Mama, play 'Lazr's'" "Mama, play 'Goodbye Dixie.'" And so on through the whole list, as soon as she has played one asking her to play another.

On April 9 her father wrote again, and for the moment Lucy's health had improved.[5]

> Lucy is sitting beside me writing. She is translating the 3rd volume of Laboulage's history of the U.S. Your mother is sitting at the other end of the table dozing and Wendell is in the Eastern parlor writing away as usual at his literary notes for the "Nation" . . . Lucy is rosy & healthy & full of life.

Lucy and Wendell's second son, Philip, was born September 28, 1869, a moment that was greeted with joy by his Boston grandfather. The news was sent to Roxbury by telegraph, and William Lloyd Garrison's congratulatory letter to Lucy and Wendell was sent the next day.[6]

> Roxbury, Sept. 29, 1869
> Dear Wendell and Lucy,
>   While we were all at the table, last evening, William came in with a telegram, announcing that to you was born another son yesterday. Of course, the gratifying intelligence was received with smiles, cheers and congratulations by the whole family. The grandparents present were especially jubilant, and felt that they had reached another stage of exultation. We all send our best wishes that all may go well with mother and child. Lloyd shall be loved none the less for the newcomer, for there is an abundance of room in our hearts

for all the little ones that may be given in this manner. Harry and Fanny are expecting a similar advent in December to bless them, and bring still more joy to our household, and should it prove to be a girl, as in the first instance, then the sexes of the grandchildren will continue to be evenly balanced. But, whether boy, or girl, it is all the same in the matter of thankfulness, and one is to be prized as much as the other. I was never anxious, as to my own children, of desiring in advance that one should prove a boy or the other a girl, but as that must be determined by an unerring law, I felt to rejoice in its operation any how . . .

The main thing now is for Lucy to be very careful, and remember it is best to "make haste slowly" as regards convalescence.

I hardly supposed that I should live to be a grandfather; yet I have now five grandchildren I shall not object if I live to see the number increased to fifty! That is a liberal margin, and I will endeavor to be content with anything short of it. . . .

Give my hearty congratulations to the grandparents at the Park

Yours in embracing love,

Wm. Lloyd Garrison

Lucy had complained to Charlie about the barrenness of his letters, but the many claims on her in the house—young Lloyd, her new baby, her responsibilities for her mother and what moments she could claim for her music—left her with little time or strength for herself. The physical problems following Lloyd's birth had intensified with Philip's delivery. She intimated in a letter to Ellen that there had been other miscarriages, and she suffered almost continuous pain with what was diagnosed as a "rheumatic complaint." The pain in her legs and knees was so severe that she had difficulty walking, and her neck, her wrists, and hands were swollen and inflamed. From her symptoms it is possible that she was suffering from what would now be known as rheumatoid arthritis. A second doctor diagnosed her difficulty as "gout," and ordered a new cure. She was only twenty-seven years old, but her body was beginning to struggle with the demands her life made on it.

On November 14 Ellen wrote to offer her sympathies and her acknowledgment that their lives were at the mercy of their childbearing. It was clear as well that their letter writing had now been sacrificed to their lives' pressures. On a visit to Roxbury to spend a precious few days with Fanny and the family there, Lucy had contracted whooping cough, and on her return to Llewellyn Park she had infected the entire family.[7]

I felt most miserable to miss all your visit in the summer, by such a paltry few days. And to think you should go & get whoop Co—and give it to all your relations! Well, I have been sorry for you—but there are times when Nature seems bent upon driving us to the wall. The *first three months* [with a new baby] is one of those periods. It was aggravating for you to be laid up while the 'boys' were at the park, but to tell the truth they did enjoy themselves.

It is refreshing to know that you are better. Nothing delights me more than to be a new Aunt. Do you want anything more than shirts?

By the fall Lucy had recovered enough to respond to letters the family was receiving from Charlie, who was discovering Europe with the same mixture of astonishment and sangfroid that many young men had experienced before him. He sent the family his drawings for a proposed casino, presenting it as a possible building project. Lucy's tone in her reply was as older-sisterly as letters like this often can be.[8]

I didn't admire particularly the nude ladies in the niches. The profuseness of it just now in New York, at the entrance of every palace of amusement, whether refined or indecent, expensive or cheap, has given me rather a distaste for it. Of course I do not condemn every kind of naked female figure in marble or plaster, but the voluptuous, meaningless, commonplace stuff that is copied and recopied is most tiresome.

In the wintry stillness, as they all felt themselves barricaded in the house by the snow and the cold, Lucy could only take Lloyd outside onto the Bramble for short walks while her mother watched Philip in his crib. In the dearth of news and meetings with friends, Charlie's European sojourn became increasingly a lively source of family entertainment. Without consciously thinking about it they had come to depend on his letters as family events to brighten the tedium of their dark evenings. The passing months were also a continuous worry to his father, who was responsible for Charlie's expenses. The family's dissatisfaction with his distance from them, with the paucity of news in his letters, and as a final disappointment his failure to account for his expenses was brought to a head by a long and what they all considered to be an unsatisfactory letter that Charlie sent them on January 3, 1870. In his answer on January 24 his father expressed his own dissatisfaction, and both Lucy and her mother added their own complaints to his father's letter, which addressed the financial situation. A friend in Paris named Bowles was responsible for disbursing Charlie's spending money and his father at least had some idea of his expenses through Bowles's accounting. Charlie also brought up in his letter the idea of continuing his stay with a year of study in Germany.[9]

> My dear Charley,
>   Your last letter dated Jan 3rd was very good as far as it went, but it gave us a very meager account of what your doings are from day to day and week to week, only the atelier.
>   The promised statement of your expenses has not yet come; but as I can make out your account stands about this.

Oct 14 arrived in Paris with	725 ft
Nov 19 Drew on Bowles for	300 "
Dec 14 " " " "	200 "
Jan 3 " " " "	500 "
	————————
	1725 "
Making in gold	$345.00
In currency	$435.00

> I suppose you must have been buying some things for presents since your return to Paris, and this accounts for your increased expenses.
>   In what you say about a year in Germany I don't take you to be serious as you would know that the cost, if there were no other reason would put it out of the question.
>   I am counting on your return on or before the middle of April . . . .

He added in closing:

> Lucy is waiting and I will add no more—except much love; and my best regards to Mr. Shaw.
>   Your ever affectionate
>   Father

Lucy added a brusque note on the back of the page, continuing to spell his nickname as ending in "ie," as his mother did.

> Dear Charlie: I did write a sheetfull, but on second thought will not send it; so look for something from me soon. Thy last meager letter, alluding to the "operas, calls, skating, dinners at Mrs Shaws", and no more, was such a

disappointment to all of us that I "over flow" a little too much about it so I tore up the sheet. Affg. Lucy

Lucy, however, hadn't torn up the sheet. She crumpled it up in a fit of annoyance and cast it into her wastebasket. Her mother retrieved it and copied out portions of it to send on to Charlie, adding her own admonitions. Charlie's situation—the family's valued son overspending on his European travels—was an aggravation, but it certainly wasn't an unfamiliar situation, and Charlie could have expected a reprimand from his father. He probably was dismayed, however, to find that at the same moment his father, his mother, and his older sister were all upset with him. His mother wrote:

> Midnight
> My dear Charlie,
> I played nurse tonight that Lucy might write to thee, but now she has finished and the evening is over she concludes Father's letter may go alone as the sheet she has written don't suit her. She has therefore just added a few lines to Father's letter and gone to bed. So was I going likewise but I don't want Father's letter which is not very loving to go alone. Neither do I like that all of what she has written should be left behind, so I shall sit up another hour & copy from hers all that I think worth sending—after first making a few remarks of my own.
> Thy last letter was received, dear and we are always delighted when Wendell comes out saying There is a letter from Charlie. We generally sit down and eat our dinner first and then hurry into the parlor and gather around the center table to enjoy our treat, Lucy mostly reading the letter aloud. But as the clock's now striking 11 & I know I should be abed—I will strike at once into a part of what Lucy says.
> "Thee speaks of being to operas, to skating ponds, out calling & dining, & at work. So for the first paragraph, & we all set our ears to hear something to [enliven] our rather dull and shut up country winter life. But not a word further! The seven pages that followed were as scrupulously devoted to architectural projects, as if they were the only projects from all our windows. Not the name of an opera. Not a syllable about the skating partners (a thing of all others that Mother likes to hear) not a mention of the persons called on, not an atom of the descriptions of the dinner parties. I know I have scolded thee a good deal in all our correspondence but sometimes I can't keep my resolutions not to break out afresh. I am so disappointed. And it is only an aggravation to hear thee perpetually hinting want of ability to write good letters as a

reason for all the reticence. Hang the manner! Thee writes well enough—as well as one needs to. It is the *intention*, and the thoughtfulness of what thy correspondents would like to hear that are wanting. . . . I don't object to the architectural parts of course—it is as interesting as anything else when it is confined to facts (and I'm sure we are all satisfied about the facts if thee is) but it does seem as if there might be a little more. I should rack my memory for incidents, supposing I hadn't such a splendid repertoire as opera, calls, & skating & dining at the Shaws. What are the Shaws anyway, besides Robert? Six sisters say? Two or three brothers? Old? Young? Pleasant? Musical? Artistic? Are other people there? Mrs. Shaw very hateful? Well, that's all, I believe I shall never bother again, but make up my mind that the masculine mind is incapable of a certain kind of productiveness unassisted by pumping in detail & *viva voce*. If there was anything to tell now I would, for all I said I wouldn't, but when one hasn't been anywhere for 5 months, further than Orange, one doesn't require much."

Her mother continued:

That's pretty much all Lucy wrote. She thought it sounded a little cross & she would try it again next week. But Charlie dear now do write the next letter full of little commonplaces. I mean the little incidents such as Lucy asks to know . . .

Then follows a page of news of friends and family members, concluding:

It is near midnight darling child and I must [run. . . .] Quantities of love to thee. I believe Annie means to come on to help us welcome thee home. She & Lucy love thee dearly. Thy name is mentioned many times a day by us all & little Lloyd rejoices in the prospect of thy coming as much as any of us . . .

It was true that seven of the pages of his letter dealt with his work, but Charlie had taken the time to send an eight-page letter to his family, and he would be justified if he were a little disappointed at their reaction. Although he was still only twenty-two, he might also have sensed the tone of desperation in Lucy's outburst. The town of Orange proper was only a mile down the slope from the house in Llewellyn Park, but with the winter weather and her painful condition even that walk was often denied her. Her mother perhaps heard the unspoken cry in her daughter's words, although it was something she might also have known well from her own years as a mother, but would never have expressed, even to herself. Lucy certainly had never realized that for a woman like herself, love, even a love as sincere as hers for her husband, could come at an almost unacceptably high cost.

Lucy had written to Ellen eight years before that "one can slowly realize that one lives in a cage, until accident sets you flying outside." Her outburst to Charlie was a cry from within her cage. How could she have known that her journey to South Carolina, with its bright discoveries and fresh adventures, would be the only journey she would ever take? Charlie, even as young as he was, could not have missed the barely concealed emotional hunger in his mother's insistence that he must reply to their lonely needs. Her half-concealed device of listing all the others besides herself who were depending on his return to remind him of his family responsibilities could play a role in whatever decisions he would make about his future life. On his return to the United States in the spring, as his father had insisted, thanks to his European training Charlie quickly found employment as a draftsman in the office of Henry Hobson Richardson, one of New York's most prestigious architects, and within a few months he moved to the city.

◆ ◆ ◆

The contrast between Lucy's life and her brother's years of study and travel in Europe only emphasized again the unyielding differences between the opportunities she would have to fulfill her own gifts and ambitions and her brother's. Within the family and with the society's support she would always be compelled to yield to their interests. The familiar rhetorical response to women's demands for a more equal role in society was that women were blessed in their nature by their sacred role of motherhood. Lucy, like so many other women, however, had found that motherhood was a complicated blessing.

For both Lucy and Ellen, the continued dependence of their young children on their mothers, virtually confining them in their homes, brought with it another unexpected trial. They both suffered cruelly from loneliness. Lucy, isolated in Llewellyn Park as her husband spent his days away from her in Manhattan, could have been a prototype for the suburban housewife who for the next century would be the typical model for a young American woman. Ellen, in Roxbury, had at least opportunities to see her sister-in-law, Fanny Garrison, who was now married to a German journalist, Henry Vuillard, and for long periods lived close by, but for

Ellen it was her crippling headaches that made it almost impossible for her to lead a fuller life.

Lucy's letters to Ellen, begging that she come for a visit, became more and more urgent, and then finally resigned as the months slipped past. A letter on July 9, 1869, thanking Ellen for a hand-sewn wrapper she had sent for Lucy's second baby, continued with fulsome congratulations to Ellen for managing a move and her illness and her own new baby. The letter then intimated that Lucy had experienced more difficulties with miscarriage, and expressed an earnest plea that Ellen come for a visit. There was some of her old banter in the letter's tone, but her life had changed so inexorably since the years before they each married. She ended with a disparaging comment on Boston's weather.[10]

> Llewellyn Park, July 9, 1869
>
> ... How you could in connection with moving, & bad cooks, & headaches, & no water, & a baby & a vivacious daughter & company & your own sewing, have succeeded in making me that dear little double (double, too!) wrapper when it was only a second baby & not at all looked for, (the *wrapper*, I mean!) & such a lovely color, & the buttonholes worked the way I never could—least ways, never would—and such a nice letter to come with it—it puzzles me to make out. And I never made a thing for Henry William Charles [Ellen's second child]! I suppose half a dozen miscarriages thrown in wouldn't make any difference to you; they'd rather give you more time to sit & knit for your friends & unborn families. I suppose this hot weather when needles stick & grate is rather pleasant to you. I don't wonder you call me "lazybones." I was only too grateful that your conscience allowed you to prefix "dear" to the term. Well, I send a thousand thanks!
>
> Don't say that you have given up your visit to the Park. Your mother gave mine the pleasant assurance that when you visited her in Auburn, she was going to keep the two children & let you run on here for a rest. Now *do* not disappoint us! For when otherwise shall I see you again. Any N. E. prospect is pretty distant for me, & except for all the Garrisons sake I am not sorry it is so. I believe I leave a year of my life every time I go there—horrible, if fascinating climate ...

A letter to Ellen a year later begged again for a visit, but the months of isolation had become so burdensome that the letter lost the occasional lightness of the year before. The immediate reason for the letter was a visit from Wendell's brother William, Ellen's husband. The Eliza mentioned in the letter is Ellen's sister, who was living close to their mother in Auburn. Ellen's gift to her this time was a hand-sewn traveling bag, which Lucy fantasizes could become her traveling bag for a visit.[11]

> Llewellyn Park Oct 9, 1870
> My dear Ellen,
> ...Would that I could put a nightgown & tooth-brush into that same bag, & run on to spend a week with you without other baggage & without children. But you know how it is. To take the young ones along is no fun for anybody, & I cannot leave them with mother. She is nervous & sleeps illy enough now, without adding a teething baby to her care. The little toad is real troublesome at night—so different from Lloyd. But you could come here. Let me proceed to show you how different is your situation from mine! Your children are older, & your sister Eliza is younger than mother. That would induce Eliza to matronize [*sic*] your household for a while? We *must* have you here, now that is certain. Everybody has been here but you, you mean thing, & I want to see you so dreadfully. I can't write letters any more – I hate 'em, though am still capable of receiving them with the old relish.... We could go to N. Y. & have larks. The season is just perfect for a visit to the Park. Come of course. What else can I say to induce you. don't wait for the way to open—open it! You shall have of our apple & quince butter too, & we won't talk a word of *Nation*.

Although in letters to Wendell's sister Fanny over the winter, Lucy wrote of occasional classical concerts on visits to New York and described her enthusiasm for the singing of the first German choirs she heard, her life continued largely to be restricted to the walks in the Bramble at Llewellyn Park. Since there is no mention of the new excitement in her letters there is no way to know of her reaction to the nation's sudden and ecstatic discovery of the St. Helena slave songs during these same months. A young African American singing group from a little-known college in Tennessee had achived unprecedented success performing arrangements of the spirituals she and the others had struggled for so long to preserve. Certainly she and Wendell must have shared their feelings about the unexpected events, but there is no way of knowing what their feelings were. The group would go on to become world renowned as the Fisk Jubilee Singers, and they would shape forever America's and the world's perception of slave songs.

The Jubilee Singers were a small nine-voice choir that had been trained to sing together at Fisk College, a struggling school committed to bringing education to the children of freedmen in Nashville, and they left on an improvised tour in October of 1871 to try to make money for their school by singing for sympathetic church congregations in the North. After some weeks of uncertainty it was their decision to add the slave songs to their concert fare that electrified their audiences. They were not the songs as Lucy and William Allen and Charles Ware had heard them in the cabins on the island, because their concert performances had been carefully arranged with European harmonies and the diction polished so that their audiences could understand every word of the stirring texts. This had been an American dream, that out of the long turmoil over slavery itself and the agony of the war would come some expression of the slaves' humanity. The Fisk Jubilee Singers were the embodiment of this dream.

◆ ◆ ◆

Lucy's life was now entirely filled with her children and her unending household tasks, and she also was still suffering complications from the birth of her second child. She must have assured herself that there would be some time later in her life when she would be able to pick up her music again, but it was now obvious to her that the days filled with household tasks were to be her life's reality. As her mother had written in her note to Charlie, intimating that Lucy was pregnant with her first child, now Lucy would be "busy." Lucy's crowded daily schedule at the time, with its hours of piano practice, her full roster of piano scholars, and the concerts in which she performed, was not something that her mother could consider "busy." That Lucy's physical suffering from problems with her body was in all probability related to her continued pregnancies was something that the society would have accepted sadly as a woman's misfortune.

The problems with Lucy's health that had been aggravated by the birth of her second son became more severe after the birth of a third baby, her daughter, Katherine, born on May 10, 1873. Now her condition began to cause alarm among the family. Wendell's father wrote him on August 14, two months after Katherine's birth, to express his concern, and to thank him for looking into his own "case" when he visited a doctor to seek advice on Lucy's situation. The elder Garrison also was suffering from similar painful symptoms, and he described Lucy's condition as "pain, inflammation and stiffness in the knees." He continued to discuss a possible remedy that he read of in an advertisement in Wendell's magazine. So little reliable medical aid was available that many people turned, as his father did, to any kind of medicine promising a miracle cure.[13]

... Dear Lucy, being afflicted in both of her knees—I only in my right—
excites a two fold sympathy in my breast. Seeing an advertisement in *The
Nation* of the Gettysburg Katalysine Water, and making inquiries concerning it of those who had used it beneficially, I have purchased a package of it
(twenty-four bottles), and mean to give it a thorough trial. It is claimed to be
singularly adapted to cases like Lucy's and mine as it dissolves the crystallized
uric acid which causes such acute pain and inflammation. Various remarkable cases are reported. If it works favorably in my case, ... I shall send some
bottles to Lucy for trials.

At the same time that Lucy was struggling with her own illness, James
McKim's health began to fail. In a letter to Lucy on May 6, 1874, Ellen
expressed her concern for his condition.[14]

> Roxbury May 6, 1874
> Dearest Sisterinlaw
>   Before I settle down to my large and ever increasing pile of sewing I want
> to write you a little word to say how grieved we are to hear of your father's
> condition, and how deeply we sympathize with you all. I have such a pleasant
> memory of him in my delightful visit to you & he looked so much better to
> me than I expected to see him, that I hoped by this he might be able to work
> in his garden again, & receive new strength ...

Lucy's father died on June 13, 1874, only a few weeks after Ellen's letter. For many in the abolitionist community it was a moment of sadness,
though they were strengthened by his own resolve in the last months as
he struggled against his illness. At the time Lucy's sister, Annie, was in
Germany, taking the waters at Bremen, hoping to find relief for her own
physical problems. Lucy wrote her a lengthy letter to bring her closer to
the scene of their father's death.[15]

> Dear Anne: I am going back a week, & try to remember what I can of each
> day. Of course I did not take the particular note of each event as I should
> have done, if I had thought it was the last one.
>   When Charlie left home to go East on the 3rd, I think it was—father was
> rather better than his ordinary fashion. He walked about the place—not only
> alone, but carrying his own stool. (It was that tall cane-sea music stand of
> yours, with a cushion tied on top of it.) There was as much expectation then
> of his lasting till Fall *at least*, as at any time. One Sunday—a week ago still

about as usual, and mother decided to go to town the next day to get hoes, a pair of fine summer blankets for father, and other much needed things. We all encouraged her going because she had been keeping at home closely for so long that she much needed a change. She went in the 9 train.

Lucy was with her father in his wheelchair and the baby in her carriage on the piazza, and later a friend came and sat with him while Lucy dressed. When Lucy returned to the piazza McKim was talking animatedly to their friend. Lucy walked with him back to his room and he needed to be helped from his chair, but as she was helping him he seemed to faint back into the chair.

It was not like any faint I ever heard of, & I thought he was going. Lloyd happened to come in and after him Phil.

She told one of her boys to send someone for the doctor and bring their cook, Hannah, up to the room.

Hannah got some whiskey & water . . . and he soon revived. After taking it he was able to step through the doorway into his big chair, & presently the Dr. came, & Hannah brought him his breakfast—a big piece of chicken, glass of ale, biscuit & plate of strawberries & cream. Under the Dr.'s cheering influence he ate more than common.

After breakfast he felt better, and blamed the fainting on not eating earlier. He shaved himself—walked into the dining room & wrote a short letter. "This was to be the last letter he ever wrote." It was to a friend and he added at the close, "They tell me I am getting better, but I do not see it so clearly."

Charlie returned after a week's absence at his work, and he was struck by the change in his father's appearance. His mother wouldn't allow anyone to sit up with her, saying it was enough to have Uncle W. next to her in case of need. In his last week there was a dreadful thunderstorm and the children had to be constantly reassured that there was no danger and the baby fretted. Wendall came from Boston bringing his father, and there was an emotional reunion between the men, recognizing that it would be their last meeting. Though they had achieved so much, they would not have time together to share what might come in the future. McKim now was receiving steady doses of morphine, but he and Garrison were able to sit on the piazza as they talked. When McKim asked the doctor what he would die of, the doctor replied, "Probably exhaustion," telling him he would probably slip away quietly. Then Father said with great feeling, "O if Heaven would only grant me such a boon."

Lucy continued:

Just after three o'clk he asked if it was not near day-light. Mother threw open the bay-window & day was just breaking, & the birds beginning to sing. It was just ¼ of 4 when he breathed his last & there couldn't have been a lovelier moment—the June day at its freshest, the room filled with the odor of the sweet grape which is in full bloom & the air full of birds' singing. We all sat perfectly quiet a while, feeling that nothing could be wished for more that we or he had not.

Then we straightened everything & went to dress. It was so blessed to have children and every baby abed—no wagons passing or people ringing at the door—just ourselves.

15

My dear Luxie

As imperceptible as Grief
The summer lapsed away—
Too imperceptible at last
To seem like Perfidy—
A Quietness distilled
As Twilight long begun,
O Nature spending with herself
Sequestered Afternoon—
The Dusk drew earlier in—
The Morning foreign shone—
A courteous, yet harrowing Grace,
As guest that would be gone—
And this, without a Wing
Or service of a Keel
Our summer made her light escape
Into the Beautiful.

Emily Dickinson

Whatever Lucy experienced, as a wife with young children, with a working husband often away and not enough money for the servants that wealthier people had to help with the children, there was never a question that she hadn't found her love for her husband and for her children fulfilling. At the end of the summer in 1871 Wendell was in Boston with his parents, and Lucy wrote him a long letter from Llewellyn Park, where Wendell's sister Fanny was staying for a visit with her young children.[1]

Llewellyn Park
Sept. 1, 1871

My dearest husband,

Is a live letter better than nothing? Then you shall have one. It is quarter
of ten, & Fanny & I have just laid down our needles, & are fully ready to
lay down our heads. I told her I should begin my letter, "Lord I have passed
another day."

If I'm not unutterably glad you're coming home then there's no use writing: Aren't we always being separated? We are, that's a fact.

Your last letter came tonight—punctually. what a good child you are. the
last news of William is most excellent for Fanny & Harry to take with them
tomorrow. Father will go with them to the steamer.

Charlie is in town tonight at the newsroom.

The children are all well.

Strike a line in everything. I am really too tired to sleep (?) to write more.
The weather is quite cold. . . .

It's a little tough to mind so many children & have not a bit of a girl [to
help]. Yesterday I was forced to go to the door & answer a ring just after
lunch & just as I was trying to dress. The callers turned out to be Annie
Townsend & her friends Mr. & Mrs. Anderson with whom she is staying in
Orange. Mother was busy in the kitchen, Fanny immersed in soapsuds in the
bathroom, her children at her skirts. Lloyd and Phil held on to me tight & let
up a howling at the prospect of my going downstairs without them. In short
it was one of those scenes of distraction of which we had several. It was too
bad that Fanny's short visit found us in such a plight. But on the whole we've
gotten along, & I could, if I would, speak in glowing terms of the behavior of
both our children. The reasonablest little things I ever did see.

Now I must go
Ever your most
loving wife—

As the years passed, however, Lucy's life became a continuous struggle
against illness, her own and the family's. In the spring of 1875 all three of
her children contracted scarlet fever. It seemed, however, to be less viru-
lent than many such attacks, and all three children quickly recovered. The
society's insistence on the primacy of the family was so strong that even
a husband like Wendell, who certainly loved his wife and was anguished
by Lucy's declining health, didn't seem to have considered that it was her
pregnancies that could be causing her condition. For a couple like them
it was unthinkable that they might adopt some measures to prevent the

dangers. What would happen was what was ordained to happen. When Wendell's father sent a sympathetic note following another miscarriage, there was more than a hint that he was as much disappointed in being denied the pleasure of a twelfth grandchild as he was upset about Lucy's condition.[2]

> December 14, 1875
> ... I was particularly grieved to hear of Lucy's miscarriage, not only on her and your account, but because I was joyfully anticipating the speedy comple- tion of a dozen grandchildren, which this untoward event postpones. (Tho' much reason there is for thankfulness that not a vacancy has yet been made in the eleven!) Following the miscarriage comes a serious attack of illness, intensifying our sympathy for dear Lucy, and very tenderly expressing our feelings toward you all; but we were greatly comforted by your letter of yes- terday to your mother, announcing that Lucy has rallied in a very hopeful manner, thus affording reasonable ground for believing that her complete convalescence will not be long deferred.

The news from Ellen was that her fourth child, William Lloyd, had been born the week before, on December 5, providing her father-in-law with the eleventh grandchild. Ellen, who had suffered from severe migraine headaches all through their school years and into her marriage, seemed at least to bear her children without problems—in its way perhaps a kind of compensation for so much pain in her ordinary life. She was one of those women who would be termed by her friends as "fortunate."

Early that same December Wendell returned from his work and found that, as he had long feared, Lucy had suffered a paralytic stroke.[3] When he reached her lying on the floor, hands clenched, she could speak only a few mumbled words, her mouth drawn and one eye fixed in an unmoving stare. After a few days she recovered most of her move- ments, even walking again, though with one leg still stiff. She attempted to rally, and later in December, to lighten the austerities of her family's Christmas she asked her brother-in-law William, Ellen's husband, for a loan of ten dollars, presumably asking that he not tell Wendell, while William told Lucy that she should not thank him but regard it as a gift. William, of course, told his brother, insisting that the ten dollars needn't be repaid, necessitating a letter from Lucy to sort out the cir- cumstances. Her letter attempted to show some of her old high spirits, and it also gave a glimpse into what she now considered as her mini- mum needs in life.[4]

Llewellyn Park, Dec. 31, 1875

My dear brother-in-law, with whom I sympathize in so many ways—dyspepsia, theatre-going, regard for one's own proper share of sleep, fondness for a little pleasant communion over affairs of human interest, admiration of your wife, etc. etc. My regard needed not the stimulation of this filthy lucre. But (the evil one prompts me to say—not Wendell this time) every little bit helps!

Can you forgive that bad joke? I never should have thought of it if I hadn't just written Ellie's name. Poor dear headachy thing! give her half the love I send to you—which is so much it will divide handsomely.

Surely you will say that I have followed your request after all, for of decent thanks I haven't said a word. But I am thankful, dear Billy, with regret that you were so kindly obstinate.

Yours gratefully

Sister Lucy

Though Wendell now realized that Lucy's illness was irreversible, by the late spring she showed some improvement and he could write to his father that Lucy "remains comfortable." She was suffering from fainting spells and a wave of debilitating headaches, and her weakened eyesight made her beloved piano beyond her capabilities. His father answered on June 25, 1876, "May her health be fully recovered soon." There was hope that there had been some change in her condition, and Lucy, Wendell, and the children attempted a two-week summer holiday at Osterville, a beach colony for summer visitors on Cape Cod. The family took two rooms in the cottage William and Ellen rented for the summer months. On August 31 Lucy wrote to the wife of one of Wendell's Harvard classmates with whom they had become friends.[5]

Osterville, Cape Cod

Aug. 31, '76

. . . Perhaps you did not know that I am considered an invalid nowadays? I thought I had about recovered from my light touch of paralysis until the children's scarlet fever came. After the boys were well; and Katherine was recovering, she started a tedious abcess behind her ear, and at that time our second girl came down with the disease. All this used me up very much. I began to be subject to unexpected faints, and it was thought best to put me under a doctor's care. I balanced for some time between the homeopathic & aereopathic, believing nothing in the former, but being afraid of the latter; so I decided on the homeopathic. Since then I have been better and worse. Never ill, never able to do much. Went to bed early, got up late—not allowed to read much, to see people, to do anything, or to think anything if I could help it. I am only lately beginning to write letters and I always make them very short. Strange to say, that fearfully hot weather agreed with me wonderfully. I had been so frozen before. This last week I began to feel the heat very much and hope it is a good sign.

Lucy's condition, instead, became more severe, and she was forced to break off the holiday and return to Llewellyn Park with her children. Wendell's father shared his concern, and he offered to come to New York to help Wendell in the office—taking over some of the onerous work like proofreading, so that Wendell could remain longer at Llewellyn Park, but Wendell assured him that he could manage the work. To compound their anxieties Lucy's mother was stricken with pneumonia in December, but recovered within a few weeks. A few weeks later it was the Garrison household that was struck with tragedy. Helen Garrison, Wendell's mother, who had been lingering for a long period with the effects of a stroke similar to what Lucy had suffered, died on January 25. Her husband was distraught and the sons and daughter struggled to ease their own loss and anxiety.

◆ ◆ ◆

In the hope that Lucy's condition might improve, Wendell made optimistic plans for her to travel to England in the summer of 1877, to accompany his father on a planned return to greet comrades from the days of their fight for emancipation. Lucy would be part of the family party in the hope that the journey and the excitement of the new experiences might bring back her strength. Lucy, however, had misgivings. She wrote to Fanny Garrison on February 18, 1877, protesting that her absence would place too much of a burden on Wendell.[6]

What would mother and Wendell do with our three precious brats? They are nice children, but being entirely natural & not precocious, they will get dirty, quarrel, get into scrapes, burst off their buttons, and need a daily attention that mother's weakened health could not give them, and a nightly and morning and Sunday attention that would give Wendell absolutely no rest.

Ellen wrote to her in the spring in some concern[7]:

April 17, 1877
My dear Luxie—
... I hear on all sides, news of your intended trip to England with our relations-in-law—& I think you must have good courage to attempt it...

Ellen then tried to persuade her instead to come with Wendell and the children to the beach cottage where they had stayed the summer before in Osterville.

> Don't you think it would do you just as much good to go there with us, & occupy that, & bathe daily in the saltsea [*sic*] waves, & inhale the fragrance of those pines, & wander through those fascinating woods. It seems so much nicer, from my point of view, than for you to be so far away among strangers—to say nothing of the horrid misery aboard ship. Wm. would jump for joy, if you and Wendell would smile upon the project—otherwise we shall let the cottage to the hotel, & search around N. H. for an inland place. I would collect all your dear old letters & scraps, & what joy it would be to look them over together.
>
> Write me soon what you think of it.

It would be her last letter to Lucy.

The journey was not to be. Lucy suffered a more severe stroke leaving her paralyzed. On April 29, William Lloyd Garrison, still sorrowing over the death of his wife, Ellen, only four months before, answered the letter with the news from Wendell, recalling with some hope that his wife, Wendell's mother, had lived for many years, after a similar stroke.[8]

> Roxbury, April 29, 1877.
>
> My dear Wendell,
>
> Your letter of yesterday, bringing the sorrowful intelligence of the paralytic stroke which has befallen your beloved Lucy, excited in our hearts the very deepest sympathy for her, for you, for the children, and for dear Mrs. McKim. I grieve in spirit with you, and know from experience how dark and depressing must be the cloud hanging over you. . . . How doubly afflicting it would have been if it had happened on the voyage to England, as it might even before we should have lost sight of land! It is the narrowest of escapes. I had a good deal of solicitude about Lucy going so far from home, on such a stormy sea, without your company, and with no female friend to minister to her necessities in case of any ill turn; yet I was hoping the trip would prove a change for the better in her condition, and so sent you no discouraging word. So let us be thankful, let the result be what it may, that she is at home, where love and affection will bend over her pillow, and all will be done that good nursing and medical skill can do for her restoration. It seemed, at first and for some time, after she was paralyzed, that your mother could hardly survive the terrible shock; yet she

lived more than twelve years after the sad event took place, and though always disabled in the use of her limbs, enjoyed general good health throughout. It may be so with Lucy. True, it is specially afflicting for a comparatively young mother to be crippled for the remainder of her days; but if in all other respects she can be herself again, much comfort remains in store for you all. I know you will exert to bear this dreaded and dreadful blow with fortitude and resignations, prepared for the worst, and hoping for the best. With the last two or three years, events have served to place a staggering load on your shoulders, which now assumes almost crushing dimensions. May you be greatly strengthened by spiritual influences and supernal powers!

In his agitation Garrison tipped his ink well onto the page and two sentences were left unreadable. He continued:

Impress for me a loving kiss upon the cheek of the stricken sufferer; and say to her sorrowing mother that my tears mingle with her own, and the pulsations of my heart beat in unison with hers. I shall wait with anxiety for further intelligence.
　　Your loving Father
Excuse this blotted page. No time to copy.

There was no improvement in Lucy's condition. She was almost entirely paralyzed, she could speak only a few words, her deafness had become worse and her vision was failing. If she lived, how could she think of caring for her children? Of her music, her piano? Her sister-in-law Fanny rushed from Boston to be with her, and to her dismay she saw that Lucy had made her own decision about what her life had become. She would not open her mouth for her mother to feed her. She held her lips closed and stiffly turned her head away when her mother tried to press food into her mouth. She would not weaken in her resolve as the family clustered around her. She could no longer speak. She lapsed into a coma and died on May 11, 1877. She was thirty-four years old.

◆　◆　◆

On May 16 William Lloyd Garrison wrote his son a distracted letter about the forthcoming trip to England, a journey in which Lucy would no longer be included in their plans. His letter ends awkwardly but with the expected assurances of love and sympathy.[9]

Fanny [his daughter] is troubled somewhat with a bronchial infection, the result of a cold which she took while with you in the Park, doing what she could in a sisterly way for the dear one who has been taken from your side, a dear one whose companionship will be missed beyond the power of utterance. I felt comforted to see how resignedly you and her loving mother had met the blow, stunning for a time as it was; and I trust it will cause no permanent depression in either of your minds, remembering that an excess of grief will avail nothing. It requires no stretch of fancy to believe that, though invisible to mortal sight, Lucy will still be with you all with her wifely and motherly love and daughterly affection, held by ties that can never be dissevered, and strengthening you by direct spiritual forces as well as by hallowed remembrance.

Your loving father.

In a society where so many experienced the early death of those close to them, Wendell's father's words were deadeningly familiar, but they would comfort, if only for their familiarity.

The following week the local newspaper gave extensive space to Lucy's funeral, under the heading "Impressive Funeral Service."[10] The opening sentences said little more than the customary announcement of the services; then the article continued, writing of her death:

Her death, on Friday morning last, was a shock to a wide circle of friends, whose attachment to her was very strong, and also awakened the tenderest sympathy for her husband and children, her venerable mother, her absent sister, her brother, and other kindred. She was stricken with paralysis in the midst of preparations for a voyage to the Isle of Wight (Eng.), where she was to spend the coming summer, in the hope of recovering from the effects of a previous illness.

In a letter in July 1862, when she was still only nineteen, Lucy had written to Ellen that "I can't wish to write finis to my history yet . . . There is too much to see, to hear, do & feel first." As the writer of the obituary went on to make clear, Lucy had not finished with her life then, though she had also accepted that "of course the end of the story always is: So they were married & lived peacefully & happily every after." The book of slave songs had been a life's dream for her at that moment, and though a handful of years were to pass, she made the dream into a reality. The writer acknowledged this in his account.

... she grew up in an atmosphere of freedom, and from her earliest childhood sympathized with the unfortunate victims of oppression, counting it an honor to suffer reproach for their sake. After the rebellion broke out and the Union armies had opened a way to the South, she went with her father to the Sea Islands of South Carolina, where she witnessed with youthful delight the joy of the emancipated slaves. Her cultivated musical ear enabled her, upon hearing the negroes sing the wild songs in which they expressed their hope as slaves, to write them down in the proper musical characters, so that they could be sung by others; and upon her return to the North they were printed in a little book which had a wide circulation and awakened a new sympathy for the people emancipated by the war ...

Among those who spoke was the Philadelphia minister who had long been a family friend, Dr. William Furness, who, "by request," read Wordsworth's "Intimations of Immortality from Recollections of Early Childhood," to which the paper gave nearly a column to print in its entirety. Wendell's father followed as one of the speakers.

Mrs. Riley followed this recital from Wordsworth by singing the exquisite solo, "Come, ye disconsolate;" after which Wm. Lloyd Garrison, the venerable father of the bereaved husband spoke a few impressive words, in which he bore fitting testimony to the character of the deceased who instead of realizing her hopes of enjoyment and bodily recuperation from a voyage across the Atlantic to new scenes of earthly beauty and loveliness, had been called to pass through the gate of death to the Summer-Land—a land whose beauties and delights were doubtless far above and beyond all this world affords, or of which our imagination can conceive.

At her burial in nearby Roseland Cemetery the writer noted that it was the day itself that was the most tender offering.

... The day was perfect. The sunshine, the tender grass, the trees in their soft, delicate foliage, the flowers lading the air with their delicate perfume, the songs of the birds, all spoke to the heart more eloquently than any speech that man could frame; and the lesson they breathed was a lesson of divine comfort and immortal hope.

16

Autumn Leaves

The leaves though thick are falling; one by one
Decayed they drop from off their parent tree,
Their work with autumn's latest day is done,
Thou see'st them borne upon its breezes free;
They lie strewn here and there, their many dyes

That yesterday so caught the passing eye;
Soiled by the rain each leaf neglected lies,
Upon the path where now thou hurriest by;
Yet think thee not their beauteous tints less fair

Than when they hung so gaily o'er thy head;
But rather find thee eyes, and look thee there
Where now thy feet so heedless o'er them tread;
And thou shalt see where wasting now they lie,
The unseen hues of immortality.

—Jones Very

For both Wendell and Lucy's mother it was clear that what they had so feared was relentlessly pressing upon them. As they realized that Lucy's death was imminent, her mother took charge of the children, managing the household so that Wendell could continue to attend to his office work at *The Nation*. Sarah McKim was sixty-seven, frail from her own illnesses, and Lucy's children still were young, only ten, seven, and four. Without complaint her mother turned to giving the children what help she could, and the family's life could go on. Many years later, at the moment of Lucy's mother's death, Wendell wrote to a friend who had recently lost someone in his family, recalling the situation he had faced when Lucy died.[1]

Jan 22, 1891

Of you I have learned through my brother Frank, & I believe on occasion of a recent affliction in your family. Well, I too have just passed through one, albeit in the regular order of nature. My wife's mother died on the 9th inst— having nearly completed her 78th year. She was of Quaker origin, a person of singular and moral beauty. She lost her husband, under this roof, in 1874, & in 1877 her daughter died. She at once took charge of my motherless children, continued to direct the house hold, & died of old age when her peculiar services were no longer necessary. As my children are beginning to be dispersed, Mrs. McKim's death threatened the destruction of my family life, but it now appears probable that I shall remain on the spot where nearly half of my life has been spent.

It seems often that when a novel ends, or a play, or a film, with the final pages its story is over. With everyday life, however, there is never any real ending. The lives that were part of the story go on. Wendell's life continued after Lucy's death, and many years later he married his sister-in-law, Lucy's older sister, Annie. She had been widowed early with her three boys and she and Wendell were married only a few weeks before his letter to his friend. Annie stepped into the household and helped fill the house's now emptying rooms with her presence until she too died only two years later.

Wendell's and Lucy's son Lloyd followed his father to Harvard, where he became popular for his verses, many of them humorous, describing life at the university. Following their graduation in 1888 his classmates arranged for a privately printed collection of the poems, which appeared as a handsomely bound volume titled *Ballads of Harvard and other Verses* in 1891. Following his unexpected death at the age of thirty-two in 1900, his friends and classmates honored his memory by establishing the Lloyd McKim Garrison Poetry Prize which is still awarded annually for the best poem submitted by a student of Harvard or Radcliffe College. Wendell eventually left Llewellyn Park, but continued to work at *The Nation* until his death in 1906. He was widely admired for his long service with the magazine, for his encouragement to his writers, and for his warmth and sympathy to his children.

Ellen's life also continued, though Lucy would never be entirely lost from her thoughts. She gave birth to her fifth child, a daughter, Eleanor, in 1880, three years after Lucy's death. She now had taken on a more public role as an outspoken advocate of women's rights, and in 1900, when she was sixty, she was made a member of the National American Woman Suffrage Association, with her membership card signed by Elizabeth Cady

Stanton, Susan B. Anthony, and Harriet Taylor Upton. Her daughter Eleanor continued to agitate for her mother's causes, and there is a classic
photo of Eleanor standing with Lucretia Mott's granddaughter Isabella
Mott, both of them wearing their suffragette sashes. Eleanor never married. She was at first enlisted for the Woman Suffrage Association as a
speaker, but her arguments were considered too radical and emotional
and she was finally employed instead as a full-time organizer. Ellen's husband, William, died in 1909. In 1925 when Ellen was in her mid-eighties
she inquired of people who had been associated with Eagleswood School
about whether someone could be encouraged to write the history of the
school. She died in 1931 at the age of ninety-one.

Lucy's young brother, Charlie, soon left the New York architectural
firm where he was employed as a draftsman. The casino that he had sent
as sketches to Lucy was built in Newport, Rhode Island, where it was
widely admired, and it led to a series of commissions for vacation homes
for wealthy New Yorkers who summered in Newport. Charlie opened his
own office in partnership with an engineer named William Mead, and
in 1879, another architect named Stanford White joined them as a third
partner. Lucy's brother, now generally known as Charles Follen McKim,
went on to become America's most distinguished architect. While Stanford White devoted much of his time to the design of leisure estates for
the wealthy, many built on Long Island, McKim, as the acknowledged
leader of the American Beaux Arts school of architecture, designed some
of America's most noted buildings. Among his achievements were the
north and south wings of the Metropolitan Museum of Art, the library
on the Morningside Heights campus of Columbia University, the Pier-
pont Morgan Library in New York, the Boston Public Library, and the
American Academy in Rome.

McKim's most celebrated achievement was the soaring Pennsylvania
Station in New York City, with its magnificent vaulted ceilings inspired,
as he said, by the Caracalla Baths of ancient Rome. It was one of the most
photographed architectural sites of the city, and was the inspiration for
innumerable artists as the subject for sketches and paintings. In the wave
of rebuilding that followed the Second World War the station was demolished and replaced with a modern structure which is one of the most
conspicuous disasters among the jumble of new buildings crowding the
streets of today's New York. He was awarded gold medals by the French
government for his work on the Paris Exhibition of 1900 and by the British government for restoration projects in the United States. There were
honorary doctorates and degrees from many universities, among them

Harvard and the University of Pennsylvania, and he spent considerable time abroad as head of international architectural groups.

Despite his success, McKim's personal life was deeply unhappy, an unhappiness compounded by the murder of his partner Stanford White by a jealous husband in 1906. In 1874, while Lucy still was living, McKim married Annie Bigelow of New York in a Newport ceremony, and the next year a daughter was born. Only four years later they were granted a divorce, after McKim had testified to "evil influences." His wife remarried and moved abroad and it would be seventeen years before McKim would see his daughter again. He died on Long Island in 1909.

Wendell's father, William Lloyd Garrison, continued to write and to agitate for social betterment, giving his attention to the issues of temperance and women's suffrage. He died in Roxbury in 1879. Lucretia Mott's husband, James, died in Philadelphia in 1868, but she continued their crusade for the rights of freedmen and for women's suffrage. Following the Civil War she was chosen as president of the American Equal Rights Association and continued to agitate for a more humane and just society until her death in 1880 at the age of eighty-seven.

In September 1869, several years after their first exchange of letters, an unknown poet named Emily Dickinson wrote to Thomas Wentworth Higginson, who had responded to poems she sent him. "Of our greatest acts we are ignorant. You were not aware that you saved my life."[2] Although in the decades following the Civil War he was one of the preeminent literary figures in the United States, as well as an active member of the American Equal Rights Association with Lucretia Mott, he is usually remembered today for his role in the discovery and encouragement of Emily Dickinson. After years of correspondence they finally met when Higginson visited her in her family's home in Amherst, Massachusetts, in 1870, a meeting which he would later describe in an unforgettable portrayal of the poet in the afternoon hours as they talked.

Following Dickinson's death in 1886 and the discovery of more than seventeen hundred poems, all but a handful unpublished, in a wooden chest at the foot of her bed, Higginson was asked to assist in editing a volume for publication. There is controversy today at the extent of his editorial revisions, but Higginson was seeking readers for her work, and the volume he helped edit marked the beginning of the discovery of her poetry. The first collection was published in 1891 and Higginson helped to introduce it with his article recounting the story of his visit with her, "Emily Dickinson's Letters," which he published in the *Atlantic Monthly*.[3] There were ten reprintings of the small gathering of the poems in the first year after its publication. Higginson died in 1911 at the age of eighty-eight, and his life and his achievement have been the subject of many articles and biographical studies.

Lucy's collaborators on their collection of slave songs, William Allen and Charles Ware, also went on with their lives. Allen remained at the University of Wisconsin until his death in 1889, at the age of fifty-nine. With his older brother John and an associate, James Bradstreet Greenough, they produced a series of translations and texts in Latin studies as the Allen & Greenough Series, which sold widely. He was also highly regarded for his insights into the teaching of history, which prefigured many of the changes in historical studies in the next decades. Ware left St. Helena in 1872 and returned to his home in Brookline, a neighborhood now included in greater Boston. Soon after Alexander Graham Bell founded the Bell Telephone Company in 1875, Ware joined the new firm, becoming a vice president of the Brookline office. He was eighty-one at the time of his death at his home in 1921.

The two women who had founded the Penn School, Laura Towne and Ellen Murray, remained on the island together, teaching and operating the school for nearly forty years. They adopted several African American children and brought them up as their own. Towne had founded the school with money from her family and she had worked without payment, preferring to live on her small income. At her death in 1901 she willed the school as a gift to the Hampton Institute in Virginia, which, like Penn School, had taken on the responsibility of instructing freed men and women in those same early years. Charlotte Forten, who had joined them a few months after the school was established and remained for almost two years until illness compelled her to leave, lived for some time in Boston before moving to Washington. There in 1878, at the age of forty-one, she married Reverend Francis Grimke, the nephew of Sarah and Angelina Grimke, assisting him in his ministry and organizing a Woman's Missionary Society in their church. She was seventy-seven at her death in 1914.

On October 29, 1885, Wendell sent a packet of materials with a letter to William Harris, the new head librarian at Cornell University in Ithaca, New York. Harris was collecting material for an archive documenting the freeing of the slaves and the emergence of the freedmen in the Reconstruction era.[4]

Dear Mr. Harris:

The enclosed letters were part of the correspondence attending the publication of the "Slave Songs of the United States," in which my wife had a share.

I am loth to destroy them, and they might deserve a place in your freedmen's collection. Some of the writers are eminent—Gens. Seymour and Savage, Kane O'Donnel, the journalist, James Schuler, the historian, one, Miss Laura Towne was and is among the *foremost* teachers on the Sea Islands.

But use your own discretion, & consign it to the waste-basket if you judge best. No acknowledgement is necessary.

Very truly yours,

W. P. Garrison

As Wendell certainly intended, the letters were not thrown away. Harris attached them inside the cover of the library's copy of *Slave Songs of the United States*, and they have continued to be part of the archive at Cornell University.

Slave Songs of the United States was virtually forgotten for many years after its publication. In W. E. B. Du Bois's acknowledgment of Lucy's place as one who had "urged upon the world the rare beauty" of these songs[5] he referred to her as "Miss McKim," as her name had appeared on the first two songs she arranged and published in 1862. On the title page of the book her name appears as Lucy McKim Garrison. Du Bois seems to have been familiar only with those first songs, and the editors of the early collections of slave spirituals published by the various jubilee choirs also may have been unaware of the book's existence. It was not until the 1920s, in the surprised discovery by mainstream American publishers of the power and the achievement of the new African American writing and music associated with the Harlem Renaissance, that the book would have a modern printing. This third edition appeared in 1929 as a facsimile of the original text. By the 1950s, with the growing interest in the folk sources of jazz, as well as the spiritual, the book became more widely known. It has remained continuously in print since that time. One publisher, in an effort to popularize the book, printed an edition with the songs arranged for singing with guitar accompaniment. The uniqueness and the immeasurable value of what Lucy and her two co-workers achieved is now recognized and it is to be hoped that in the future there will be a wider understanding of the achievement of the book.

As to the songs themselves, the great body of slave spirituals that Lucy McKim Garrison dedicated a part of her life to preserve have become so woven into the American spirit that sometimes they seem to be taken for granted. They will, however, continue to be heard and to be sung, with new audiences moved and inspired by the glory of their music and the wrenching sorrow of their human story. The songs have become as well known

and loved throughout the world as they are to audiences in the United
States. In the rich texture of African American music their "rare beauty"
will never be lost, and their message will continue for untold decades to
nourish all that follows after them.

APPENDIX A

Slave Songs of the United States

A Description and Commentary

When *Slave Songs of the United States* was published in late November 1867 it was not only the first book devoted to slave music to appear in the United States; it was the first book to take African American culture as its subject. There was not a strong response in the nation's press. The most lengthy review appeared in *The Nation*. As Wendell wrote his father on November 30, it was "patchwork" that he and Lucy had pieced together, and Lucy wrote a review of her own for the *Independent*.

Slave Songs of the United States is a small volume. Its 38-page introduction, its 136 songs, the list of the songs, the "Directions for Singing," and an "Editor's Note," fill only 159 pages. It is an attractive volume, simply bound, with gold stamping on the spine and the front of the light tan cloth cover. It contains almost all of the songs that the editors had managed to gather that had both words and melodies. Many of the people who had been interested enough to collect songs hadn't the musical training to notate the melodies, and the editors were often frustrated in their efforts to find a version with a melody to some songs. Also they found that many of the songs they received were duplicated, since much of the material came from the southeastern states and the Sea Islands. Although the total number of songs in the book is small, they have been carefully documented, and arranged systematically. They are separated into four geographical areas:

Part I. South-Eastern Slave States, including South Carolina, Georgia and the Sea Islands
Part II. Northern Sea-board Slave States, including Delaware, Maryland, Virginia, and North Carolina
Part III. Inland Slave States, including Tennessee, Arkansas, and the Mississippi River
Part IV. Gulf States, including Florida and Louisiana: Miscellaneous

Part IV includes among the miscellaneous songs further examples from Port Royal, Georgia, Maryland, and North Carolina. In his "Editor's Note" Wendell acknowledged the irregularities in the presentation and the lack of conformity in the collection's geographical divisions, but offers as explanation:

... That the division into parts is not strictly geographical was caused by the tardy arrival of most of the songs contained in Part IV. Should a second edition ever be justified by the favor with which the present is received, these irregularities will be corrected.

In his article on slave spirituals that had appeared in *Atlantic Monthly* a few months before, Thomas Wentworth Higginson had begun by noting the similarity between the appearance of the Scottish border ballads in the work of Sir Walter Scott and his own experience of the slave songs of South Carolina. Wendell acknowledged Higginson's assistance in his introduction.

Through him we have profited by the cheerful assistance of Mrs. Charles J. Bowen, Lieut.-Colonel C. T. Trowbridge, Capt. James S. Rogers, Rev. Horace James, Capt. Geo. S. Barton, Miss Lucy Gibbons, Mr. William A. Baker, Mr. T. E. Ruggles, and Mr. James Schouler. Our thanks are also due for contributions, of which we have availed ourselves, to Dr. William A. Hammond, Mr. Kane O'Donnel, Mr. E. J. Snow, Miss Charlotte L. Forten, Miss Laura M. Towne, and Miss Ellen Murray.

Wendell then went on to name nineteen others who had either contributed advice or unused material. It was, if not a Gideon's army, at least a Gideon's band.

The greatest number of contributions came from the editors themselves. Only four of Lucy's transcriptions were included, but Ware contributed fifty-three songs and Allen thirty-four. Many of the songs were evanescent, forgotten soon after they were copied down by their listener, but others—in the pages of a book for the first time—are among the classic spirituals that have been heard and sung in innumerable new versions and arrangements since their discovery.

Only a handful of books presenting songs or ballads from the folk tradition had appeared earlier in England and America, which meant that the editors of *Slave Songs* had few models for their volume. The three partners, however, understood the most important elements that had to be present for the book to be of use to anyone seriously interested in the slaves' musical expression. As folklorist and blues historian David Evans has commented, "It was also, I believe, the first book-length collection of American folksongs of any kind, using remarkably good collecting and reporting methods for the time."[1]

In the list of the book's contents the collector of each song is named, with the place that the song was heard. Since the collectors had heard the songs for themselves and none of them had conceived of a plan to perform or to introduce the songs to a popular audience, there was no attempt to harmonize the songs. The songs were sung without harmony on St. Helena Island and the three editors never suggested that they heard the songs sung in harmony. Other visitors to the South who described slave songs also noted that the singing by groups was in unison. The collection opens with both Charles Ware's and Lucy McKim's transcription of "Roll, Jordan, Roll," but her arrangement for voice and piano is not included. The same decision was made for her "Poor Rosy."

◆ ◆ ◆

It was this conscious decision to document the songs as they were found that gives their small volume its importance today. *Slave Songs of the United States* was not only the first collection of slave songs; it was the only one to present them as an integral element of the slave culture. Later, following the enormous success in the early 1870s of the Fisk Jubilee Singers and other groups inspired by their example, there was a steady stream of songbooks presenting "jubilee songs" or "plantation melodies," as the spirituals were generally called. When the first pamphlet of the Fisk songs appeared in the summer of 1872, only five years after the appearance of *Slave Songs*, virtually all of the songs were heavily arranged to suit the musical tastes of their new audiences. The melodies were harmonized for vocal quartet singing, one of the most popular entertainments during those decades. Without exception all of the spiritual collections that followed—the almost yearly new editions of the Fisk songs, as well as the song collections of the Hampton Institute Singers, among many others, the first in 1875—continued this recasting of "plantation melodies" for vocal quartet, and similar publications followed this pattern.

Occasional songs were arranged for voice with accompaniment as Lucy McKim had done with her two songs in 1862, but it was some years before the solo arrangements of the spirituals overtook the quartet arrangements in popularity. It was the publication of the spiritual arrangements by African American composer H. T. Burleigh, first appearing in 1916 and 1917, that led to the acceptance of the spirituals in the concert repertoire. In 1925 the very successful collection *The Book of American Negro Spirituals* appeared, with a valuable introductory text by James Weldon Johnson and sensitive arrangements by J. Rosamond Johnson, and in 1937 the arrangements by the best-known African American composer William Grant Still were published by the well-known blues composer and music publisher W. C. Handy as *Twelve Negro Spirituals*. For each of these collections the music was presented for solo voice with piano accompaniment.

It is an interesting connection that a major gathering of Sea Island spirituals published in 1942, *Slave Songs of the Georgia Sea Islands* by Lydia Parrish, was collected on the islands only an easy day's drive south of St. Helena, where much of the *Slave Songs* material was collected, and that Mrs. Parrish also was from the Quaker community in Philadelphia that had sent Lucy, Laura Towne, Ellen Murray, and Charlotte Forten to the island.

◆ ◆ ◆

The lengthy introduction to *Slave Songs* in 1867 was signed by all three of the people involved, Allen, Ware, and Lucy McKim Garrison. However, the thirty-six pages that form the material itself was signed with the initials W. F. A., and it is clear that it was Allen who wrote it, though the others certainly read it and perhaps made suggestions themselves. Allen included passages from Higginson's article in the *Atlantic Monthly* as well as Lucy's pioneering description of slave songs that appeared in *Dwight's Journal* in

1862. It is a useful document, and it makes clear what lay behind their concern to preserve the songs, as well as the difficulties in transcribing what they were hearing. Allen quoted from a number of sources, including the letter received from Lucy's uncle John McKim, whose admonition that the purest "negro" songs he heard were the work chants he heard along the docks, which he described to Lucy when he wrote her in the spring. Allen's own experience gave him insights into the song processes that were unique for their time. His understanding of the transient nature of the songs and their familiarity among different groups of singers could only have been possible by someone like himself or Charles Ware, who had spent considerable time in one place. Allen wrote:

> The wealth of material still awaiting the collector can be guessed from a glance at the localities of those we have, and from the fact . . . that of the first forty-three of the collection most were sung on a single plantation, and that it is very certain that the store of this plantation were by no means exhausted. Of course there was constant intercourse between neighboring plantations; also between different States, by the sale of slaves from one to another. But it is surprising how little this seems to have affected local songs, which are different even upon adjoining plantations. The favorite of them all, "Roll, Jordan" (No. 1), is sung in Florida, but not, I believe in North Carolina.

With Ware at Coffin Point, working on the plantation adjoining the Fripp plantation where Allen and his wife were conducting their school, there was the opportunity for the two men to compare the songs they were hearing. Allen commented on what he felt was the slowness of songs to travel:

> As illustrations of the slowness with which these songs travel, it may be mentioned that the "Graveyard" (No. 21), which was frequently sung on Capt. Fripp's plantation in the winter of 1863–4, did not reach Coffin Point (five miles distant) until the following spring. I heard it myself at Pine Grove, two miles from the latter place, in March. Somewhere upon this journey this tune was strikingly altered . . .

Allen also noted that it had already become difficult to find new songs. He found that the plantation singers were adopting the practice of the white churches known as "deaconing," in which two lines of a hymn were recited, and then the same lines were sung slowly. Nowhere did any of those collecting the songs find any examples of "part-singing," and this was another of the reasons that they printed only the melody of the songs in the collection.

◆ ◆ ◆

The songs were presented with as much information as the editors had been able to gather about their sources, often with variant melodies or texts. It is this effort to place the songs geographically and to include some hint of the people who sang them that gives their modest collection its much broader significance. An example is No. 74, "Nobody

Knows the Trouble I've Had," which William Allen had collected in Charleston, where
he'd been teaching in the last year of the Civil War. He was aware that the song was also
sung as "Nobody Knows the Trouble I See"—as it is performed today—and he added this
as an alternative version of the first line with an asterisk. A verse was taken from another
source, which Allen acknowledged, and he identified the source. He also noted that an
alternate melody for four bars of the notation was sung on St. Helena Island. His note
appended to the song was in itself sufficient to give the song a specific identity within the
rich gathering of so much other diverse music:

> This song was a favorite in the colored schools of Charleston in 1865; it has since that
> time spread to the Sea Islands, where it is now sung with the variation noted above.
> An independent transcription of this melody sent from Florida by Lt. Col. Apthorp
> differed only in . . . certain measures, as has also been noted above.

Allen continued his note to relate an anecdote about the song that describes more
fully its meaning for the singers in their daily lives, and the anecdote itself was repeated
by other writers later, among them W. E. B. Du Bois in his *The Souls of Black Folk*. The
General Howard named by Allen was the commanding officer of the Union Forces stationed in Beaufort and the coastal islands.

> Once when there had been a good deal of ill-will excited, and trouble was appre-
> hended, owing to the uncertain action of the Government in regard to the confiscated
> lands on the Sea Islands, Gen. Howard addressed the colored people earnestly and
> even severely. Sympathizing with them, however, he could not speak to his own satis-
> faction; and to relieve their minds of the ever-present sense of injustice, and prepare
> them to listen, he asked them to sing. Immediately an old woman on the outskirts
> of the meeting began "Nobody knows the trouble I've had," and the whole audience
> joined in. The General was so affected by the plaintive words and melody, that he
> found himself melting into tears and quite unable to maintain his official sternness.

The notes appended to the songs, like this example, often gave as vivid a sense of
the immediacy and vitality of the songs. Some of the readers of the book probably also
would have been aware that because of the protests and the determined opposition by
the teachers and supervisors active on St. Helena to plans to delay a promised sale of the
confiscated lands to the freed slaves, the government had reconsidered its position, and
substantial areas on the island were ultimately sold to the freedmen.

◆ ◆ ◆

There has never been any question that music and song were among the most important
expressions of the slaves' culture, most significantly in the songs of worship and praise,
but also in the secular melodies of the dance and the work song chants. In her study of
the early years of the Port Royal experiment[2] Willie Lee Rose wrote:

Even while they pondered the "extravagant" practices in Negro worship, the Gide-
onites (the name the soldiers gave to the teachers and missionaries on St. Helena)
understood that religion was the central fact in the lives of most of the colored people.
"Not only their soul, but their mind finds here," wrote young Gannet [a visitor to the
island], "its principle exercise, and in a great measure it takes the place of social entertainments and amusements." When Gannet asked the Negroes for their scriptural
authority for the "shout," they replied plausibly that "the angels shout in heaven!" There
was nothing whimsical about such justifications, for all the Sea Island slave songs
reveal a conception of a heaven as tangible as the next plantation and as desirable as
freedom. . . . Composed in infinite variety and freely improvised upon, the religious
songs of the slaves were a fine creative expression, an art requiring no expenditure of
two items the slaves could not call his own, time and money. Songs were also infinitely
portable. Rowing, hoeing cotton, grinding corn, or at prayer, the Negroes sang of the
heavenly home and of their Savior, who was as real as their master, and more kind.

In his introductory discussion of some of the difficulties the people working on the
island faced in collecting the songs, William Allen also mentioned the infinite variety and
the continual rephrasing of any melody and verses:

The difficulty experienced in attaining absolute correctness is greater than might be
supposed by those who have never tried the experiment, and we are far from claiming
that we have made no mistakes. I have never felt quite sure of my notation without a
fresh comparison with the singing, and have then often found that I had made serious
errors. I feel confident, however, that there are no mistakes of importance. What may
appear to some to be an incorrect rendering, is very likely to be a variation; for these
variations are endless, and very entertaining and instructive.

Allen also included in his introduction a summary of the comprehensive notes he had
been making in his island letters and journals on the speech of the St. Helena slaves. As he
noted in his introduction:

A stranger, upon first hearing these people talk, especially if there is a group of them
in animated conversation, can hardly understand them better than if they spoke a foreign language, and might, indeed, easily suppose this to be the case. The strange words
and pronunciations, and frequent abbreviations, disguise the familiar features of one's
native tongue, while the rhythmical modulations, so characteristic of certain European languages, give it an utterly un-English sound. After six months residence among
them, there were scholars in my school, among the most constant in attendance,
whom I could not understand at all, unless they happened to speak very slowly.

Allen followed this paragraph with a twelve-page discussion that represented an invaluable introduction to the island's slave "creole" speech.
Wendell concluded the volume with an editor's note, encouraging the public's
response and support in the event that there should be a second edition. He also cited

the failure to separate the handful of secular songs from the religious songs as further justification for another edition. Since the editors had been told of other well-liked songs that others had heard and asked to be included, Wendell could only hope that a second edition would make these additions possible:

> These certainly are songs to be desired and regretted. But we do not despair of recovering them and others perhaps equally characteristic for a second edition: and we herewith solicit the kind offices of collectors into whose hands this volume may have fallen, in extending and perfecting our researches. For fully a third of the songs recorded by Colonel Higginson we have failed to obtain the music, and they may very well serve as a guide for future investigations. We shall also gratefully acknowledge any errors of fact or of typography that may be brought to our attention, and in general anything that would enhance the value or the interest of this collection. Communications may be addressed to Mr. W. P. Garrison, Office of *The Nation* newspaper, New York City.

For someone turning to the musical examples of the book today, there will probably be difficulties with the notation of many of the songs. With the easy availability of sound recordings in recent decades, these melodies on the printed page may present considerable obstacles, but they are the earliest examples that have come down to us of slave songs at just the moment they were first heard by serious listeners; so it is crucial to make the effort. It is of considerable help to become familiar with the two arrangements that Lucy McKim made from her St. Helena notations, since they make it possible to *hear* the melodies with some sense of the ambiguity of what she has written as major and minor modes. In the introduction to the book and in Ware's letters to Allen, as well as Lucy's article in *Dwight's Journal*, the editors ruefully admit the near impossibility of capturing the elusive turns and phrases of the singing. Their admonitions can serve as a guide to hearing what the notation is attempting to indicate.

It is best to approach the songs in the book with the sense of *interpreting* them, rather than *reading* them as notes on the diatonic scale. Intervals of a third will generally be altered, as will the sixth and seventh tones of the scale. The octaves generally will hold, as well as intervals of a fifth. The singers themselves were not hearing the intervals of the European scale as they sang, but the familiar tonic and dominant tones remain the most constant elements of their own scale. The rhythms of individual notes also should be sung freely, especially since, as Allen noted, when he tried to have a song repeated he usually was sung a melody that was different from what he had already notated. It is the flow of the texts over the bar-lines that gives life to the verses themselves.

The texts of the songs give such a useful insight into the emotions and the attitudes of the slave singers that they may be studied without reference to the melodies. Any discussion of the texts will also have to consider the questions that have been raised from the first encounters of slave songs—how much of the texts and melodies are original and how many have been adapted from European sources. None of the melodies in the book can be said to have purely African origins, but all of them have elements that set them apart from the widespread religious songs of the white churches that have been identified as a source of many of the slave melodies and verses. It is also useful to remember that though there were a number of people who annotated the examples in the book, the general forms of their melodies show so many similarities that it is obvious that slave songs had their own distinctive character, whatever the origins of the original songs they had heard. Certainly the audiences of their own times heard them as different—and in an era of almost universal church-going these listeners certainly were familiar with the common liturgical materials.

In these texts, unlike much of the standard hymnology, the voice that is singing is intensely personal. The singers express their suffering or their hopes with an immediacy that is often harsh and painful. It is this individual testimony that gives the spirituals their power. A spiritual like the well-known No. 64, "Many Thousand Go," springs directly from the experience of slavery, whoever might have been the first person to sing it.

> No more hundred lash for me,
> No more, no more;
> No more hundred lash for me,
> Many tousand go.

It is perhaps most helpful to consider that the musical expression of the slaves was an adaptation of music around them, but that the nature of the adaptations is so consistent and so distinctive in its musical elements that it should be recognized as a distinct musical tradition. Some of the melodies the editors of *Slave Songs* notated share a similar outline with clearly African-derived chants, but each of the examples ends with a tonic cadence, which clearly show a degree of acculturation. The slave culture at this point had developed in the North American colonies for more than two hundred years, and even if new arrivals had been brought onto the plantations, they were quickly absorbed into a slave culture that had already developed its own habits of speech as well as its religious convictions.

◆ ◆ ◆

A short introduction to the book by noted folklorist Harold Courlander is included in several current editions, and it recognizes the difficulties of the transcriptions. Courlander's studies of African American music, first in Haiti and then later in Alabama, with his own song notations, are essential to our understanding of the development of vernacular African American music in the 1930s and 1940s, the time when he did much of his field work. He wrote:

> The notations in the book, and of course the words, were set down mouth-to-ear by hand, the only way then known. Allen, Ware and Garrison put down what they heard or seemed to hear, usually trying to fit the rhythms into our established measures, frequently ignoring those purposive (not accidental) tones that were higher or lower than our usual scales allowed. In their earnest efforts to get everything "right," they

often had a singer repeat a song, only to find that a second singing was a little different. It was the beginning of an understanding that the tradition allowed the singer
to perform a piece a little differently if he wished. The small improvisations here and
there might even enhance group singing. Melodies, as well as timing, were not set in
stone. . . .

Some of the pieces in *Slave Songs of the United States* did not come directly from
mouth-to-ear, however. They might have been memorized by one enthusiast and re-
sung for another. The authors were aware of, and apologized for, possible inaccuracies
during the process. They need not have done so, however, for the overall collection
opened the gates for a long line of investigators who followed over a period of more
than a century, producing an abundant treasury of what this writer, at least, regards
as probably the largest and richest single body of so-called "folk-music" in the United
States.[3]

Anyone who spends any time with *Slave Songs of the United States* will quickly realize
that it is, as its title suggests, a world of song. There are songs from virtually every area
of slave life, and in them there are several strains of tradition and age evident. Two corn
songs, No. 86, "Shock Along, John" and No. 87, "Round the Corn, Sally," the second collected by William Allen, come from Maryland and Virginia, and their sound is chant-like,
suggesting African origins, hinting that they might be older songs that had been handed
down by aural tradition among the slaves themselves in these long-established rural
areas. In others, like No. 11, "There's a Meeting Here, Tonight," in two versions collected in
the Port Royal Islands by Mrs. Charles J. Bowen and Charles Ware, there is clearly a newer
harmonic sophistication. In No. 12, "Hold Your Light," collected by Ware on St. Helena,
the responding voices of the typical call and response of a congregation are sketched in.
Some of the songs seemed to be sung freely: others, like the great spiritual "Rock My Soul
in the Bosom of Abraham"—No. 94, titled here "Rock o' My Soul," collected by William
Allen in Virginia—move with the resistless energy of the earth's turning.

The songs gathered in the book also suggest some of the social complexity of the
southern states, the examples concluding with a lately arrived collection of seven songs
from the French-speaking areas of Louisiana. The collector is identified in the note
accompanying the songs only as "a lady who heard them sung before the war on the
'Good Hope' plantation, St. Charles Parish, Louisiana." Among these examples is one of
the classics of today's Cajun and zydeco musical traditions, No. 134, "Calinda" with its
classic chorus "Dansé, calinda . . ."

Since its rediscovery in the 1920s, *Slave Songs of the United States* has continued to add
an invaluable dimension to our understanding of the roots of African American music.
The book is a freely flowing, irreplaceable spring from which so much has already been
drawn. What is clear today is that its pages still have more to teach us.

Selected Songs

SLAVE SONGS OF THE UNITED STATES.

I.

1.   **ROLL, JORDAN, ROLL.**

1. My brudder* sit-tin' on de tree of life, An' he yearde when Jor-dan roll; Roll, Jor-dan, Roll, Jor-dan, Roll, Jor-dan, roll! O march de an - gel march, O march de an - gel march; O my soul a - rise in Heaven, Lord, For to yearde when Jor-dan roll.

2 Little chil'en, learn to fear de Lord,
    And let your days be long;
      Roll, Jordan, &c.

3 O, let no false nor spiteful word
    Be found upon your tongue;
      Roll, Jordan, &c.

* Parson Fuller, Deacon Henshaw, Brudder Mosey, Massa Linkum, &c.

[This spiritual probably extends from South Carolina to Florida, and is one
of the best known and noblest of the songs.]

11. THERE'S A MEETING HERE TO-NIGHT.

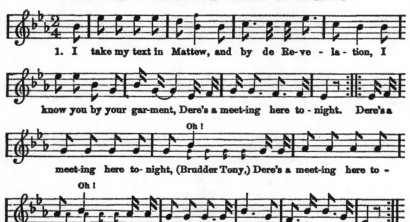

1. I take my text in Mattew, and by de Re-ve - la - tion, I
know you by your gar-ment, Dere's a meet-ing here to - night.   Dere's a
Oh!
meet-ing here to- night, (Brudder Tony,) Dere's a meet-ing here to -
Oh!
- night, (Sister Rina,) Dere's a meeting here to-night, I hope to meet a - gain.

2 Brudder John was a writer, he write de laws of God;
Sister Mary say to brudder John, "Brudder John, don't write no more."
   Dere's a meeting here to-night, Oh! (Brudder Sandy,) (*bis*)
   Dere's a meeting here to-night,
   I hope to meet again.

[Mrs. Bowen gives us the following beautiful variation, as sung in Charleston:]

I see brudder Mo-ses yon-der, And I think I ought to
know him, For I know him by his gar-ment, He's a blessing here to -
- night; He's a bless-ing here   to- night, He's a bless-ing here to -
- night, And I think I ought to know him, He's a bless-ing here to - night.

28.   **JINE 'EM.**

On Sunday mornin' I seek my Lord; Jine 'em, jine 'em oh!   Oh

jine 'em, be - lie - ver, jine 'em so;   Jine 'em, jine 'em oh!

[For other words see "Heaven bell a-ring," No. 27. The following were sung at Hilton Head, probably to the same tune:

> Join, brethren, join us O,
> Join us, join us O.
> We meet to-night to sing ann pray;
> In Jesus' name we'll sing and pray.

A favorite rowing tune: apparently a variation of "Turn sinner," No. 48.]

29.   **RAIN FALL AND WET BECCA LAWTON.**

Rain fall and wet * Becca Lawton, † Oh.......   Rain fall and

wet Bec - ca Law - ton,   Oh!   Brudder ‡ cry   ho - ly!

1. Been § back ho - ly, I must come slow - ly; Oh! Brudder cry   ho - ly!

2 Do, Becca Lawton, come to me yonder.

3 Say, brudder Tony, what shall I do now?

4 Beat back hely, and rock salvation.

* Sun come and dry.   † All de member, &c.   ‡ We all, Believer, &c.   § Beat, Bent, Rack.

["Who," says Col. Higginson, "*Becky Martin* was, and why she should or should not be wet, and whether the dryness was a reward or a penalty, none could say. I got the impression that, in either case, the event was posthumous, and that there was some tradition of grass not growing over the grave of a sinner; but even this was vague, and all else vaguer."

Lt. Col. Trowbridge heard a story that "*Peggy Norton* was an old prophetess, who said that it would not do to be baptized except when it rained; if the Lord

39

50.   **JOIN THE ANGEL BAND.**

1. If you look up de road you see fa-der Mose-y,

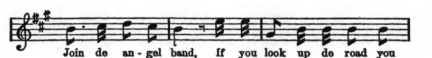

Join de an-gel band, If you look up de road you

see fa-der Mose-y, Join de an-gel band.

2 Do, fader Mosey, gader your army.

3 O do mo' soul gader togeder.

4 O do join 'em, join 'em for Jesus.

5 O do join 'em, join 'em archangel.

The following variation of the first line, with the words that follow, was sung in Charleston :

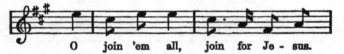

O join 'em all, join for Je - sus.

O join 'em all, join for Jesus, Join Jerusalem Band.

Sister Mary, stan' up for Jesus.

Sixteen souls set out for Heaven.

O brudder an' sister, come up for Heaven.

Daddy Peter set out for Jesus.

Ole Maum Nancy set out for Heaven.

[" The South Carolina negroes never say Aunty and Uncle to old persons, but Daddy and Maumer, and all the white people say Daddy and Maumer to old black men and women "—A. M. B.

This is no doubt correct as regards South Carolina in general. I am sure that I heard " Uncle " and " Aunty " at Port Royal, and I do not remember hearing " Daddy " and " Maumer."—W. F. A.]

41

52. SHALL I DIE?

1. Be - liev - er, O shall I die? O my ar - my, shall I die?

2. Je - sus die, shall I die? Die on the cross, shall I die?

3 Die, die, die, shall I die?
Jesus da coming, shall I die?

4 Run for to meet him, shall I die?
Weep like a weeper, shall I die?

5 Mourn like a mourner, shall I die?
Cry like a crier, shall I die?

[This shout was a great favorite on the Capt. John Fripp plantation; its simplicity, wildness and minor character suggest a native African origin. Sometimes the leading singer would simply repeat the words, mournfully: "Die, die, die,"—sometimes he would interpolate such an inappropriate line as "Jump along, jump along dere."]

53. WHEN WE DO MEET AGAIN.

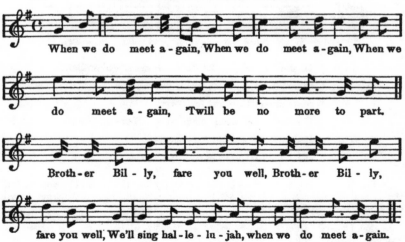

When we do meet a - gain, When we do meet a - gain, When we

do meet a - gain, 'Twill be no more to part.

Broth - er Bil - ly, fare you well, Broth - er Bil - ly,

fare you well, We'll sing hal - le - lu - jah, when we do meet a - gain.

55

74. NOBODY KNOWS THE TROUBLE I'VE HAD.

No-bod-y knows de trouble I've had,* No-bod-y knows but

Je-sus, No-bod-y knows de trouble I've had, (Sing)

Glo-ry hal-le-lu! 1. One morning I was a-walking down,

O yes, Lord! I saw some ber-ries a-hanging down,

Variation on St. Helena Id.

O yes, Lord! O yes, Lord! I saw some berries hanging down.

2 I pick de berry and I suck de juice, O yes, Lord!
Just as sweet as the honey in de comb, O yes, Lord!

3 Sometimes I'm up, sometimes I'm down,
Sometimes I'm almost on de groun'.

4 What make ole Satan hate me so?
Because he got me once and he let me go.

* I see.

[This song was a favorite in the colored schools of Charleston in 1865; it has since that time spread to the Sea Islands, where it is now sung with the variation noted above. An independent transcription of this melody, sent from Florida by Lt. Col. Apthorp, differed only in the ictus of certain measures, as has also been noted above. The third verse was furnished by Lt. Col. Apthorp. Once when there had been a good deal of ill feeling excited, and trouble was apprehended, owing to the uncertain action of Government in regard to the confiscated lands on the Sea Islands, Gen. Howard was called upon to address the colored people earnestly and even severely. Sympathizing with them, however, he could not speak to his own satisfaction; and to relieve their minds of the ever-present sense of injustice, and prepare them to listen, he asked them to sing. Immediately an old woman on the outskirts of the meeting began "Nobody knows the trouble I've had," and the whole audience joined in. The General was so affected by the plaintive words and melody, that he found himself melting into tears and quite unable to maintain his official sternness.]

60

80. SHOUT ON, CHILDREN.

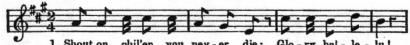

1. Shout on, chil'en, you nev - er die; Glo - ry hal - le - lu!

You in de Lord, an' de Lord in you; Glo - ry hal - le - lu!

2 Shout an' pray both night an' day;
How can you die, you in de Lord?

3 Come on, chil'en, let's go home;
O I'm so glad you're in de Lord.

81. JESUS, WON'T YOU COME BY-AND-BYE?

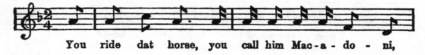

You ride dat horse, you call him Mac-a-do-ni,

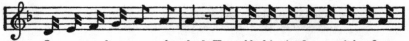

Je - sus, won't you come bumby? You ride him in de mornin' and you

ride him in de evenin', Je - sus, won't you come bumby? De

| 1st. | 2d.

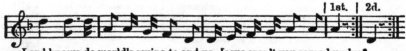

Lord knows de world's gwine to end up, Jesus, won't you come bumby?

94. **73**

ROCK O' MY SOUL.

1, Rock o' my soul in de bosom of Abraham, Rock o' my soul in de

bo - som of A - braham, Rock o' my soul in de

bosom of A - braham, Lord, Rock o' my soul. (King Jesus.)

2 He toted the young lambs in his bosom, (ter)
And leave the old sheep alone.

95. WE WILL MARCH THROUGH THE VALLEY.

1. We will march thro' the val - ley in peace, We will

march thro' the val - ley in peace; If Je - sus himself be our

lead - er, We will march thro' the val - ley in peace.

2 We will march, etc.
    Behold I give myself away, and
    We will march, etc.

3 We will march, etc.
    This track I'll see and I'll pursue;
    We will march, etc.

4 We will march, etc.
    When I'm dead and buried in the cold silent tomb,
    I don't want you to grieve for me.

APPENDIX B

"Poor Rosy, Poor Gal" and "Roll, Jordan Roll" for Voice and Piano; Collected and Arranged by Miss Lucy McKim, 1862

From correspondence at the time it is known that Lucy McKim completed settings for voice and piano for at least six slave spirituals within a few weeks of her return from St. Helena Island in June 1862. Only these two were published, however, the first in the autumn of 1862 and the second a few weeks later, probably in January 1863. The other settings, with their piano accompaniments, have not been found. In her article in *Dwight's Journal* at the same time she wrote that she would decide if there was sufficient interest in the songs for the publication of the other settings, and poor sales may have been the reason for her decision not to continue. In these same weeks a young officer in the Union army whom she had known from childhood and to whom she had become deeply attached was killed in a skirmish in Tennessee, and her shock at his death may also have led to her decision.

It is not known how many copies of each song were published, or which of the songs W. E. B. Du Bois was familiar with—perhaps he had seen both of the settings. The distribution through the antislavery journals was probably poor, and the winter of 1863 was a wrenching period for the nation. Three copies of "Poor Rosy" are on deposit with the Garrison family papers at the Sophia Smith Collection at Smith College in Northampton, Massachusetts, while only a single copy of "Roll, Jordan Roll" is also there, which is perhaps an indication of the relative popularity of the two songs.

Songs of the

FREEDMEN

OF

Port Royal.

Collected and Arranged by

MISS LUCY McKIM.

1. POOR ROSY, POORGAL.   2.
3.   4.
5.   6.
7.   8.

Geo. Swain.

Philadelphia.

Ent. according to Act of Congress A.D. 1862 by Miss Lucy McKim in the Clerks Office of the Dist. Court of the Eastn. Dist of Pa

POOR ROSY, POOR GAL.

Nº 1.

Arranged by Miss LUCY McKIM.

Andante.

2ᵈ ver: Got hard &c.

Poor   Rosy, poor gal!   Poor   Rosy, poor gal!   Poor   Rosy, poor gal!

Poor Rosy, poor gal!   Poor Rosy, poor gal!   Poor Rosy, poor gal!   Heab'n shall a be my home.

2.

Got hard trial in my way!
Hard trial in my way,
Hard trial in my way,
    Heab'n shall a be my home
O! when I talk I talk wid God.
    Heab'n shall a be my home
O! when I talk I talk wid God.
    Heab'n shall a be my home
    Poor Rosy, poor gal!
    Poor Rosy, poor gal!
    Poor Rosy, poor gal!
    Heab'n shall a be my home.

3.

I dunno what de people want o' me,
Dunno what de people want o' me,
Dunno what de people want o' me,
    Heab'n shall a be my home.
O! dis day no holiday,
    Heab'n shall a be my home.
O! dis day no holiday,
    Heab'n shall a be my home.
    Poor Rosy, poor gal!
    Poor Rosy, poor gal!
    Poor Rosy, poor gal!
    Heab'n shall a be my home.

4.

A singin' an' emb'acin, talkin' too,
Singin' an' emb'acin' talkin, too,
Singin' an' emb'acin' talkin too,
    Heab'n shall a be my home.
O! when I walk, I walk wid God!
    Heab'n shall a be my home.
O! when I sleep, I sleep in God!
    Heab'n shall a be my home.
    Poor Rosy, poor gal!
    Poor Rosy, poor gal!
    Poor Rosy, poor gal!
    Heab'n shall a be my home.

Poor Rosy. 3.

ROLL, JORDAN ROLL.

2.

March, angels, march!
March, angels, march!
My soul am rise to heaven, Lord,
Where de heav'n e Jording roll.
Parson Fuller settin' on de Tree ob Life
Where de heav'n e Jording roll,
Oh! roll, Jording, roll, Jording, roll, Jording, roll!

3.

March, angels, march!
March, angels, march!
My soul am rise to heaven, Lord,
For to hear de Jording roll.
Little chil'en learn to fear de Lord,
Au' let yore day be long.
Oh! roll Jording, roll Jording, roll Jording, roll!

4.

March, angels march!
March, angels march!
My soul am rise to heaven, Lord,
Where de heav'n e Jording roll.
Let no false or spiteful word
Be found upon yore tongue.
Oh! roll, Jording, roll, Jording, roll Jording, roll.

Roll, Jording roll!
Roll, Jording roll!
Oh! Lord, I wish I been dar,
To hear de Jording roll!

APPENDIX C

Unsigned Reviews by Lucy McKim Garrison, Lucy McKim Garrison and Wendell Garrison, and Charlotte Forten

Lucy McKim Garrison
Unsigned review from *The Independent*, November 28, 1867, p. 2

THE HYMNODY OF THE BLACKS

Ever since the occupation of a Southern port by our troops, the fame of the music of the negroes has been straggling slowly northward through all sorts of channels—through newspaper letters, magazine articles, through private description, and, occasionally, through illustration. Specimens of the words of the songs have frequently been printed; specimens of the music, with but three or four but illy [*sic*] known examples, never till now. If only in the light of a curiosity, therefore, we welcome the volume before us—the first collection of songs, words and music, that has ever been attempted; and before opening its lids, we may thank the editors for their efforts to save from oblivion a portion of this wild and unique minstrelsy that is now rapidly passing away under the influence of the new civilization. The names of the editors of the collection are sufficient vouchers for its genuineness. All have spent more or less time at the South, and two of them, Messrs. Allen and Ware, were superintendents of Port Royal plantations for protracted periods.

The songs are introduced by an essay from the pen of Professor Allen. This, which is both vivacious and exhaustive, tells all of the history of the songs that is known, describes the manner of their singing, and closes with an account of the dialect of the Sea Island negroes. Most of the songs are religious—"sperichills" (spirituals), as the colored people call them—and of these Port Royal furnishes the largest part. "I never," says Mr. Allen, "fairly heard a secular song among the Port Royal freedmen, and never saw a musical instrument among them. In other parts of the South, 'fiddle-songs,' 'devil-songs,' 'corn songs,' 'jig-tunes,' and what not, are common; all the world knows the banjo, and the 'Jim-Crow' songs of thirty years ago. We have succeeded in obtaining only a very few songs of this character. Our intercourse with the colored people has been chiefly through the work of the Freedmen's Commission, which deals with the serious and earnest side of the negro character. It is often, indeed, no easy matter to persuade them to sing their old songs, even as a curiosity, such is the sense of the dignity that has come with freedom." These "sperichills" have been described by people who have heard them as breathing the very history of slavery. "The wild, sad strains tell, as the sufferers themselves never could, of crushed hopes, keen sorrow, and a dull, daily misery, which covered them as hopelessly as the fog from the rice swamps. On the other hand, the words breathe a trusting faith in rest for the future—in 'Canaan's air [fair] and happy land,' to which their eyes seem constantly turned." *The World* recently said that the contentment of the slaves in their condition was deductible from these very words. It evidently knows equally little of the religion and the music of the miserable.

The essay relates: "One of their customs, often alluded to in the songs (as in No. 19), is that of wandering through the woods and swamps, when under religious excitement, like the ancient bacchantes. To get religious is, with them, to 'fin' dat ting.' Mollay described thus her sister's experience in searching for religion: 'Couldn't fin' dat leetle ting; hunt for 'em—huntin for 'em all de time; las' foun' 'em!' And one day, on our way to see a 'shout,' we asked Bristol whether he was going: 'No, ma'm; wouldn't let me in—hain't foun' dat ting yet—hain't been on my knees in de swamp!'" No. 19 referred to we find to be "Go in the Wilderness," the second part of which will have been already familiar to many. It is not the only one in the collection that savors strongly of the Methodist hymn-book; yet, as the editors suggest, who can pronounce them imitations? Who can tell whether many of the quaint camp-meeting tunes which now obtain everywhere did not originate with the blacks? What are presented of their kind, however, if they are imitations, have been restramped with the negro characteristics.

It would be easy to quote much from the introduction; in fact, it is difficult to quote a little, the interest being so equally kept up. There is a lively description of the "shout"— that odd, religious dance, which consists of shuffling round in a circle to the music of rhythmic clapping of hands and a chorus of voices. And there is an account of the rowing songs, and the songs preferred in church and praise-house, and those sung in imitation of "white, genteel worship."

In speaking of the dialect, Prof. Allen says that the ordinary Negro-talk in books has very little resemblance to that spoken on the Sea Islands. "A stranger, upon first hearing these people talk, especially if there is a group of them in animated conversation, can hardly understand them better than if they spoke a foreign language." "*Cuss* is used with great latitude, to denote any offensive language. 'Him cuss me, git out.' 'Ahvy (Abby) de cuss me,' was the serious-sounding but trifling accusation made by a little girl against her seat-mate. "'Me one, and God,' answered an old man in Charleston to the question whether he escaped alone from his plantation." "*Talk* is one of their most common words, where we should use *speak* or *mean* . . . 'Talk lick, sir? nuffin but lick,' was the answer when I asked whether a particular master used to whip his slaves."

In quoting from this Introduction, we describe the songs, in part. To give an adequate idea of them in words is out of the question. Every one will be curious to find for himself—as nearly as it is possible from the notes—how the often spoken-of "Poor Rosy" and "Roll, Jordan, Roll," sound, as well as the unfamiliar "Rain fall and wet Becca Lawton," and "Jericho, da worry me," and "God got plenty o'room"; what the songs of Col. Higginson's regiment are like—the words of which he has already published in the *Atlantic Monthly*; and what, also, the Louisiana songs, "Aurore Bradaire," "Lolotte," with their negro-French patois. We abstain from transcribing any verses; for, although the collection exhibits many new and odd phrases, our readers have been already made familiar with the general style of them through their frequent publication in the newspapers.

In recommending the book as a curiosity in literature, as a valuable bit of history, and as a collection of remarkable musical ideas,* we feel that we do not go beyond the truth.

◆ ◆ ◆

*"The high voices, all in unison, and the admirable time and true account with which their responses are made, always make me wish that some great traditional composer could hear these semi-savage performances. With a very little skillful adaptation and instrumentation, I think one or two barbaric chants and choruses might be evoked from them that would make the fortune of an opera."—*Mrs. Kemble's "Life on a Georgia Plantation,"* p. 218.

◆

—Lucy McKim Garrison and Wendell Garrison
Unsigned review from *The Nation*, November 21, 1867, p. 411

SLAVE SONGS OF THE UNITED STATES

This book, of which we had the pleasure of announcing the inception, is a remarkable proof of the stringent separation of North and South, in consequence of slavery before the war. Not a few of the songs, contributors testify, are at least a quarter of a century old, and the greater part of the collection may easily be older. A very small proportion belong to the Jim Crow category, the remainder being religious hymns or "spirituals." If intercourse between the two sections had been unrestricted; if the Tract Society and the Bible Society had performed their mission as faithfully in South Carolina as Timbuktoo; if other ministers than the South-Side Adamses could have gone to the plantations to pray or to preach the Gospel of Christ, we should have had something beyond the gospel of Christy. But the whites who attended the negro camp meetings were present for other motives than a love of harmony; the planter's guest was naturally content to hear from a distance, and to cherish as simply a pleasant recollection the airs that floated up to the house from the "nigger" quarter; and as for the wanderer who would have stopped to listen and to note down, the suspicion of tampering with happy but credulous laborers was not to be incurred with impunity. Moreover, most men are curious, many and many again have a fondness for music, but those who are musically educated are comparatively rare, and those who are capable of notation by ear are very seldom to be met with. To know two in one's circle of acquaintances (which may embrace several who can sing from notes at sight) is a rare thing. But given this capacity, without a certain amount of sympathy for the slave, and the courage to endure the odium of abolitionism, you lack the impulse necessary to an undertaking of this character. And having all these qualities, there would be wanting an opportunity. We do not speak positively, but our impression is that on the plantation the slaves were obliged to be quiet in their cabins after a certain hour of the evening, and their greatest license in singing was on Sunday nights and during the Christmas holidays. If this be the case, their freedom has produced a striking reaction, and the "praise-meeting" now keeps hours which would wear out the *habitué* of the most fashionable belle. At Port Hudson it was not uncommon to retire for the night, leaving such a meeting in full blast, and to wake at sunrise to the same monotonous beat that was last heard before closing the eyes. Indeed, some of the offices were compelled, in order to get their rest, to procure an order prohibiting these unseasonable performances.

These remarks were suggested by the opening sentence of the preface, and their length warns us that we must not enlarge upon an essay which is full of suggestiveness. Putting aside the Zip Coon or "secular" period as out of the province of the present research, although it overlaps it at a few points, Professor Allen relates the history of various collections which are here united, and discusses the nature of the music, the source of the words, and the religious significance of the "spiritual;" describes the "shout," and indicates the "shouting" tunes, and offers some evidence as to the spontaneity of these compositions. There follows, from the same pen, a valuable and amusing monograph on the dialect of the Sea Islands, for which we bespeak the attention of philologists; and at last—the reader, we believe will say too soon rather too tardily—after some directions for singing, the songs are reached. They are one hundred and thirty-six in number, divided under groups of states to four parts, and exhibiting characteristically the music of each group. By far the greater number (eighty-eight) belong to South Carolina, Georgia, and the Sea Islands—the result plainly of accident, though possibly this region was more fertile in musical expression than any other part of the South. The remainder were obtained from States among which Alabama, Mississippi, Texas, Missouri, and Kentucky alone do not figure. In two or three instances the editors have been able to present varieties of the same tune as sung in different States.

We utter no new truth when we affirm that whatever of nationality there is in the music of America she owes to her dusky children. Negro minstrelsy sprang from them, and from negro minstrelsy our truly national airs, of which "Yankee Doodle" and "The Star Spangled Banner" are *not* specimens. The negroes in their turn imitate the whites, but they show their peculiar musical genius as much in their imitations as in their compositions. A "white tune," so to speak, adopted and sung by them—in their own way—becomes a different thing. The words may be simply mangled, but the music is changed under an inspiration; it becomes a vital force. Hence the difficulty in according authorship: to say how much is pure African, how much is Methodist or Baptist camp-meeting. Where did the camp-meeting songs come from? Why may not they as likely emanate from black as white worshippers? Doubts such as these, in the absence of certain proof, can alone account for the admission into this collection of songs like "The Old Ship of Zion," "Almost Over," and several others of the same stamp. Suggestive as they are, they are the least interesting of the collection. The host of unmistakably negro compositions, of which "Poor Rosy" and "Becca Lawton" are two pertinent examples, are a reward to the slowest decipherer of notes and the most backward conceiver of tempo. The opening songs are rich in illustrative variety. What better adaptation of music to words than in "Jehovah—Hallelujah"—"De foxes have a hole, and de birdies have a nest"? What more rousing then "Blow your Trumpet, Gabriel" and "Praise, Member"? What more truly spiritual than "The Lonesome Valley"? Then there is the quaint "O deat' he is a Little Man," which we remember ourselves to have heard sung by a crew rowing across the ferry from St. Helena to Beaufort. The fugle [sic] man of that occasion—a fellow of inky blackness, with the sweat of a summer's day streaming from every pore, and his eyes squinted under the sun's glare—can never be forgotten as he poured forth, energetically, "O Lord, remember me; do, Lord, remember me!"

A great deal has been said about the predominance of the minor key in the songs of the slaves, attributable, it has been supposed, to their misery. The misery, surely, was not wanting; the minor key, on the contrary, to anything like the extent supposed. The mistake has possibly arisen from the latitude with which the term has been applied, by persons who did not understand its technical use, to all those strains which sounded wild or mournful; as, for instance, "The Graveyard," p. 15. There is also a theory that barbaric (or, as some call it, natural) music is always minor. But if these views are mistaken, equally so is the opinion that these negro songs evince the easiness of the yoke of bondage. They are, rather, the embodiment of the mental and physical anguish of a bruised race—the safety-valve of their complaining and revolt against oppression. "Heaven" is to the slave not merely nor principally a reward of virtue, but a refuge from the lash. "Heab'n shall-a be my home" is the solace of "Poor Rosy, poor gal." And it is no moral conflict, no striving of conscience that is alluded to in

"Nobody knows the trouble I've had,
Nobody knows but Jesus."

It was trouble with "massa," trouble with the driver, trouble with the government halting in its policy of confiscation. But in these considerations we must not indulge. Let us be permitted to point out some of the songs with which we have been particularly struck, first premising that the average excellence of the collection is surprising, and that no one who has not explored it to the end will be acquainted with all its beauties. At the very close, in fact, are the Louisiana negro creole songs, with an obscure patois but delightful melodies. We specify: "Meet O Lord," p. 48, "Day of Judgement," p. 53, "Nobody Knows," p. 53, "Let God's saints come in," p. 76, "The Gold Band," p. 83, "I want to die like a Lazarus die," p. 98, and "God got plenty o' room," p. 105. The illustrative and exegetical notes and the parallel versions make the book thoroughly readable. We shall be disappointed if many of the airs do not become popular, and the effort of the editors to make that permanent which is now transient be not crowned with signal and merited success.

◆

—Charlotte Forten

Unsigned review from *The Freedmen's Record*, December, 1867, p. 185–86

SLAVE SONGS OF THE UNITED STATES

A volume bearing this title has recently been published by Messrs. A. Simpson & Co., New York. It is edited by Prof. W. F. Allen, C. P. Ware, and Mrs. L. Mc.K. Garrison, and contains a valuable and interesting collection of "Negro Spirituals," words and music. These are mainly from the Sea Islands of South Carolina, from Georgia and Florida, and, from personal knowledge, we can testify to their faithfulness. There is also a large number from Virginia, and some from several other Southern and Southwestern States. We are very glad that these songs, which are too rapidly losing favor among the freedmen—are thus collected and preserved; for they make a most striking, curious, and valuable addition to the history of slavery in this country. Professor Allen says: "Our title, 'Slave Songs,' was selected, because it best described the contents of the book. A few of those here given (Nos. 64, 59), were, to be sure, composed since the proclamation of emancipation, but even these were inspired by slavery. All, indeed, are valuable as an expression of the character and the life of the race which is playing such a conspicuous part in our history. The wild, sad strains, tell, as the sufferers themselves never could, of crushed hopes, keen sorrow, and a dull, daily misery, which covered them as hopelessly as the fog from the rice swamps. On the other hand, the words describe a trusting faith in rest for the future, 'in Canaan's fair and happy land,' to which their eye seems constantly turned."

To those who have been fortunate enough to hear these songs sung by the freedmen themselves, this collection is one of peculiar interest, and recalls vividly the many and varied occasions on which the sweet, wild melodies, have touched and charmed them. The sunset row from island to island, when we first arrived, in the golden glow of October, with our crew of sturdy boatmen; their jet black faces, strongly relieved by scarlet shirts, and in some cases, by white kerchiefs tied over the head, the more effectively to protect them from the heat; the joyous, eager crowd of expectant little faces, collected for morning school; the sad, solemn burials at night; the gay weddings at church, when, sometimes four couples, were united at one ceremony, and brides appeared radiant in "ole missus's" cast-off finery; the great gatherings under the grand, moss-draperied old oaks, on the Fourth of July, and on the glorious "Emancipation Day," that celebration which has so often been described, but whose sublime significance, whose deep and soul-thrilling interest can never be fitly spoken; the midnight "shout," in the roughly boarded "praise-house," lighted only by the red glare of a single pine knot, which, indeed, did *not* light, but only served to "render more visible" the darkness embodied in the weird forms, flitting through their strange, barbaric dance; these are a few of the never-to-be-forgotten pictures which rise before us, and awaken almost irresistible longings to behold again the realities, as we glance over the familiar words, and listen to the familiar airs of these songs.

In his very interesting preface, Professor Allen tells us all that is known or conjectured about the origins of the "Spirituals;" gives us an excellent description of the "shout;" and some amusing specimens of the negro dialect. The Sea Island Songs are largely based on the valuable collection of Colonel Higginson, in the "Atlantic Monthly," and to him the editors acknowledge their great indebtedness.

At the close of the collection, are several melodious Louisiana songs, in the "Negro French" dialect, which is very curious and amusing, and which is said to be "more difficult for persons who speak French to interpret, than it is for those who speak English to understand the most corrupt of the ordinary negro talk." The specimens of Louisiana songs, are all "seculars," being, in this respect, unlike the Port Royal songs, which are, almost without exception, of a religious character.

This valuable book will, doubtless, be much in demand. We are informed that the first edition is already very nearly, if not entirely, sold. The publishers are about to issue a second edition, which will, we hope, find as speedy a sale.

NOTES

Abbreviations

SS/SC—The Garrison Papers at the Sophia Smith Research Collection, Smith College
NYPL—The Maloney Collection of McKim Garrison Family Papers at the Manuscripts and Archives Division of the New York Public Library, New York City
Cornell—The Division of Rare and Manuscript Collections, Cornell University Library, Ithaca, NY

Chapter 1

1. Du Bois, p. 180.
2. SS/SC.
3. NYPL.
4. SS/SC.
5. Ibid.
6. *Dwight's Journal of Music*, Nov. 8, 1862.
7. *The Nation*, Nov. 21, 1867.

Chapter 2

1. Hollowell, p. 115.
2. Ibid., p. 128.
3. Ibid., p. 193.
4. Bremer, pp. 400–1.
5. Ibid.
6. Ibid.
7. Ibid.
8. SS/SC.
9. Hollowell, p. 310.
10. NYPL.
11. SS/SC.

Chapter 3

1. NYPL.
2. Alonso, p. 183.

3. Ibid., p. 184.

4. SS/SC.

5. NYPL.

6. Harding/Bode, pp. 439–40.

7. SS/SC.

8. Ibid.

9. Ibid.

10. Ibid.

11. Ibid.

12. Ibid.

13. Ibid.

14. Ibid.

Chapter 4

1. SS/SC.

2. Ibid.

3. Ibid.

4. Ibid.

5. Rasmussen/Tilton, p. 40.

6. Periodicals/Microforms Division, New York Public Library.

7. NYPL.

8. Ibid.

9. Ibid.

10. William L. Garrison, Jr., n.p.

11. *Dwight's Journal*, "Who Wrote the Negro Songs," 1856.

12. *North American & US Gazette*.

13. NYPL.

14. Rasmussen/Tilton, p. 91.

15. SS/SC.

16. Ibid.

17. Ibid.

18. Ibid.

Chapter 5

1. Epstein, *Sinful Tunes*, p. 317.

2. SS/SC.

3. Alonso, p. 191.

4. SS/SC.

5. NYPL.

6. Hollowell, p. 398.

7. SS/SC.

8. Stackhouse, p. 22.

9. Ibid., p. 9.

10. SS/SC.

11. Ibid.

12. Epstein, *Sinful Tunes*, p. 244.

13. Ibid., p. 244.

14. Ibid., p. 245.

15. SS/SC.

16. Ibid.

17. Ibid.

18. Stackhouse, p. 23.

Chapter 6

1. Epstein, *Sinful Tunes*, p. 247. Epstein added the former slaveholder's response in her discussion: "When these exciting chants were sung in his hearing, he acknowledged that so long as the Union forces remained the Carolinians were in danger from their slaves."

2. Rose, p. 12.

3. SS/SC.

4. Ibid.

5. Rose, p. 77.

6. NYPL.

7. Towne, p. 3.

8. SS/SC.

9. Ibid.

Chapter 7

1. SS/SC.

2. Ibid.

3. Ibid.

4. Towne, p. 40.

5. Ibid., p. 62.

6. Ibid., p. 63.

7. Ibid.

8. SS/SC.

9. NYPL.

10. SS/SC.

11. Towne, p. 65.

12. Ibid.

13. SS/SC.

14. Towne, p. 66.

15. Ibid., p. 67.

16. SS/SC.
17. Ibid.
18. Towne, p. 69.
19. SS/SC.
20. Ibid.

Chapter 8

1. SS/SC.
2. Ibid.
3. Ibid.
4. Epstein, Offprint, p. 539.
5. Ibid.
6. SS/SC.
7. Ibid.
8. The well-known general John C. Fremont, who had been dismissed by Lincoln, and John "Jesse" Cochrane were nominated for president and vice president by the Radical Republicans, a splinter party launched by Republicans dissatisfied with the progress of the war. Fremont withdrew before the election, fearing that he might split the Republican vote, allowing the "peace" Democrats to win.
9. SS/SC.
10. Ibid.
11. Ibid.
12. Ibid.
13. NYPL.
14. *Dwight's Journal*, Nov. 8, 1862, Vol. XXI, pp. 254–5.
15. Forten, May 1864, pp. 588–9.
16. Ibid.
17. Ibid., June, 1864, pp. 666–7.

Chapter 9

1. Forten, June 1864, p. 668.
2. Ibid.
3. SS/SC.
4. *Nosce te ipsum*—from the Latin, "Know thyself."
5. *Terque quaterque beati*—from the Latin, "Thrice and four times blessed."
6. SS/SC.
7. Ibid.
8. Ibid.
9. Kemble, p. 163.
10. Alonso, p. 200.
11. Ibid., p. 194.

12. Ibid., p. 163.
13. SS/SC.
14. NYPL.

Chapter 10

1. SS/SC.
2. Ibid.
3. Ibid.
4. Ibid.
5. Ibid.
6. Ibid.
7. Ibid.
8. Ibid.
9. Ibid.
10. Ibid.
11. Ibid.
12. Ibid.
13. Alonso, pp. 210–11.
14. Ibid.
15. Ibid.
16. SS/SC.
17. Ibid.
18. Ibid.
19. Ibid.
20. Ibid.
21. Forten, May 1864, p. 590.
22. Ibid.
23. Towne, p. 122.
24. Ibid., p. 125.
25. Ibid., p. 137.
26. SS/SC.
27. Ibid.

Chapter 11

1. SS/SC.
2. Ibid.
3. Ibid.
4. Towne, p. 145.
5. Ibid., p. 142.
6. Ibid., p. 144.
7. SS/SC.

8. Epstein, Offprint, p. 542.

9. Hollowell, p. 416.

10. Ibid., p. 482.

11. SS/SC

12. Epstein, Offprint, p. 543.

13. Ibid.

14. NYPL.

15. Ibid.

16. Ibid.

17. Ibid.

18. Ibid.

19. Moore, pp. 18–19.

20. NYPL.

21. SS/SC.

Chapter 12

1. NYPL.

2. Towne, p. 181.

3. William F. Allen Papers, Library Archives, Wisconsin Historical Society, Madison, WI.

4. Cornell.

5. Wisconsin.

6. SS/SC.

7. Alonso, p. 245.

8. Epstein, p. 331.

9. Ibid.

10. Cornell.

11. Ibid.

12. Forten, June 1864, p. 669.

13. Ibid.

14. *Dwight's Journal,* July 20, 1867, p. 71.

15. SS/SC.

Chapter 13

1. See text in appendix C.

2. Ibid.

3. Ibid.

Chapter 14

1. SS/SC.

2. Ibid.

3. Moore, p. 32.
4. SS/SC.
5. Ibid.
6. Ibid.
7. Ibid.
8. Ibid.
9. NYPL.
10. SS/SC.
11. Ibid.
12. Ward, p. 100.
13. NYPL.
14. SS/SC.
15. Ibid.

Chapter 15

1. SS/SC.
2. Ibid.
3. Alonso, p. 251.
4. SS/SC.
5. Ibid.
6. Ibid.
7. Ibid.
8. Ibid.
9. Ibid.
10. *The Orange Journal*, May 19, 1873.

Chapter 16

1. SS/SC.
2. *Atlantic Monthly*, October 1891.
3. Cornell.
4. Op. cit.
5. Chapter 1.

Appendix A *Slave Songs of the United States:* A Description and Commentary

1. Letter to the author.
2. Rose, p. 93.
3. SSUS, Dover Edition, 1995, "Preface to the Dover Edition," unpaged.

BIBLIOGRAPHY

Manuscripts and Rare Printed Materials

The correspondence of Lucy McKim Garrison and Ellen Wright Garrison, as well as additional family papers, is included in the Garrison Collection at the Sophia Smith Library at Smith College, Northampton, MA.

The correspondence relating to John Brown between James Miller McKim, Brown, and Thomas Wentworth Higginson is on deposit at the Manuscripts and Archives Division of the New York Public Library. Also in their holdings is the family correspondence between McKim and his wife and children.

The correspondence relating to the gathering of musical examples for *Slave Songs of the United States* is on deposit in the Samuel J. May Anti-Slavery Collection at the Kroch Library, Cornell University, Ithaca, NY.

The papers of William Francis Allen, including the unpublished diary of his months on St. Helena Island and his daily journal from the spring of 1867, are deposited in the Library Archives at the Wisconsin Historical Society, Madison, WI.

The Samuel and Ann Charters Archives of Blues and Vernacular African American Musical Culture, Dodd Research Center, University of Connecticut. Storrs holdings include pamphlets and editions of the Fisk Jubilee histories and spiritual arrangements, as well as early "plantation song" collections and other nineteenth- and twentieth-century spiritual collections listed below.

Books and Articles

Alonso, Harriet Hyman. *Growing Up Abolitionist: The Story of the Garrison Children.* Amherst: University of Massachusetts Press, 2002.

Armstrong, Mrs. M. F., and Helen Ludlow. *Hampton and Its Students, by Two of Its Teachers with Fifty Cabin and Plantation Songs arranged by Thomas F. Fenner.* New York: G. P. Putnum's Sons, 1874.

Ballanta, Nicholas George Julius. *St. Helena Island Spirituals.* St. Helena: The Penn Normal Industrial and Agricultural School, 1925. "Printed at the press of G. Schirmer, New York."

Barton, William F. *Old Plantation Hymns*. Boston and New York: Lamson, Wolffe and Company, 1899.

Billington, Ray Allen, ed. *The Journal of Charlotte L. Forten*. New York: The Dryden Press, 1953.

Blockson, Charles L. *The Underground Railroad*. New York: Prentice-Hall, 1987.

Bontemps, Arna. *Chariot in the Sky: A Story of the Jubilee Singers*. Philadelphia: John C. Winston, 1951.

Bordewich, Fergus M. *Bound for Canaan: The Epic Story of the Underground Railroad*. New York: HarperCollins Publishers, 2005.

Bremer, Fredrika. *The Homes in the New World: Impressions of America*. Vols. 1 & 2. Translated by Mary Howitt. New York: Harper & Brothers, 1853.

Cabin and Plantation Songs as sung by the Hampton Students. Arranged by Thomas P. Fenner, Frederick G. Rathbon, and Mrs. Bessie Crawford. New York: G. Putnam's Sons, 1901. The third edition, which has been expanded by the addition of forty-four songs.

Cain, William E., ed. *William Lloyd Garrison and the Fight against Slavery*. Boston: Bedford/St. Martins, 1995.

Courlander, Harold. *The Drum and the Hoe: Life and Lore of the Haitian People*. Berkeley: University of California Press, 1960.

———. *Negro Folk Music U.S. A*. New York: Columbia University Press, 1963.

Cromwell, Otelia. *Lucretia Mott: The Story of One of America's Greatest Women*. Cambridge: Harvard University Press, 1958.

Du Bois, W. E. B. *The Souls of Black Folk*. Chicago: McClure Publishers, 1903.

Epstein, Dena J. *Lucy McKim Garrison*. Offprint from the *Bulletin* of the New York Public Library, Vol. 67, October 1963, pp. 529–546.

———. *Sinful Tunes and Spirituals*. Urbana: University of Illinois Press, 1977.

Fisher, Miles Mark. *Negro Slave Songs in the United States*. Ithaca: Cornell University Press, 1953.

Forten, Charlotte. "Life on the Sea Islands." Published in *The Atlantic Monthly*, May–June 1864, Vol. XIII, Nos. 79–80.

Garrison, Lloyd McKim. *Ballads of Harvard and Other Verses*. Cambridge: Privately printed, 1891.

Garrison, Wendell Phillips. *Letters and Memorials*. Cambridge: Printed at the Riverside Press, 1908.

Garrison, William Lloyd, Jr. *In Memoriam of Sarah A. McKim*. Privately printed and read at the funeral service, 1891.

Guy, William E. *The Message of the Negro Spirituals*. Springfield: The Williamson Press, 1946.

Harding, Walter, and Carl Bode, eds. *The Correspondence of Henry David Thoreau*. New York: New York University Press, 1958.

Higginson, Thomas Wentworth. *Army Life in a Black Regiment*. Boston: Fields, Osgood & Co., 1870.

———. "Negro Spirituals." Published in *The Atlantic Monthly*, June 1867, Vol. XIX, No. CXVI, pp. 685–694.

Holland, Rupert Sargent, ed. *Letters and Diary of Laura M. Towne.* Salem: Higginson Book Co., 2007 (reprint of 1912 edition).

Hollowell, Anna Davis, ed. *James and Lucretia Mott: Life and Letters.* Boston: Houghton, Mifflin & Co., 1884.

Hopkinson, Deborah. *A Band of Angels: A Story Inspired by the Jubilee Singers.* New York: Atheneum Books, 1999.

Jackson, George Pullen. *White Spirituals in Southern Uplands.* Chapel Hill: University of North Carolina Press, 1933.

Johnson, James Weldon and J. Rosamond Johnson, with Lawrence Brown. *The Book of American Negro Spirituals.* New York: Viking Press, 1925.

Jubilee Songs: Complete as Sung by the Jubilee Singers of Fisk University. New York: Biglow & Martin, 1872.

Kemble, Francis Anne. *Journal of a Residence on a Georgian Plantation in 1838–1839.* NY: Harper & Sons, 1863.

Kennedy, R. Emmet. *Mellows: A Chronicle of Negro Singers.* New York: Albert and Charles Boni, 1925.

Krehbiel, E. H. *Afro-American Folk Songs: A Study in Racial and National Music.* New York: G. Schirmer, 1914.

Marsh, J. B. T. *The Story of the Jubilee Singers, with Their Songs.* "Eighty-Seventh Thousand" with additional material. Boston: Houghton, Mifflin and Company, n.d.

——, with F. J. Loudin. *The Story of the Fisk Jubille Singers, with the Story of their Six-Year Trip Round the World.* "New Edition Completing One Hundred and Thirty Thousand." Cleveland: The Cleveland Printing and Publishing Company, 1892.

Moore, Charles. *The Life and Times of Charles Follen McKim.* Boston: Houghron Mifflin Co., 1929.

Odum, Howard W. *Folk-Song and Folk Poetry, As Found in the Secular Songs of the Southern Negro.* Bound offprint from the *Journal of American Folklore,* July–September–October–November 1911.

——, and Guy B. Johnson. *The Negro and His Songs: A Study of Typical Songs in the South.* Chapel Hill: University of North Carolina Press, 1925.

——. *Negro Workaday Songs.* Chapel Hill: University of North Carolina Press, 1926.

Parrish, Lydia. *Slave Songs of the Georgia Sea Islands.* New York: Creative Age Press, 1941.

Pike, Gutavus D. *The Jubilee Singers and Their Campaign for Twenty Thousand Dollars.* Boston: Lee & Shepard, 1873.

Rasmussen, William S., and Robert S. Tilton. *The Portent: John Brown's Raid in American Memory.* Richmond: Virginia Historical Society, 2009.

Religious Folk Songs of the Negro, as Sung on the Plantations. Hampton, VA: The Institute Press, 1909. "Arranged by the musical directors of The Hampton Normal and Agricultural Institute from the original edition by Thomas P. Fenner."

Rose, Willie Lee. *Rehearsal for Reconstruction: The Port Royal Experiment.* Athens: University of Georgia Press, Brown Thrasher Books, 1999.

Scarborough, Dorothy. *On the Trail of Negro Folk-Songs.* Cambridge: Harvard University Press, 1925.

The Songs of the Jubilee Singers. London: Hoddard and Stoughton, 1875.

Stackhouse, Eugene G. *Germantown in the Civil War.* Charleston: History Press, 2010.

Taylor, Marshall W., D.D. *A Collection of Revival Hymns and Plantation Melodies.* Cincinnati: Marshall W. Taylor and W. C. Echols Publishers, 1888.

Thomas, W. H. *Some Current Folk-Songs of the Negro.* Offprint. College Station, Texas: The Folk Lore Society of Texas, nd. "Read before the Folk-Lore Society of Texas, 1912."

Thurman, Howard. *Deep River: Reflections on the Religious Insight of Certain of the Negro Spirituals.* New York: Harper & Brothers, 1955. Revised and enlarged edition.

Ward, Andrew. *Dark Midnight When I Rise.* New York: Farrar, Straus & Giroux, 2000.

White, Newman I. *Negro Folk Songs.* Cambridge: Harvard University Press, 1928.

Work, Frederick J., ed., and John Wesley Work, introduction. *Folk Song of American Negro* [*sic*]. Nashville: Self-published, 1907. A ninety-six-page stapled volume containing ninety-one spirituals arranged for vocal quartet.

———. *Folk Songs of the American Negro.* Nashville: Work Brothers & Hart Co., nd. A sixty-four page stapled volume containing sixty-one spirituals arranged for vocal quartet. The arrangements were included in the earlier publication by the Work brothers.

Work, John Wesley, A. M. *Folk Song of the American Negro.* Nashville: Press of Fisk University, 1915. One-hundred-thirty-two page study with musical examples.

Work, John Wesley, III. *American Negro Songs and Spirituals.* New York: Bonanza, 1940.

INDEX

Printed in the USA
CPSIA information can be obtained
at www.ICGtesting.com
JSHW020514030224
56306JS00004B/7